Landscapes of Christianity

Bloomsbury Studies in Religion, Space and Place

Series editors: Paul-François Tremlett, John Eade, and Katy Soar

Religions, spiritualities, and mysticisms are deeply implicated in processes of place-making. These include political and geopolitical spaces, local and national spaces, urban spaces, global and virtual spaces, contested spaces, spaces of performance, spaces of memory, and spaces of confinement. At the leading edge of theoretical, methodological, and interdisciplinary innovation in the study of religion, Bloomsbury Studies in Religion, Space and Place brings together and gives shape to the study of such processes.
These places are not defined simply by the material or the physical but also by the sensual and the psychological, by the ways in which spaces are gendered, classified, stratified, moved through, seen, touched, heard, interpreted, and occupied. Places are constituted through embodied practices that direct critical and analytical attention to the spatial production of insides, outsides, bodies, landscapes, cities, sovereignties, publics, and interiorities.

Christianity in Brazil
Sílvia Fernandes

Global Trajectories of Brazilian Religion
Edited by Martijn Oosterbaan, Linda van de Kamp, and Joana Bahia

Religion and the Global City
Edited by David Garbin and Anna Strhan

Religious Pluralism and the City
Edited by Helmuth Berking, Silke Steets, and Jochen Schwenk

Singapore, Spirituality, and the Space of the State
Joanne Punzo Waghorne

Towards a New Theory of Religion and Social Change
Paul-François Tremlett

Urban Religious Events
Edited by Paul Bramadat, Mar Griera, Julia Martinez-Ariño, and Marian Burchardt

Landscapes of Christianity

Destination, Temporality, Transformation

Edited by
James S. Bielo and Amos S. Ron

BLOOMSBURY ACADEMIC
LONDON • NEW YORK • OXFORD • NEW DELHI • SYDNEY

BLOOMSBURY ACADEMIC
Bloomsbury Publishing Plc
50 Bedford Square, London, WC1B 3DP, UK
1385 Broadway, New York, NY 10018, USA
29 Earlsfort Terrace, Dublin 2, Ireland

BLOOMSBURY, BLOOMSBURY ACADEMIC and the Diana logo are trademarks of
Bloomsbury Publishing Plc

First published in Great Britain 2023
This edition published 2024

Copyright © James S. Bielo, Amos S. Ron and contributors, 2023

James S. Bielo and Amos S. Ron have asserted their rights under the Copyright,
Designs and Patents Act, 1988, to be identified as Editors of this work.

Cover image © Thomas M. Scheer / EyeEm / gettyimages.co.uk

All rights reserved. No part of this publication may be reproduced or transmitted
in any form or by any means, electronic or mechanical, including photocopying,
recording, or any information storage or retrieval system, without prior
permission in writing from the publishers.

Bloomsbury Publishing Plc does not have any control over, or responsibility for, any
third-party websites referred to or in this book. All internet addresses given in this
book were correct at the time of going to press. The author and publisher regret any
inconvenience caused if addresses have changed or sites have ceased to exist,
but can accept no responsibility for any such changes.

A catalogue record for this book is available from the British Library.

Library of Congress Control Number: 2022934947.

ISBN: HB: 978-1-3500-6289-4
PB: 978-1-3503-4181-4
ePDF: 978-1-3500-6290-0
eBook: 978-1-3500-6291-7

Series: Bloomsbury Studies in Religion, Space, and Place

Typeset by Deanta Global Publishing Services, Chennai, India

To find out more about our authors and books visit www.bloomsbury.com and
sign up for our newsletters

Contents

List of Figures	vii
Foreword	ix
Introduction: Landscape Processes in the Making of Christianities *Amos S. Ron and James S. Bielo*	1

Part 1 Destinations

1	Galactic shrines and the Catholic Cult of St. Padre Pio of Pietrelcina *Michael A. Di Giovine*	19
2	Sacralizing the Landscape: Water and the Development of a Pilgrimage Shrine *John Eade*	45
3	Crucifix and Dirt: Catholic and Indigenous Origins of the Holy Earth of the Santuario de Chimayó *Brett Hendrickson*	60
4	Captivating Landscapes: Gender and Religion in Mormon Captivity Narratives *Sara M. Patterson*	77

Part 2 Temporalities

5	From the Messiah's Glade to the Gods' Mountains: Christian Landscapes of Africa and Asia *Jonathan Miles-Watson and Sitna Quiroz*	101
6	Geography as Eschatology: Moral Freedom and Prophecy Fulfillment on Land and at Sea *Joseph Webster*	121
7	Imagining an Ethnic Ecumene: Evangelical Landscapes as Gentile, Jewish, and Native in the American South *Rebekka King*	136

Part 3 Transformations

8	Landscape as Expressive Resource in Materializing the Bible *James S. Bielo*	157
9	When Mountains Move: Athonite Processions, Sacred Performance, and Overlapping Topographies *Veronica della Dora*	176
10	The Garden of Eden in an Era of Over-Tourism: (Managing) New Testament Sacred Groves in the Holy Land *Amos S. Ron*	201

Afterword: The Work that Landscape Does: On Placing and Displacing in Christianity *Simon Coleman* 220

Notes 231
References 238
List of Contributors 265
Index 267

Foreword

It is an honor to write the foreword to this wonderful edited volume on "Landscapes of Christianity." The importance of this topic first cannot be underestimated, since it is through these landscapes that people become engaged and enmeshed with Christianity, that the past, present, and future are made visible side by side.

The spatial practices of Christians have fascinated me ever since I visited Nigeria in the spring of 2007 with two of my colleagues. We traveled through Nigeria, visiting several of the mega-churches there and interviewing their leaders while getting acquainted with the ways these churches were creating new "geographies of conversion" through their missionary efforts aimed at Europe. The Christian landscape of Nigeria is very impressive, materially, in terms of infrastructure and buildings in terms of the concentration of people, power, and finances as is also highlighted in the chapter by Miles-Watson and Quiroz describing Canaanland in this volume. Along the Lagos–Ibadan highway, several other churches have established campgrounds, which have become mini-cities: with banks, schools, a university and housing, resort-style accommodation and its own electricity, sewer supply, and so on. This is in sharp contrast with conditions elsewhere in the cities such as Lagos and Ibadan, where electricity is erratic, traffic is a nightmare, and public facilities are underfunded.

It is also, in a different way, in contrast with the landscape of Christianity in Europe. Whereas Pentecostal churches in Nigeria have become key players in Nigerian society: they are perceived, if they are perceived at all, as quite marginal from northern European perspectives, and Christian landscapes are becoming heritage sites. The main concerns among government officials and national organizations of mainline churches in northwestern Europe are what to do with all the churches that are now standing empty, how to convert them for new use, how to desacralize them, or whether to choose to keep them open as heritage sites which creates all sorts of new "Post-Christian" dynamics of sacralization. Meanwhile, "migrant churches" (driven by missionaries from the Global South) choose to locate in empty office buildings, although increasingly they now take over church buildings as well.

This first visit to Nigeria and the contrast with European Christian landscapes convinced me that in order to study Christianity in the twenty-first century, we need to attend to spatial practices: mapping, place-making, ways of using the landscape, and ways of orienting oneself. Especially when there is a strong missionary impulse, the whole world is opened up as a territory to be claimed, a landscape to be marked and shaped. Even more, we need to attend to the ways that these spatial practices are, or become, political, both implicitly and explicitly, as the editors and the authors of several chapters in this volume also note. Thus, through a focus on spatial practices not only subtle dynamics of power but also personal empowerment and disempowerment can be made visible on different scales.

The genius of a focus on landscapes and spatial practices is that it allows for the recognition of the existence of several different processes, structures, narratives, and dynamics taking place at the same time, observing whether and how they interact: both secularization *and* the emergence of new and dynamic religious landscapes.

Through the focus on landscape, this edited volume develops the emerging literature on spatial practices in the study of religion in fascinating new directions, engaging fully with the notion that landscapes are always an interaction between what is given and what is made, viewing landscape as a process rather than a static horizon of what is visible from one particular viewpoint. Thus, new questions are engaged with: What histories are made present materially, which ones are pushed away and forgotten? How does the material presence of buildings, or theme parks such as described by Bielo, establish a public fact that must be engaged with somehow? Questions of empowerment and disempowerment also recur in the fascinating chapter on Christians engaging with Jewish and Native American history in the American South by Rebekka King, the chapter on imageries of civilization and wilderness in abduction narratives of Mormon women by Patterson as well as in the fascinating chapter on Scottish Fishermen. In this case, the subject of landscape also includes a reflection on seascapes of their livelihood and their changeable nature, which are seen as instantiations of an eschatological promise, which will eventually deliver them from the pressures of the top-down EU bureaucracy that is seen as constraining their lives.

Some chapters trace the transformations of landscapes through sacralizing practices, always fascinating to read, such as the chapter by della Dora on how the landscape is inscribed through the practice of processions. Although such practices seem to create only momentary divisions, they can be likened to the notion of trans-substantiation: a mundane piece of bread becomes the body of

Figures

1.1	Stained glass image of Pio's invisible stigmata experience	28
1.2	Map of Pio sites in Southern Italy	30
1.3	Map of Pio's shrine in San Giovanni Rotondo	32
1.4	The shrine complex as created by Padre Pio	33
1.5	The Casa Sollievo della Sofferenza towering over the shrine complex	33
1.6	National Center for Padre Pio, Barto, PA	37
1.7	The faithful venerate Pio's heart in Boston's Cathedral	38
1.8	Map of the global system of Padre Pio shrines	43
3.1	Pilgrims queue to enter the Santuario	67
3.2	Señor de Esquipulas crucifix on the main altar of the Santuario	73
5.1	Canaanland	105
5.2	The Eagle of Shiloh	107
5.3	The House of Ancestors	109
8.1	Hilltop cross at Holy Land USA (Waterbury, CT)	158
8.2	Garden Tomb replica at the Garden of Hope in Covington, Kentucky	168
8.3	Welcome sign, with city skyline in backdrop	171
8.4	Sermon on the Mount Statue at the Garden of Hope	172
8.5	Jesus weeping at the Garden of Hope	173
9.1	Procession of the miraculous icon of the Mother of God Quick to Hear around the *katholikon* of Docheiariou monastery, Mount Athos	184
9.2	Procession of the miraculous icon of the Mother of God Axion Estin in Karyes, Mount Athos	186
9.3	Route of the procession of the icon of the Mother of God Axion Estin around the village of Karyes, Mount Athos	187
9.4	Engraving of Docheiariou monastery, Mount Athos	189
9.5	General view of Mount Sinai, by anonymous engraver	190
9.6	Reception of the miraculous icon of the Mother of God Quick to Hear outside of the church of Saint George in the village of Sochos, northern Greece	194
9.7	Procession of the miraculous icon of the Mother of God Quick to Hear moving through the village of Sochos	195

9.8	Procession of the miraculous icon of the Mother of God Quick to Hear on the way to Docheiariou's dependency	196
9.9	Procession of the miraculous icon of the Mother of God Quick to Hear approaching Docheiariou's dependency	198
9.10	Procession of the miraculous icon of the Mother of God Quick to Hear approaching Docheiariou's dependency at dusk	199
10.1	A group of American pilgrims at the Mount of Beatitudes	210
10.2	The tomb of Jesus at the Garden Tomb	211
10.3	The Garden of Gethsemane	212
10.4	Communion request form, indicating fourteen individual spots for the use of groups, at the Garden Tomb	214
10.5	The bus parking lot at the Mount of Beatitudes	214
10.6	The Mount of Beatitudes	215

Christ and is ingested. Similarly, landscapes may become something else through the imaginative practices that are material and spatial, but also embodied and lived experientially: the landscape of poverty and the failed state of southwestern Nigeria becomes a landscape of hope, and the certainty of God's fulfillment of his covenant.

Thus, the focus on landscape brings into view the concrete and practical ways the work of the imagination interacts with the given-ness of the world (both human-made and natural) in which Christians find themselves and how these worlds are (partially) remade, materially and in narratives, for themselves and for others to engage with. It is my hope that this volume will inspire researchers to continue tracing how Christianity is enacted spatially and materially.

Kim Knibbe

Introduction

Landscape Processes in the Making of Christianities

Amos S. Ron and James S. Bielo

Christianity is widely reckoned as a scriptural religion and Christians as a "people of the Book." Christians are writers, readers, interpreters, and users of diverse texts—from different biblical canons and translations to prayer books, concordances, tracts, study guides, popular literature, comics, and much more. In this volume, we propose a complementary lens through which to examine the making and changing of Christian identity and community: landscape. How would our comparative understanding of Christianity advance if we focus on Christianity as a territorialized religion of land, and Christians as producers, consumers, preservers, and occupiers of landscapes?

We pose this question in response to the spatial turn in the study of religion. As Knott (2010) outlines, this turn broadly emphasizes the "poetics and politics" of place-making. The former highlights the phenomenological experiences of place, such as dwelling and cultivating "senses of place" (Feld and Basso 1996). A central commitment here is on discovering the affective and meaningful attachments that religious adherents and communities invest in places. The latter highlights the political, economic, and discursive conditions that structure the identification, claiming, shaping, and management of places. A central commitment here is on dynamics of power, and how religious adherents and communities interact with place in ways that create exclusive boundaries and reinforce conflictual social orders. Throughout this volume, contributors engage these emphases not as mutually exclusive alternatives but as mutually defining processes that structure Christian(ized) landscapes.

The chapters collected here engage a central question: How do Christians make relationships with land central to projects of faith? This question does not assume the ontological priority of either nature or culture. It seeks to discover the entangled forms of agency between nature and culture that are at work as Christians produce, consume, experience, imagine, inhabit, manage, and struggle over landscapes. How have the blunt realities of materiality, geography, and ecology shaped Christian territories of belonging and theologies of territory? How have Christians reworked, fashioned, dominated, and coexisted with those blunt realities? And, what social-economic-political conditions engulf these exchanges among religion and nature?

To address these questions, the chapters explore patterns of Christian theological and ideological practice vis-à-vis landscapes, including planning, settling, cultivating, dwelling, gazing, commodifying, destroying, extracting, salvaging, worshiping, memorializing, commemorating, mapping, historicizing, dispossessing, privatizing, and making public. In this introductory chapter, we focus on some foundational touchstones for this reframing of Christianity as a religion of land(s), primarily from the fields of cultural geography and the anthropology of religion. To conclude, we review the chapters to come and their orienting themes: destinations, temporalities, and transformations.

Religion and Landscape: Scholarly Foundations

Geography of Religion: Founding Figures

An established ideology for Christians about the relationship between the Bible and the land of the Bible is that the Holy Land is the fifth gospel. This was perhaps first expressed in the 1860s by Ernest Renan, a French philosopher and scholar of religion:

> To the perusal of documentary evidences I have been able to add an important source of information—the sight of the places where the events occurred.... The striking agreement of the texts with the places, the marvelous harmony of the Gospel ideal with the country which served it as a framework, were like a revelation to me. I had before my eyes a fifth Gospel, torn, but still legible, and henceforward, through the recitals of Matthew and Mark, in place of an abstract being, whose existence might have been doubted, I saw living and moving an admirable human figure. (1863: 22; cf. Rogers 2011; Kaell 2014; Feldman 2016)

Renan's statement can be interpreted as an indication of the significance of the landscape to theologians, and the significance of theology to landscape researchers; unfortunately, for decades the two entities existed mostly separately. Other relationships between the Bible and the land were more informal, based on revelations, visions, apparitions, and emotions. Almost a century after Renan, Pierre Deffontaines, a French human geographer, wrote a thick book called *Géography et Religion* (Deffontaines 1948). His research was perceived by peers as both pioneering and comprehensive, but in the Francophone academic milieu it came to be understood as a "standalone" project that generated minimal interest. The significance of Deffontaines' book is that it changed the "attitude of ignoring" and paved the road for geographers and other social scientists. While other scholars have provided thorough outlines of work in the geography of religion (e.g., Knott 2005), we wish to elaborate on the works of two lesser-known US scholars and on the relationship between religion and geography.

Wilbur Zelinsky

Wilbur Zelinsky (1921–2013) was a prominent cultural geographer from Chicago, who worked mainly in the north and northeast United States. One of his specialties was the geography of religion. His publications included studies of church membership patterns (Zelinsky 1961), cemeteries (Zelinsky 1976), pilgrimages (Zelinsky 1990), the American religious landscape broadly (Zelinsky 2001), and the churchscape more specifically (Zelinsky 2001).

His methodology was more quantitative than qualitative and included data collection and its display in maps and diagrams. For example, in his article on church membership patterns (Zelinsky 1961) he produced thirty maps and five tables that displayed population spread patterns of various religious groups, including twenty-nine Christian denominations, in a given year (1952). As an example, the analysis of the relevant maps clearly identifies the "Bible Belt" (reported members of Baptist bodies, p. 172) and the "Book of Mormon Belt" (reported members of Latter-day Saints, p. 179).

In another project Zelinsky (2001) displayed and analyzed eleven photographs of American religious landscapes (a partial list includes an Islamic bookstore, an African American shop specializing in gospel music, a residential unit converted into a Buddhist temple, a sign showing the way to an otherwise hard-to-find church embedded in a residential neighborhood, and a huge billboard sign suggesting that we need to choose between heaven and hell through Jesus) (Zelinsky 2001). These analyses are more qualitative than the maps' analyses—such thick descriptions and interpretations of photographs as texts were quite common among prominent American cultural geographers, such as Donald Meinig and J. B. Jackson (Ballesta 2016; Meinig 1979).

Richard V. Francaviglia

Richard Francaviglia (b. 1943) is a cultural geographer and historian specializing in the western United States. His numerous publications include studies of

Mormon cultural landscapes (Francaviglia 1969, 1970, 1971a, 1978a, 1978b), cemeteries (Francaviglia 1971b), Catholicism (Treviño and Francaviglia 2007), spiritual geography broadly (Francaviglia 2003), and Mormon sacred cartography (Francaviglia 2015).

Like other geographers, Francaviglia's methods are visual observations in the field itself and mapping. Both methods are considered fundamental among geographers (Stoddard 1982), but Francaviglia's works are also inspired by the qualitative landscape theory known as landscape interpretation (Duncan and Duncan 2010; Ron 1989), and by prominent landscape interpreters, such as J. B. Jackson. For example, in his book *The Mormon Landscape* (1978a), the first chapter provides an introduction to the Mormon landscape by describing a "typical" Mormon village. Francaviglia uses the imaginary community (Canaanville) as a vehicle for describing the Mormon landscape. According to Richard Jackson, "The landscape is described in stereotypes of lombardy poplars, irrigation ditches, block letters on mountainsides, mountain-valley relationships, hay derricks, scripturally based place names, dilapidated fences and farm buildings, wide streets, and unique architectural style for church and home" (Jackson 1979: 441).

This method, of portraying an imaginary community, was used twenty-five years earlier by J. B. Jackson in his classic piece, *The Westward Moving House* (Jackson 1953), but with one fundamental difference. Jackson's imagined family (Nehemia and Submit Tinkham and their six children, in seventeenth-century New England) was very religious during the pioneering days, whereas in later generations they have become secularized. Francaviglia's Canaanville community was very much a reflection of an ongoing Latter-day Saint culture and theology. For example, the very wide roads (132 feet) reflect the civic order inscribed by the prophet Joseph Smith in his city plan to the City of Zion (Eddy 1999: 24).

The research themes developed by Zelinsky and Francaviglia anticipate the eleven chapters to come, but their primary relevance for this volume is several fold. First, this introduction does not introduce only the chapters in this volume, it also aims to introduce the academic and intellectual context of religion and space. Second, by doing so, some of the differences between the geographical and anthropological views regarding space in general, and the religious use of space in particular, will be clarified. Third, the evolution of research methodologies in the context of environment and belief systems will be better understood.

The Spatial Turn and the Cultural Turn

Decades ago, there used to be a very clear distinction, division, and even tension between anthropology and geography (Lins 2019). Anthropologists were researching societies with minimal references to space, while geographers were researching places and spaces (Claval, Alberti, and Scaini 2005; Ellen 1988:230). This polarized situation changed when a number of social science disciplines developed an understanding regarding the relevance of spaces and landscapes: what has come to be called the spatial turn (Knott 2010).

This process gradually led toward a higher degree of interdisciplinary activity and to an understanding among human geographers regarding the relevance of culture and cultural studies: of a need for a cultural turn. As taken up by geographers, this has been a social-intellectual movement that emphasizes the experiential and affective aspects of life. Compared to other approaches in geography, it is more qualitative and interpretive. The following extract is an example of how geographers perceive the cultural turn:

> The cultural turn, which started in the 70s and gathered full momentum in the 90s, relied on an enlarged vision of the forms of causality working in the world: what we discover around us, see and live, does not result only from past or present forms of causality; it reflects the way people dreams their future. The world we observe has been built out of human decisions. People try to shape the environments they live in according to their aspirations: they do not accept it passively. This is the fundamental idea of the cultural approach. (Claval, Alberti, and Scaini 2005: 9)

On the other hand, anthropologist Roy Ellen perceived the cultural turn as follows:

> geography was for a long time a practice without an underlying methodology or philosophy. . . . But perhaps more importantly, the central identifying and epistemological role accorded to *ethnography* has made it possible for anthropologists to define themselves untautologically in terms of what they do. Some geographers too appear to see a similar pragmatic solution to their soul searching through an emphasis on "doing geography." (1988: 230–1)

The importance and relevance of the geographical contribution is the historical context or evolution of methodologies, or in other words, from data collection "the old way" to data collection "the new way." The old way involved data collection which could take place even without meeting people. The new way requires people-oriented methodologies such as participant observation and ethnography.

To conclude, one of the outcomes of this methodological-disciplinary tension and the mutual "search for turns"—both spatial and cultural—is the assimilation of anthropologists and cultural geographers to a degree that nowadays it is difficult to distinguish between anthropological and geographical writing on spatial perspectives and contexts regarding space and religion. Examples for this advanced state of assimilation are evident in the writings of Lily Kong, Nimrod Luz, and Veronica della Dora (geographers) (della Dora, in this volume; Napolitana, Luz, and Stadler 2015; Qian and Kong 2018) and Kim Knott and Simon Coleman (anthropologists) (Knott 2010; Street and Coleman 2012).

Other Academic Traditions and Geography of Religion

Despite the abovementioned scholarship, geography of religion is still a comparatively neglected area of interest. According to Park (2004: 439), "geography rarely appears in books on religion, and religion rarely appears in books on geography." Similarly, Dwyer observes that "re-reading Jackson's (1989) *Maps of Meaning* . . . I was struck by the absence of religion. For cultural geographers writing in the late 1980s religion was studiously avoided, belonging to the traditions of earlier cultural geographies and absent too in the cultural studies of race from which Jackson's new cultural geographies drew inspiration" (2016: 758).

Therefore, it is not surprising that other academic disciplines picked up on this intellectual absence and contributed significantly to the body of knowledge that has developed around space and religion. Anthropologists of religion are primary contributors, and this tradition binds most of the authors in this volume.[1]

Included among the non-geographers that research these issues are pastors and Christian theologians. An interesting example for this category would be Eric Jacobsen's book *Sidewalks in the Kingdom: New Urbanism and the Christian Faith* (2003). The book is defined by one of the reviewers as the intersection of Christianity and urban planning and starting from the first chapter we see the critical approach. In the chapter entitled "Broken Promises: Sprawl and the American Experience," Jacobsen exposes one of the greatest challenges of Christianity in an era of over-size-ness, where people worship in mega-churches that are often located in megalopolises, such as Los Angeles. The promises are individualism, independence, and freedom, and the price for the broken promises is the negative effect on community life, alienation, and the constant and endless moving through spaces of zoning.

Landscape as Process

The chapters in this volume focus on Roman Catholic, evangelical and charismatic Protestant, Mormon, and Eastern Orthodox Christianities in settings ranging from northern New Mexico to northern India. Contributors examine how Christians make relationships with land central to projects of faith. The nature of these relationships oscillates from case to case, and at times within cases, from material to imagined, practical to ideological. Throughout, this volume demonstrates landscape to be a "cultural process" (Tilley and Cameron-Daum 2017: 5): that is, its meaning, function, and materiality can change over time as land forms exist in relationship with practices of human settlement. In particular, five processes are foregrounded in the analyses that follow: sacralization, contestation, relationality, mediation, and accumulation.

First, this volume engages an enduring theme in the interdisciplinary study of landscape and religion, the process of sacralization (e.g., Chidester and Linenthal 1995). Broadly, this refers to the ways in which space becomes sacred space. Sacralization encompasses human engagements with space that are historically formed, collectively managed, and ideologically saturated. While certainly a socially constructed phenomenon with extensive capacity for human agency, the production and maintenance of sacred space is not totally unbound. The socio-historical formation of sacred space always unfolds in relation to the "topography and material character" (Lane 2001: 58) of places, structuring possibilities for human creativity. John Eade's chapter on aquatic infrastructure and the healing waters of Lourdes provides an exemplary case of sacralization as a cultural process. Eade explores how human acts of attempting to control nature are an expression of physically altering landscapes for sacred purposes.

The second process this volume engages is also well established among scholars of landscape: contestation (e.g., Esplin 2018). Landscapes host multiple forms of human presence, meaning-making, and claims to territory over time. As co-present settlements and as remembered histories, the result is that landscapes exist as contested phenomena, illustrations of power dynamics such as dominance, erasure, appropriation, and resistance. In the context of Christian(ized) landscapes, contestation can occur as both an inter- and intra-religious process. The robust scholarship on missionary colonialism is replete with cases of Christian claims to land subverting those of other traditions (e.g., Klassen 2018), while others have amply demonstrated how intensely multiple Christian traditions can compete to claim landscapes (e.g., Bowman 1991). Brett Hendricksen's chapter on the sacred dirt of Chimayó, New Mexico, is a fascinating analysis of how contestation can operate over time. He explores the multiple claims to sacredness in the Chimayó region, from the indigenous Tewa Pueblo sacred geography to the colonial Hispano Catholicism.

Third, this volume engages the cultural process of relationality: that is, the interdependent and coconstitutive ties that develop among places in a contiguous or non-contiguous landscape region. The emphasis here is on how multiple spaces can become linked over time, with the status of spaces themselves and spaces vis-à-vis each other contingent on broader social configurations. Relationality in this sense can operate on micro, meso, and macro scales, possible in both highly localized and thoroughly transnational contexts. As multiple spaces develop relations over time, they can incorporate spaces into related processes of sacralization and contestation. Michael Di Giovine's chapter on the Padre Pio cult, centered on a series of Italian Catholic pilgrimage shrines but resonant globally, addresses this process directly. He argues that a shifting relationality among core and periphery shrines develops over time, shaping local geographies and global imaginaries.

The fourth process that this volume engages centers on the potential for landscape to be mobilized as theological media. In step with the media turn in the study of religion, this process fits among the myriad of other ways in which different material and sensory channels mediate religious experience, communication, and learning (Engelke 2010). Religious actors use materiality—from landscapes to objects, architecture, and human sensory capacities—to address the fundamental problems that animate their religious traditions, such as authority, belonging, and spiritual intimacy. Joseph Webster's chapter on a Brethren fishing community in northeast Scotland illustrates how immediate and distant landscapes can be used to mediate theological commitments, namely an apocalyptic future time. The Brethren we meet through his ethnography integrate local seascapes and the biblicized landscape of contemporary Israel-Palestine into their vision of how the world will end and eternity will commence.

Finally, this volume engages a cultural process wherein landscapes work as palimpsests for local communities (Mitchell 2020). This process recognizes a significant fact about place-making over time more generally, which is that social action and its residues accumulate over time in place (Badone 2007). Places accrue objects, stories, rituals, labor, and discourses as human settlements come, develop, stay, go, and return. This process of accumulation both leaves traces and is prone to erasures and elisions, as competing narratives and narrators emerge. Veronica della Dora provides a compelling case of how the process of landscape palimpsest can work in her chapter, as she analyzes Eastern Orthodox rituality over time at the Greek monastery at Mount Athos.

Introduction 9

Volume Overview

The volume's core chapters are arranged in three parts: "Destinations," "Temporalities," and "Transformations." The parts reflect this volume's orientation that landscape exists as a dynamic, often contested, cultural process and, each in their own way, engage the five particular processes outlined in the previous paragraphs.

In Part I, "Destinations," contributors examine case studies in which particular places have become focused sites of Christian travel, devotion, and pedagogy. Engaging core issues in the interdisciplinary study of tourism and pilgrimage, these chapters advance the effort to conceptualize Christianity as a religion of land by highlighting how processes of change and contestation are central to managing attachments to landscape over time.

Michael Di Giovine's chapter, "Galactic Shrines and the Catholic Cult of St. Padre Pio of Pietrelcina," deals with Catholic shrines that have life histories that see their influence and importance ascend and descend over time, in contraposition with that of other, competing cult centers. Such a phenomenon challenges the dominant, Weberian understanding of Vatican organization as bureaucratic and hierarchical when it pertains to pilgrimage destinations. Drawing on anthropologist Stanley Tambiah's concept of "galactic polities" in the Buddhist kingdoms of Southeast Asia, this chapter argues that the global landscape of popular Catholicism is better conceived of as existing in overlapping systems of "galactic shrines" organized around a core power center and more peripheral, satellite shrines that orbit it. Based on long-term ethnographic research at pilgrimage sites associated with twentieth-century Catholic stigmatic and saint Padre Pio of Pietrelcina—who is considered by many as "the Catholic world's most popular saint"—the chapter traces the development of Pio's shrine of San Giovanni Rotondo as a devotional center from a peripheral satellite of a major medieval cult center to a dominant center in its own right, drawing satellites from Europe (primarily Italy and Ireland), Asia (especially the Philippines and Singapore), and the Americas (especially eastern United States and Canada). Toward the end, the chapter offers a more cartographic and sociopolitical model for understanding the pressures pilgrimage site managers must negotiate to remain relevant in the ever-shifting sacred landscape of global Catholicism.

John Eade's chapter, "Sacralizing the Landscape: Water and the Development of a Pilgrimage Shrine," examines the case of Lourdes, France: one of the most highly visited Roman Catholic shrines in the world. Emerging during the nineteenth century, its fame for "miraculous" healing also spread around the world with replications of the grotto in Africa, Latin America, North America, and even within the Vatican. The process of bathing in the spring water associated with these miracles became highly regulated and concealed from public view. Moreover, the grotto and other key sites within the sanctuary have been gradually domesticated leaving few reminders of the original "wild" place beyond the old town. While procedures associated with healing the physical body became privatized, rituals celebrating the healing of social bodies were highly public and were facilitated by the drastic reordering of the landscape. Although a clear physical boundary was quickly established between the sanctuary and the rapidly growing "pilgrim town" outside that boundary, these two areas of Lourdes were intimately tied together through the same process of domesticating the landscape. The sacred and the secular were interdependent, and this interdependence was expressed through the physical changes taking place within this Marian healing shrine from the nineteenth century to the present day.

Brett Hendrickson's chapter, "Crucifix and Dirt: Catholic and Indigenous Origins of the Holy Earth of the Santuario de Chimayó," explores one of North America's most popular Catholic shrines in northern New Mexico, the Santuario de Chimayó. Since its completion in 1816, visitors to the church have processed down its nave, gazed upon the Cristo de Esquipulas behind the altar, and turned left to enter a low-slung room that features a small hole in the floor. The faithful believe that dirt from the hole has miraculous healing properties, and they rub it on their bodies and occasionally ingest it. Today, hundreds of thousands of pilgrims and visitors extract tons of dirt from the site every year, which is replenished continuously by Santuario staff. This chapter traces the origins of this unique and popular devotion, with particular focus on two narrative elements: the prevalence of holy earth and geography in Esquipulas, Guatemala, where the crucifix which is replicated in Chimayó originated, and on the stories of miraculous mud that Tewa Pueblo people ascribe to the area of Chimayó itself. The chapter argues that these relatively well-known origin stories for the Santuario's holy dirt have been strategically managed by various constituencies to either promote or downplay the Santuario's status as a Catholic Church as well as a spiritual hub for health-seekers and devotees of alternative and holistic medicine. The interplay of indigenous and Christian origins at the Santuario provides a dynamic narrative setting for visitors of every stripe.

Sara Patterson's chapter, "Captivating Landscapes: Gender and Religion in Mormon Captivity Narratives," compares two memoirs of Mormon women who narrate an escape from oppressive patriarchal religion. The first, written by Ann Eliza Webb Young in the late nineteenth century, presents a critique of Mormon polygamy based on the experiences of a former wife to prophetic figure Brigham Young. The second, written by Elizabeth Smart in 2013, recounts Smart's abduction, suffering, and escape when she was a teenager in 2002–3. Smart's family were mainline Latter-day Saints (LDS) members in Salt Lake City, while her abductors were outcast fundamentalist Mormons driven by apocalyptic visions. In both accounts, the imagined and ideological landscape of the frontier American West played a pivotal role in how the authors narrated their respective journeys into and out of moral and spiritual danger.

In Part II, "Temporalities," contributors explore case studies in which Christian communities make land integral to relations with time, using land (and sea) to imagine past, present, and future conditions. Moving across scriptural, national, and political temporalities, these chapters advance the effort to conceptualize Christianity as a religion of land by keeping space-time welded as a single experiential category.

In their co-authored chapter, "From the Messiah's Glade to the Gods' Mountains: Christian Landscapes of Africa and Asia," Jonathan Miles-Watson and Sitna Quiroz build a dialog about two sacred landscapes based on their respective fieldwork. The authors present and contrast accounts of two sites of Christian "pilgrimage" and the communities that shape/inhabit them: Christ Church Cathedral, located in the Indian Himalayas, and Faith Tabernacle Church, located in Nigeria, West Africa. Taking landscape as a verb (cf. Ingold 2000) they argue that the landscapes of Christ Church and Faith Tabernacle Church are powerful sites of becoming that maintain their relevance because of the traumas of history. Special attention is paid to the way that these landscapes are engaged with and remade by the postcolonial pilgrims who flow over and knot around them, making them at the same time as they are made by them. Through this consideration, they seek to demonstrate the way contemporary Christian pilgrims (in these distinct regions) engage with shared myths, local, historical expressions of worship, and contemporary political agendas. The distinct strategies that are taken for reckoning with Christian landscapes in the region are united by a shared concern with collapsing three time periods into the present landscape: postcolonial (Christian: own), colonial (Christian: other), and pre-colonial mythic (Christian and non-Christian) action. In this chapter, they aim to reconfigure the debate, pointing to the possibility of an anthropology of Christianity that operates from a phenomenological, inductive basis and in so doing rethinks the boundaries of both academic and "popular" discourses.

Joseph Webster's chapter, "Geography as Eschatology: Moral Freedom and Prophecy Fulfillment on Land and at Sea," reflects upon fieldwork among Brethren deep sea fishermen in Gamrie, NE Scotland. He explores how two sources of authority—biblical apocalyptic prophecy and the agentive acts of individual Christians—came to be located within and constituted by their experience of geography. More specifically, by using the term "eschatological agency," this chapter considers how local Christian fishermen placed themselves at the center of "end-times" events by first reading and then fulfilling such prophecy within the materiality of different landscapes and seascapes. How, in this context, are we to understand what it means to be a moral actor or a free agent? These questions are made more complex still by attending to the ways in which Gamrie's Christian fisher-families obfuscated their own agency by attributing all human actions to either God or the devil, while at the same time working tirelessly to identify and enact various "signs of the times" that collectively evidenced the nearness of the end of the world. Here, "self-fulfilling prophecy" is given a new double meaning; it creates not only the semiotic conditions necessary for its own apocalyptic realization but also the geographical conditions necessary for the apocalyptic realization of the Brethren self and community, for example, in afforestation, or in stormy seas. This chapter offers an ethnographic sketch of that self and community in relation to material place and space, and, in so doing, attempts to query recent anthropological pairings of freedom and morality through a re-examination of the notion of authority.

Rebekka King's chapter, "Imagining an Ethnic Ecumene: Evangelical Landscapes as Gentile, Jewish, and Native in the American South," explores real and imagined landscapes in the social lives of Jewish Affinity Christians. She examines the case study of the relationship between an evangelical congregation in rural Tennessee and a Messianic rabbi, Larry Mallet, from Oklahoma, who promotes a version of the Prosperity Gospel which forges a new Christian identity that is simultaneously Jewish, Gentile, and Native American, with Jewish and Native American identities privileged for what is perceived to be their cultural antiquity, uncontaminated spirituality, and their respective claims to being original inhabitants of Israel and North America. Based on ethnographic fieldwork in both Tennessee and Oklahoma, she discusses the ways that Jewish and indigenous religio-ethnic landscapes are extrapolated into an evangelical Christian imaginary and made accessible through a focus on their absence, exoticism, and lack of familiarity. Furthermore, she sees at work a form of deterritorialization in which Christian American spaces gain authenticity by virtue of their failure to resemble Jewish and indigenous ones. She further argues that this process is as much about economic concerns as spiritual ones. The amalgamation of a Prosperity Gospel which purports to reverse their current economic situation and yield unexpected financial capital is accompanied by a new, hybrid variety of Christianity which is compounded with a spiritual capital that is simultaneously local and translocal, distant and proximate, and immediate and eternal.

In Part III, "Transformations," contributors explore case studies in which we find Christians immersed in projects of asserting and reframing relationships with nature. Through analyzing ritual practices of dwelling, touring, narrating, and replicating, these chapters advance the effort to conceptualize Christianity as a religion of land by examining how Christians define and negotiate tradition by imagining and transforming lands.

James Bielo's chapter, "Landscape as Expressive Resource in Materializing the Bible," deals with the ways in which the material and symbolic affordances of local landscapes are mobilized as an expressive resource in contexts of Christian tourism. Throughout the world there are hundreds of sites that materialize the Bible: that is, represent written scripture as experiential, choreographed environments. He examines how landscape features are used to bolster the performative ambitions of these sites. Drawing on multiple examples, from diverse Christian traditions, he explores how local geographies are mobilized, how land forms are reshaped by built environments, and how landscape elements are imported and integrated into sites. Ultimately, he argues that features of landscape function as a powerful expressive resource for Christian projects that promise access to the biblical past through material environments.

Veronica della Dora's chapter, "When Mountains Move: Athonite Processions, Sacred Performance, and Overlapping Topographies," elaborates on the tension between the macro-scale of global redemption and the micro-scale of the sites in which biblical events took place. Alongside these sites, a number of non-biblical places have long constelled the sacred geographies of various Christian denominations. Holy mountains are the most characteristic topographic features of Byzantine spiritual culture. Mount Athos, a peninsula culminating in a 2,033-meter peak, was the first Byzantine holy mountain to be established in Greece. It was also the most isolated and hardest to reach. Described as "the Holy Mountain" par excellence since the mid-tenth century, Athos is the only surviving Byzantine holy mountain to have experienced uninterrupted occupation to our days, and, with its twenty monasteries and a population of nearly 2,000 monks, it is currently the largest monastic community in the Orthodox world. Its survival has been ascribed to its seclusion and to its ability to control external forces. Yet, as with other holy mountains and famous Christian holy sites, Athos has always transcended its physical boundaries. This chapter focuses on *litaneies,* or open-air processions performed by Athonite monks on major liturgical feasts, or as part of special petitions (e.g., relief from a drought). Recorded since the tenth century, *litaneies* on Mount Athos have been closely intertwined with the topography of the peninsula. Some monasteries, however, periodically also hold processions in their dependencies outside of the peninsula. By replicating the practice outside of Athos and adjusting it to new topographies, the Holy Mountain is transposed outside of its physical boundaries, even for a day. Athonite *litaneies* can thus be interpreted as mobile intersections between different scales. In bringing the church outside of its walls and Mount Athos outside of its perimeter, they temporarily turn villages into churches, hills into holy mountains, and the earth itself into a cosmic temple.

Finally, Amos Ron's chapter, "The Garden of Eden in an Era of Over-Tourism: (Managing) New Testament Sacred Groves in the Holy Land," examines the ambiguous and ambivalent view of gardens in Christianity. On the one hand, the garden is the origin of what is good and godly and represents an oasis at the heart of the spiritual and physical desert that surrounds us; on the other hand, the garden is full of temptations, contrary to the wilderness, which is pure and metaphorically speaking, this is where the true garden lies. Historically, both approaches have left their mark on the landscapes of Christianity. This chapter elaborates on the first approach and highlights three contemporary sacred groves in the Holy Land: the Mt. of Beatitudes, the Garden of Gethsemane, and the Garden Tomb. The chapter will interpret the "gardenscape'" of the three sacred groves and will elaborate on these sites on two different levels of reference: the instrumental-tangible level, as pilgrimage centers in an era of over-tourism, and the symbolic-intangible level, as centers of meaning for Christian individuals and denominations.

Conclusion

From physical altering land forms (Eade) to creating imagined connections between distant lands (King, Webster), this volume examines how Christians make relationships with land(s) central to projects of faith. "Landscape" can take diverse forms and be named in diverse ways, and the expressions presented here—from gardens to mountains to dirt to seas—only graze the myriad possibilities. In organizing this collection, our ambition has not been to create an encyclopedia of Christian(ized) landscapes but to help establish an approach that makes *landscape* a central category for the comparative study of Christianity.

Given the scope of this ambition, there are many opportunities for scholars to take up this call and develop this framework further. Following the model set by Hendrickson (this volume), scholars working ethnographically and historically are inspired to trace forms of belonging and assertions of ownership over time, drawing out the entanglements of power and meaning that shape contested and changing landscapes (cf. Farmer 2010). Interdisciplinary scholars seeking to explore the ways in which religious architecture is built out of, into, and in spite of local landscapes can take inspiration from the chapters by Bielo, Eade, Miles-Watson and Quiroz, and Ron (cf. Carter 2015; Grubiak 2020). Numerous chapters examine cases of pilgrimage and religious tourism (Di Giovine, Eade, Hendrickson, Bielo, and Ron), highlighting a promising intersection where other scholars may expand on how landscapes are imagined, altered, and inhabited in the production of pilgrimage routes and centers (cf. Maddrell et al. 2014).

Why landscape? Each in their own way, contributors address this question by illuminating the rich engagements that develop between Christians and land(s). Throughout, we find landscapes to be potent and active resources in and for Christian communities, never merely an empty stage. The geopolitical histories and materialities of landscapes help shape the contours of local Christian life, irrespective of physical location or if "land" is much discussed within the Christian community. This volume invites readers to grapple with an argument that there is an enduring dynamic between religion and land: in short, that lived Christianity is always constituted in and through landscapes.

Part One

Destinations

1

Galactic shrines and the Catholic Cult of St. Padre Pio of Pietrelcina

Michael A. Di Giovine

On March 17, 2018, Pope Francis made his first papal visit to the major Italian pilgrimage sites associated with St. Padre Pio of Pietrelcina (1887–1968)—a once polarizing, yet extremely popular, figure in modern-day Catholicism. Born Francesco Forgione in the small Southern Italian town of Pietrelcina, Pio was a highly ascetic Capuchin friar whose ministry spanned the end of the First World War through the culmination of the Second Vatican Council (Vatican II). Pio was thought to be a living saint by the tens of thousands who annually flocked to him at his friary in San Giovanni Rotondo, thanks to the stigmata he bore for fifty years—bleeding wounds of Christ's crucifixion on his hands, feet, and side—as well as his otherworldly visions, supernatural power of bilocation (of being in two places at once), and his famously honest and oft-gruff behavior in the confessional; he was said to have known people's transgressions before they confessed them and would cast out those who omitted them without absolution. Pio's cult grew after his death in 1968, thanks to the mobilization of a network of prayer groups operated through the cutting-edge research hospital he founded with the many ex-voto donations he received from the faithful. Despite the Vatican's notoriously ambivalent stance toward Pio that resulted in him twice being barred from publicly celebrating the Eucharist, he was canonized by Pope St. John Paul II, a devotee, in 2002. Known today as the "Catholic world's most popular saint"—to whom Italians and Irish pray more than to Jesus, Mary, or St. Francis (Bobbio 2006; Keane 2008: 200)—Pio is at the center of a worldwide cult whose power radiates out of Italy and into Southeast Asia (particularly the Philippines), North and South America, and sub-Saharan West Africa.

Pope Francis' half-day visit in March 2018 began early in the morning at Pio's farmhouse in Piana Romana, the countryside outside of Pietrelcina, where the saint had experienced childhood visions of Jesus, Mary, and his guardian angel, and suffered what has been known as the "invisible stigmata": painful red welts on his hands and feet. After praying an hour in the small chapel built over the site where Pio received the invisible stigmata, Pope Francis then proceeded directly by helicopter 132 kilometers west to San Giovanni Rotondo atop the forbidding Gargano Peninsula to venerate Pio's body and then to celebrate a papal Mass in the Basilica of St. Pio, a hotly contested modernist mega-church designed by famed architect Renzo Piano, which briefly held the body of the saint. By 2:00 p.m., the pope was back at home in Vatican City, some 380 kilometers away.

The brief papal "pilgrimage" (Bosco 2018) was exceptional on many levels: it was done to commemorate both the hundredth anniversary of Pio's stigmata and the fiftieth anniversary of Pio's death, it was Francis' first visit to Pio's shrine at San Giovanni Rotondo, and it was the first time a sitting pontiff visited Pio's hometown. However, from a geographic standpoint, Francis' visit is also notable for what was left out. Flying from one site to another, Francis did not stop at numerous Catholic shrines and pilgrimage sites; his was a precision-oriented visit, pinpointing a select set of Pio-specific places that he deemed most important. Francis also eschewed a stop at Monte Sant'Angelo, an immensely historic shrine that played a major role in the Christianization of Europe in Late Antiquity and was a pilgrimage hub for devotees and Crusaders in the Middle Ages, and which is now a UNESCO-designed World Heritage site. Emanating a dark and mysterious air, the shrine was built into a cave supposedly on the orders of St. Michael the Archangel himself, and to this day remains one of the only churches never to have been consecrated by a bishop (Accrocca and Curto 2008: 73). The sanctuary was considered so sacred in medieval times that St. Francis of Assisi—Pope Francis' namesake—deemed himself unworthy of setting foot inside (120–5). In that era, San Giovanni Rotondo was nothing more than a shepherd's outpost, a small settlement named after its sole church, a circular edifice ("Rotondo") that scholars believe was originally dedicated to the Roman god Jove ("Giove" = "Giovanni").

Lying 27 kilometers outside of San Giovanni Rotondo, Monte Sant'Angelo is literally the next town over from Pio's shrine and a common half-day excursion for international pilgrims (particularly from Ireland) overnighting in San Giovanni Rotondo. Yet despite its historical importance, integration on international pilgrimage itineraries, and proximity to Pio's shrine, only 9 percent of the visitors to San Giovanni Rotondo are from Monte Sant'Angelo. According to 2016 statistics, while San Giovanni Rotondo welcomes around 250,000 pilgrims a year, Monte Sant'Angelo counts 21,809; this is a significant downturn from 6 million pilgrims who flocked to Pio's shrine during the tumultuous years of the saint's exhumation, exhibition, and interment in the Basilica (2008–10) of which St. Michael's church saw but 65,000 during the same period (Anon 2017).

How can one explain the shift in power and importance between Monte Sant'Angelo and San Giovanni Rotondo over the centuries? At first glance, the answer may seem simple: saints to whom these pilgrimage centers refer are social beings, created for people other than themselves (Delooz 1983: 199), and, as such, have life histories of their own; they ascend and descend in favor and in power over time. And this may certainly be true; one can think of numerous local saints' shrines in Italy alone that were active centers of devotion, but yet have waned in visitation. In Pio's time, for example, pilgrimages to an image of a "black Madonna" at Montevirgine outside the provincial capital of Avellino and to the relics of San Pellegrino in Altavilla Irpina were immensely popular—Pio himself had been to the latter as a boy (Ruffin 1991: 33)—but today have fallen out of favor, ironically, as contemporary pilgrims prefer to travel to Pietrelcina or San Giovanni Rotondo. Yet unlike San Pellegrino, who is a rather localized saint in a particular part of Italy, St. Michael continues to be popular across the world. He is one of those relatively rare universal, "doctrinal" saints that theologically and culturally transcends distinct locales (see Catechism 330-1, Mt. 18:10). Indeed, if the proliferation of names after popular saints is also indicative of the saint's power (see Wilson 1983: 14–15; Hertz 1983: 84), then this is also the case; variations on "Michael" remain a popular choice for newborns (Anon 2019).

In this chapter, I argue that we must look not only at pilgrimage visitation numbers but at the political organization and juxtaposition of the shrines themselves to understand how they gain and lose significance over time. Like the saints to whom they are dedicated, Catholic shrines also have life histories that see their influence and importance ascend and descend over time, in contraposition with that of other, competing cult centers. Furthermore, as I will show through the example of San Giovanni Rotondo, these shrines also tend to exert differential influence over other holy sites, and, in an effort to stave off hagiographic entropy that ultimately could foster their downfall, site managers often look to expand their reach, simultaneously creating satellite shrines and co-opting holy sites under the influence of other devotional centers. To understand this, I draw on anthropologist Stanley Tambiah's concept of "galactic polities" in the Buddhist kingdoms of Southeast Asia to argue that the global landscape of popular Catholicism may be better conceived of as overlapping systems of sanctuaries organized around core power centers and more peripheral, satellite shrines that orbit them. Dynamic and relational, these "galactic shrines" shift in composition over time as the devotional center integrates or loses power over peripheral satellite shrines. Based on long-term ethnographic research at Padre Pio devotional centers in Europe and the United States, this chapter ultimately offers an integrative ethno-historical and geopolitical model for understanding the interconnectedness and relationality of saints' shrines in modern-day Catholicism.

Conceptualizing "Galactic" Political Organization

The concept of "galactic polity" was introduced by the great scholar of Buddhist religion, politics, and culture and anthropologist Stanley Jeyaraja Tambiah, as a model for understanding traditional Southeast Asian geopolitical organization. Inspired by the *mandala*—a repetitive geometric design consisting of a core and concentric enclosing elements, which is a key symbol in many branches of Hinduism and Buddhism—Tambiah envisioned the galactic polity to be a composite or "totalizing" topographical, cosmological, and political-economic system in which satellite states surround, and are linked in varying strengths to, a core political entity (Tambiah 1976: 69). Mandalas, Tambiah points out, can be roughly translated as "galaxy" in the Indo-Tibetan tradition; they at once symbolize the arrangement of the human body, of consciousness and associated mental phenomena, of the cosmos, and of the kingdom (69). Like the Milky Way, or even our solar system, the galactic polity is organized into a series of concentric circles: at the center is the capital and the area under the authority's direct control; it is surrounded by vassal provinces ruled or overseen by princes or governors from the center; and these are themselves surrounded by more independent tributary entities. Each satellite is autonomous, yet it replicates the center in organizational and ritual forms; and each is increasingly more independent the farther from the center it lies. Just as our solar system consists of a gravitational axis—the sun—around which planets and their satellite moons revolve, so too are the polities in Tambiah's galactic model tied together through a type of centripetal force (79). But mandalas also symbolize the paradoxes of daily life: while they may seem stable—organized as they are around a defined core—such stability is illusory; each individual satellite is susceptible to outside influence and the centripetal forces of other nearby systems (see Dellios 2003: 4).

Tambiah's concept emerged at a time in which World Systems Theory—a model of the economic interconnectedness of global systems consisting of a core colonial power and peripheral/semi-peripheral vassals (Wallerstein 1974)—grew in increasing favor in anthropology. Yet as Robinson and Lechner point out

(1985), World Systems Theory may not adequately take into account the complex role of culture and cultural responses to colonialism. Tambiah's model, while nevertheless presenting a generalized view, was informed by ethnography and a close reading of history, and pushed back on reductionist thought. A galactic polity is a totalization of politics and economics, of myth and cosmology, and of topography and geography. More importantly, it challenged the dominant Weberian view of bureaucratic political organization that emanates from the top down (Tambiah 1977: 79), as well as territorial definitions of nation-state. While Sino-Western states are defined by geographic borders, the galactic polity is defined by its center, see boundaries as more fluid, and can be made up of a number of other entities that pay tribute to the central authority without being integrated into its administrative bureaucracy (Dellios 2003: 2). They do not keep the system together exclusively through exercises of power, then, but rather through symbolic mechanisms.

Represented as a centripetal force, the glue of this system is a series of cosmological, mythological, and ritual symbols intended to bond periphery to core. Symbolically, the center ideologically represents the totality of the system and embodies the unity of the whole; this is conveyed through its architecture and architectonics, as well as the central rituals of the polity, which "in a ripple effect" are replicated by the provincial centers on a diminishing scale (Tambiah 1976: 79). As they extend farther from the center, they will replicate less and less the center's symbols and ideologies. Change is therefore built into this model, and the system is in near-constant flux—either in the midst of strengthening its pull and adding more satellites to the system or loosening its hold on them and risking loss and even disintegration. This depends on the charismatic power of the central authority, how faithfully the rituals are carried out in the provinces, and how closely the satellites continue to replicate the center. Thus, galactic polities take on what Michael Fischer calls a "snow-flaky" dynamic: they are "ephemeral, loose, disappearing, with new ones constantly forming" (2013: 243; see also Dellios 2003: 4).

Elements of Galactic Shrines

We can already see how the Vatican fits in here. The Holy See was a recognized political entity by the Middle Ages. Even before the 1929 Lateran Treaty, which created Vatican City as an independent city-state within the Republic of Italy, it has possessed defined political borders and armies to defend them. Yet in actuality its political power extends far beyond any temporal boundaries through its network of bishoprics, its parishes and local religious organizations, and sacred sites and authorized shrines (including basilicas, which are technically Vatican territory) that replicate the worldviews, theological narratives, and rituals of the Vatican despite their embeddedness in vastly different nation-states throughout the world today. Bound together through a common liturgy, and through a bureaucracy led by local bishops invested with symbolic power that replicates that of the pontiff, the Bishop of Rome, these geographic entities create a galactic political organization that radiates its power out across the world, mapped onto a global landscape of traditionally bounded nation-states. If the Catholic world can be conceived of as the Milky Way, and the Vatican its center, then individual networks of shrines within a particular saint's cult can each be considered a solar system: they replicate the Vatican in form and function, and have their own satellites—individual worlds themselves—that are linked to them.

The galactic concept lends itself well to understanding the interconnectedness of Catholic shrines, though curiously Tambiah (2013) wrote on comparative saints' cults but did not link the two. First, anthropological theory has long asserted the paradoxical core-periphery nature of pilgrimage sites. While on the temporal plane Catholic shrines often lie at the geographic periphery of the society's political center (Turner 1973), ontologically they are seen as the true center, or axis mundi, of the social world—a place where cosmological perfection "irrupts" into the chaos of humankind's existence (Eliade 1959). Thus, while pilgrimage is inherently social—it is a collective and repetitive movement toward the sacred—and therefore is frequently built on, and induced by, contested narratives and behaviors (Eade and Sallnow 1991), it nevertheless often creates an anti-structural sensation of *communitas* that temporarily enables participants to transcend the divisive baggage of social life as dictated and symbolized by the center (Turner 1973; Turner and Turner 1978; Di Giovine 2011). Even when this so-called spontaneous communitas does not necessarily occur, both spiritual leaders and the pilgrims themselves at the shrines explicitly seek to rhetorically and performatively harness the anti-structural nature of pilgrimage (Di Giovine 2013), at least in ideology if not also normatively (see Turner 1969).

Tensions are inherent in the system. These tensions are not simply between sacred and profane but also between bounded geographic authority and diffuse sacred power—a phenomenon that is quite complex given the historical reality that Catholic shrines play a temporal, as well as spiritual, role in Catholic life. This blurring of the boundaries between sacred and profane creates, on the one hand, the imposition of the profane on the sacred; Turner points out that "spontaneous communitas," which bubbles up in the collective effervescence of pilgrimage, often becomes enshrined in ideology and norms (Turner 1969) when it is coopted by the efforts of religious authorities who wield temporal spiritual power. Indeed, officially recognized shrines—dedicated to officially recognized saints—are themselves as exertion of authorized control from a central power over the potentially destabilizing practices of popular religion (see Badone 1990).

Second, although they may officially be organized around a central authority, shrines nevertheless continue to maintain a certain level of autonomy of their own. They have their own managers, though often they are answerable to higher-up representatives of the center, such as bishops and Provincials. Sometimes pilgrims visit them on their own accord, and therefore they build up their own set of prescribed practices; sometimes they are seen as complementary to other shrines with greater appeal, share in common rituals and worldviews, and are visited together on a common pilgrimage itinerary. These all, in turn, ultimately revolve around the most central authority—the Vatican—and do replicate symbols and ritual forms of the Holy See, but the power it wields, particularly in this contemporary era, is not coercive. Rather, they are bound through the centripetal force of the center, as played out by the pilgrims who, espousing religious imaginaries of the saint and the place (Di Giovine 2014; Salazar and Graburn 2014), are often drawn to them en masse.

Third, the glue that binds these shrines together are the symbolic narratives, images, and rituals that outline a common cosmology, and "accrete rich superstructures" of mythological representations (Turner and Turner 1978: 23). Pilgrimage sites emerge from very local movements; they have their own local histories and play roles in the local sociocultural, political, and economic milieus. Yet as they grow in power and prestige, moving closer to the core of a cult, they assume more regional, national, and even international import, and the devotional culture associated with it becomes more generalized, more like the center. But conversely, local, peripheral shrines may fall under the influence of other cult centers as these sanctuaries assume narratives and rituals that may serve to incorporate the minor shrine into its cosmology. This phenomenon is what occurred between Monte Sant'Angelo and San Giovanni Rotondo: while the former was at the center of a galactic organization of shrines dedicated to St. Michael in the Middle Ages, the ascendency of Padre Pio's shrine had not only eclipsed Monte Sant'Angelo but increasingly coopted it as part of a Pio-centric hagiography that posited that the twentieth-century saint as a devotee to St. Michael. Today, images of St. Michael as they are portrayed at Monte

Sant'Angelo are everywhere in San Giovanni Rotondo, and, likewise, images of Pio are ubiquitous at St. Michael's shrine (including in the souvenirs sold). And replicating a common story that Pio entreated devotees to go to Monte Sant'Angelo in penance for their sins, today many pilgrim groups come from Pio's shrine for a quick visit and Mass at St. Michael's cave church.

Padre Pio Pilgrimage Sites as Galactic Shrines

It is argued here that the pilgrimage sites dedicated to Padre Pio are organized into a system that I call "galactic shrines," in much the same way the Southeast Asian polities—and the Holy See itself—were arranged. In this system, the center is the shrine-town of San Giovanni Rotondo—the place in which Pio lived for his entire fifty-year ministry; it is the site of his stigmata, his burial place, and central shrine, and the headquarters of both his powerful network of global prayer groups and a multi-million-dollar media empire that diffuses his cult across the world. Under its political and religious influence are a number of localized shrines associated with Pio that are increasingly more autonomous in nature the farther from the center they lie, yet are tied to San Giovanni Rotondo in their replication of the center's worldview, narratives, and rituals. These processes represent the "centripetal force" of the galactic shrine system, which developed over time in a historical process that ultimately saw San Giovanni Rotondo attain primacy within the cult itself, and able to exert its influence onto sometimes oft-competing narratives and views of Pio, his life history, and his legacy. This system developed in three stages: (1) the emergence of a landscape of sites directly connected to Pio's youth before he moved to San Giovanni Rotondo in 1918, never to leave again; (2) the development of San Giovanni Rotondo during Pio's lifetime; (3) San Giovanni's ascendency to power as the center of a saint's cult and the creation of new shrines outside of Italy.

Toward the Creation of a Landscape of Galactic Shrines: The Emergence of Sites Associated with Pio's Youth (1887–1918)

The landscape of Padre Pio shrines in Southern Italy is primarily composed of those historical sites in which Pio visited in the years leading up to his stigmata experience in 1918. The anchor in this landscape is undoubtedly Pietrelcina, the small village outside the provincial capital city of Benevento, in which Pio was born and raised, convalesced in many periods of illness, and hosted several of Pio's core followers. From about age five, Pio saw visions of Jesus, the Virgin Mary, and his guardian angel, and experienced violent torments by the devil in his hometown of Pietrelcina. It was also at this time that a young, bearded friar from a nearby Capuchin monastery would systematically roam the countryside begging for alms and distributing religious medals and candy to the local children. This left an impression on Pio, who wanted to join the ascetic order and become a "friar with a beard" (Ruffin 1991: 35). His father and brother made multiple long-term trips to the United States for work to raise money for Pio's education, and when he was of age, he entered into the Capuchin friary in Morcone, about 30 kilometers outside of Pietrelcina. It was here that, despite dedication and promise, Pio fell inexplicably ill; this chronic illness would threaten his ability to complete his formation, as he would be sent home to Pietrelcina to recover, only to fall ill when he entered a different friary. In the span of three years, from 1907 to 1910, he was sent to San Egidio di Montefusco, Campobasso, Gesualdo, and visited doctors in Naples whose diagnoses ranged from tuberculosis to neuroses. Because this constant back and forth threatened his formation, and it was assumed he would not ultimately survive the illness, his spiritual advisor, Padre Benedetto, arranged for him to be ordained in the cathedral of Benevento, 12 kilometers from Pietrelcina, on August 10, 1910. Pio subsequently celebrated his first Mass in Pietrelcina's main church, and, in autumn of that year, received what hagiographers call the "invisible stigmata" while praying under an elm tree at his family's farmhouse in Piana Romana; he experienced a vision of Jesus and Mary that left him with "fiery red spots in the palms of my hands, accompanied by extremely sharp pains that lasted several days" (Raffaele da S. Elia a Pianisi 1967[1978]: 358) (Figure 1.1).

When the invisible stigmata seemed to recede a year later, in 1911 Pio was sent to a monastery in Venafro, where he fell sick again; both his Capuchin advisor at Venafro and an outside psychiatrist would observe him engaging in mystical ecstasies (see Di Flumeri 1977: 80). He was again sent back to Pietrelcina to convalesce, where he produced a rich series of letters from his studio in a little tower (*la torretta*) near his family's home (see Pio da Pietrelcina 2008a); then he was sent onto the friary of Sant'Anna in Foggia and to San Giovanni Rotondo in 1916 before he was drafted into military service in the First World War. Although priests often served as chaplains, he was drafted as a cleric-soldier and made to don a uniform, but because of his illness was moved between barracks in Caserta and Naples before being discharged. In 1918, he was sent to San Giovanni Rotondo, never to leave again.

Figure 1.1 Stained glass image of Pio's invisible stigmata experience, Santa Maria degli Angeli, Pietrelcina. Photograph by the author.

On the official website of Pio's cult, produced through the Capuchin Order at the friary-cum-sanctuary at San Giovanni Rotondo, all of these places are listed simply as "the other sites" (*gli altri luoghi*) of Padre Pio, with only a few lines of description given for each (Frati Minori Cappuccini n.d.). This minimizes the individual spiritual value of these places in favor of San Giovanni Rotondo, which would quickly become the center of this galactic organization. Apart from Pietrelcina and Piana Romana, these sites are all minor pilgrimage destinations; while they are directly connected with Pio's life, they have generally not been of interest to most pilgrims. But particularly as curiosity in Pio's life before the stigmata grew in the latter half of the twentieth century—when the Vice-Postulator for the Cause of Canonization was researching this period of Pio's life—site managers would begin turning them into what can be considered religious heritage sites, publicizing them as connected with Pio's life history. As with other heritage sites, they began to be set apart, restored, valorized, designated, and marketed as integral to the life of Pio. For example, Morcone boasts several large roadside signs, in the typical brown color reserved for marking heritage destinations in Italy, publicizing the town as a *luogo di Padre Pio* ("Padre Pio site"), even though it also contains a rich history of pre-Roman and Lombard archeological remains. A few mainly Southern Italian pilgrim groups make a stop there.

An exception to this is Pio's hometown of Pietrelcina and Piana Romana, which toward the end of Pio's life boasted a certain level of regional visitors. As early as 1958, a small chapel was built over the remains of the elm tree in Piana Romana under which Pio had his first invisible stigmata experience, and visitors would leave ex-votos on nearby stones upon which Pio liked to sit as a boy. It was here that Pope Francis would visit in 2018. Likewise, in the village of Pietrelcina itself, the edifices that are directly associated with Pio's life had similarly been set aside and preserved as pilgrimage sites. Since the 1980s, they have been marked by large placards in four languages—an accommodation for foreign visitors that his shrine in San Giovanni Rotondo still does not have: these include his birth home, the home of his brother, the church of St. Anna where he was baptized, the *torretta*, and *'a morgia*, ("the large stone" in Pietrelcinese dialect) in front of his home. This last piece is of great importance; Pio was said to always finish meetings with Pietrelcinesi with the phrase, "*Salutami 'a morgia*" ("Say hi to the Morgia for me"). Speaking in Pietrelcina's dialect and referring to a geographic formation only locals would know about, Pio's repetition of this phrase is believed to reveal the saint's special, intimate relationship with his townspeople, who were largely marginalized from the economic development that he would bring to San Giovanni Rotondo (Di Giovine 2012) (see Figure 1.2).

The Development of the Center: San Giovanni Rotondo (1918–68)

Shortly after Pio arrived at San Giovanni Rotondo in 1918, Pope Benedict XV urged all Catholics to pray for the end of the war. News of heavy losses of Italian soldiers, coupled with the death of thousands of families on the homefront from the Spanish flu that swept through Pietrelcina and San Giovanni Rotondo, led Pio to offer himself in prayer as a sacrificial victim for the end of the war. In August, while confessing the young Capuchin novices, Pio suddenly saw a terrifying vision of a seraphim with a long, fiery sword that pierced his heart in what theologians call the transverberation. When the intense pain ceased in September, Pio prayed in thanksgiving in front of a crucifix in the choir loft, when, according to his diaries, the crucifix transformed itself "into a great being, all blood, from which there came forth beams of light with shafts of flame that wounded me in the hands and feet. My side had already been wounded on the fifth of August that same year" by the same being (Raffaele da S. Elia a Pianisi 1967: 357). In another letter he recalled, "All my insides rained blood and more

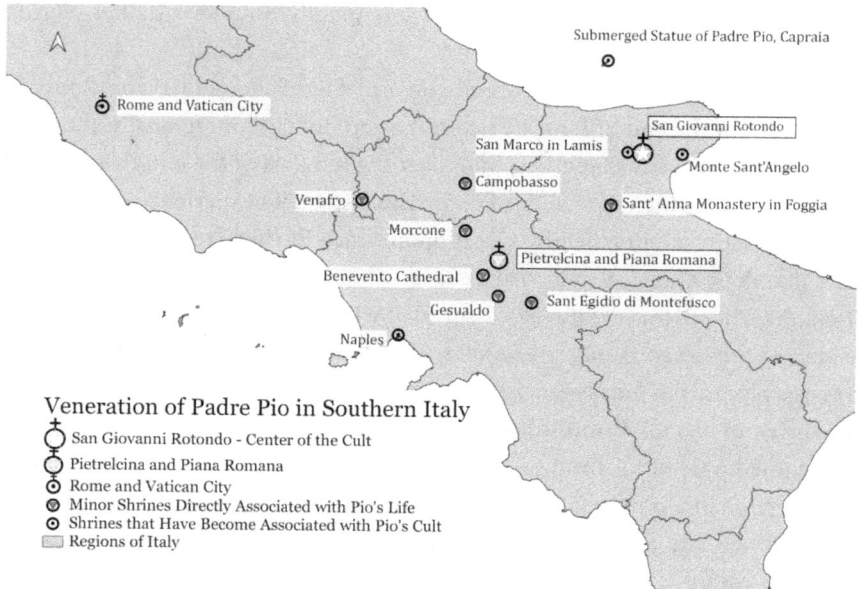

Figure 1.2 Map of Pio sites in Southern Italy. Created by Aaron Gallant.

than once my eyes were made to watch it pour out. . . . I was afraid I would bleed to death" (Pio da Pietrelcina 2008b: 1090, 1094). When he awoke in a pool of blood, he was in extreme pain, but quickly was filled with joy: his desire to imitate the sacrificial nature of Jesus was materially manifested in his body as the stigmata. He would have these bleeding marks for fifty years without interruption; one week before he died, they disappeared, leaving no trace of the holes and wounds that doctors had attested to during his lifetime (see Marianeschi 1988 for an in-depth medical examination).

Word spread quickly of the stigmata experience. Within a year, the town averaged 500 pilgrims a day (Luzzatto 2009: 38, 42); this number grew exponentially as images and stories of Pio and his miraculous abilities to cure the sick spread throughout the international press. By the 1920s, pilgrimage was an international phenomenon. For example, between 1920 and 1921, the friary registered pilgrims from Spain, France, Cuba, Argentina, Uruguay, and Chile; in 1920, up to thirty letters per day arrived from Chile alone (Saldutto 2001: 126). Considering Pio a living saint, devotees were frenzied, some armed with scissors to cut pieces of his clothing, which they perceived of as relics (Allegri 1998: 185). They were drawn by word of mouth, aided by the swift distribution of *santini*, wallet-sized prayer cards emblazoned with an image of his bleeding hand on them. A year after the stigmata experience, the Provincial head of the Capuchin

Order wrote a letter to his Minister General decrying "the fanaticism, pride and, I'd even say, the commercialism of that population" (qtd. Luzzatto 2009: 57). This also attracted the attention of Vatican authorities, who were shocked by the "wheeling and dealing" of San Giovanni Rotondo's citizenry and tried to move him away from the town. Locals rose up; one even ran at Pio with a pistol shouting, "Better dead among us than alive for others!" (Pio 2008b: 398–9)—a clear indication of locals' recognition of the benefits of his seductive power. The Vatican gave up, but twice barred him from celebrating the Eucharist and seeing the faithful. Yet they still came, and by the time of his death on September 23, 1968, such a crush of mourners were present that the Italian military police were called in to prevent rioting, and police helicopters dropped flowers and leaflets on the crowd during the funeral (Da Ripabottoni and Parente 1996: 252–3).

San Giovanni Rotondo developed materially and economically during Pio's lifetime. Once only accessible by foot or oxcart, Pio's small friary 2.5 kilometers outside of town soon was connected with roads, public transportation, and taxis; local families quickly built hotels and rest houses; and hundreds immigrated to the town in search of work. By the 1950s, the distance between Pio's church and the center of San Giovanni Rotondo was completely built up with houses where entrepreneurs and devotees lived in close proximity to Pio (Gaudiose 1993: 126–7). To manage the crush of pilgrims and gawkers who came to confess their sins to Pio—he was believed to know one's sins before they confessed them, and would publicly cast insincere visitors out without absolution—the friary instituted an innovative reservation system based on the distribution of different colored tokens for locals, religious, Italian, and foreign visitors. And to better spread out the masses of people, it used donations from the faithful to build different religious sites. In 1922 the monastery bought nearby land to construct a home and a recreation complex for Third Order Franciscans (lay people who take a vow to live as Franciscan friars and nuns), in 1925 a former convent belonging to the Poor Clares was transformed into the first pilgrim hospital in San Giovanni Rotondo, named after St. Francis of Assisi, and in 1939 the convent constructed a Via Crucis (Stations of the Cross) along the roadway linking the center of San Giovanni Rotondo to Pio's small friary and church, Santa Maria delle Grazie.

Major constructions were initiated by Pio himself, who capitalized on his charisma to successfully gain political and economic support for a number of ambitious projects in the 1950s, including the development of a new Via Crucis replete with modern sculpture that visually linked Pio with Jesus' crucifixion; a new pilgrimage church designed to accommodate the mass of pilgrims (and to eventually hold Pio's tomb); and an immense hospital, the Casa Sollievo della

Sofferenza ("Home for the Relief of Suffering"). These initiatives were funded by the many donations Pio would receive in the form of money and jewelry from supplicants; they would be given directly to Pio in face-to-face meetings, or enclosed in letters, as many of my Italian and Irish informants testified doing (see Di Giovine 2012b). At the cost of over 2 billion lire, the hospital also secured funds from European royalty, American businessmen, and the United Nations Relief and Rehabilitation Administration (UNRRA). Dominating the landscape, the hospital was built into the side of a mountain in front of the Capuchin monastery and today remains one of the premiere research hospitals in Italy.

Placed next to Pio's friary, the Casa Sollievo della Sofferenza was part of a larger shrine-creation complex that also included the building of a new church, Santa Maria delle Grazie, next to it. Adorned with images of Capuchin saints, as well as those of Padre Pio, the new church could hold hundreds of pilgrims and included a small crypt where Pio would eventually be interred. The stated goal in these constructions was to create a holistic pilgrimage landscape, a destination to cure mind, body, and soul through the most spiritually advanced priests and technologically advanced doctors. But it also serves to diversify the offerings of the shrine for pilgrims, particularly after Pio passed away (see Figures 1.3–1.5).

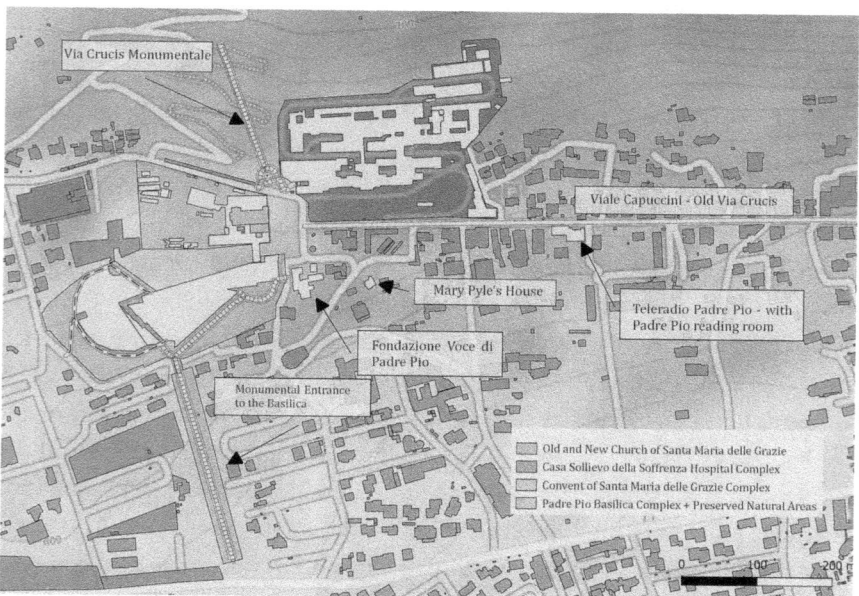

Figure 1.3 Map of Pio's shrine in San Giovanni Rotondo. Created by Aaron Gallant.

Galactic Shrines

Figure 1.4 The shrine complex as created by Padre Pio. This includes the original convent and church of Santa Maria delle Grazie (left) and Padre Pio's new church (right). The Casa Sollievo della Sofferenza (not pictured) is adjacent to the right. Photograph by Josep-Maria Garcia-Fuentes.

Figure 1.5 The Casa Sollievo della Sofferenza towering over the shrine complex. Photograph by the author.

The Creation of Satellites Further Afield (1968–2002): Consolidating and Diffusing the Power of the Center

The power of San Giovanni Rotondo as the center of a galactic organization of shrines did not wane after Pio's death; rather, it grew in the decades leading up to Pio's canonization. On the one hand, the structures that were in place to accommodate interpersonal social interactions between pilgrims and Pio himself were repurposed for new devotional-memorial rituals, as they were at the ancillary shrines scattered throughout Southern Italy. Pilgrims continued to arrive to venerate Pio's body, celebrate liturgical feasts in his honor, and visit the places that were associated with his life and ministry. In addition to attending Mass in Pio's dual churches of Santa Maria delle Grazie, the shrine has gradually been transformed into a museum in which pilgrims can see and interact with the choir stall and crucifix where Pio received the stigmata, various cells Pio inhabited, the altars upon which Pio celebrated Mass, Pio's confessional, and galleries in which various relics are displayed, including Pio's mundane personal effects (tooth brushes, soap-on-a-rope, books), collections of Pio's hairs and scabs (first-class relics), bloodied tunics and bandages, and ex-votos. Such "museumification" of artifacts related to Pio gradually was replicated in other satellite shrines, such as Pietrelcina, Piana Romana, Morcone, and Venafro. While these serve to link satellites to the center through a centripetal force of shared processes, it is important to note that these shrines exercise their own autonomy, emphasizing their role in Pio's life story—something that was increasingly stifled by authorities in San Giovanni Rotondo as Pio's official hagiography was solidified in this time period.

On the other hand, San Giovanni Rotondo became the center of a formable missionary movement that raised awareness of Pio across the world, solidified a particular hagiographic narrative that celebrated the shrine, and fostered the creation of new shrines directly in the shrine's own image. This grew out of the very real need to promote Pio's cause for canonization, which was driven by three important Capuchin friars in San Giovanni who had already written biographies about Pio when he was still alive. The cause for canonization is a canonical legal process (Woestman 2002); it is intended to make the case for a nominee's saintliness by providing a thorough treatment of his life, mental and physical capacities, and morality. To make the most compelling case, the Vice-Postulator solicited testimonials from devotees and supported the publication of biographies and memoirs by those connected to Pio in San Giovanni Rotondo. Indeed, by the 1970s, the Vice-Postulator for the Cause of Canonization founded the publishing house Edizione Padre Pio to publish books on the friar. In 1990, the publisher constructed a "Padre Pio Reading Room," which attempted to serve as a definitive library for all books published on Pio; by 2000, it contained 35,000 books, 5,000 brochures, 2,500 manuscripts, and 60 periodicals (Villani 2000: 42–3).

The publishing house works in synergy with the Voce di Padre Pio Foundation, which originally was founded as an Italian-language magazine in 1970. As its name, "The Voice of Padre Pio" suggests, it was not only positioned to be the authorized voice for the movement, but it positioned its publishers in San Giovanni Rotondo as the authorized spokespeople for Pio himself. It disseminated information about the shrine and Pio, provided updates on the canonization process, and collected testimonials in an effort to both raise awareness of Pio and combat alternative voices, according to its official website (Voce di Padre Pio n.d.). This was a global endeavor, and soon it was published in six (European) languages and spread throughout the world. By 2008, the magazine had some 130,000 subscriptions in Italy and over 50,000 in Europe alone (Neirotti 2008). Today, the foundation also operates Teleradio Padre Pio, an Italian radio station; Padre Pio TV, a satellite TV station broadcasting internationally; and internet sites. It has grown to become a media conglomerate netting over 250 million euros annually (anon. 2008).

Perhaps the most effective means of exerting the power of the center are the thousands of individual prayer groups founded not by the Capuchins but rather by Pio himself under the aegis of the Casa Sollievo della Sofferenza in 1947. These began as a loose collection of devotees from twenty-three different Italian cities that would meet monthly to pray for Pio's ministries; they now memorialize Pio and build in social interactions that serve to bond devotees together. They are formed under the consent of the local bishop, coordinated by lay people who took a vow to become Pio's "spiritual children," and run with a local priest present (Grottola 2009). This localism ensures not only that they were autonomous from the Capuchin Order, which had sometimes contested Pio's power, but also that they had the autonomy to adapt themselves to local needs and ways of praying, while at the same time directing them generally on forms of prayer and ritual prescribed by Pio in the center of the system. As of 2009, there are 2,711 groups in Italy alone, and 646 others in 40 nations (Grottola 2009: 40).

The construction of satellite shrines and devotional centers ultimately were the product of physical missionizing and social interaction, initially by Capuchins but later led by devotees and prayer group members. For example, the Irish are exceptionally devoted to Padre Pio; like Italians, they pray to Pio more than to Jesus, Mary, or their indigenous saints, Brigid and Patrick (Keane 2008: 200). Curiously, however, they did not come to know Pio until after his death, when Pio's personal caregiver, the charismatic Padre Alessio, made numerous trips to the country, speaking on national TV and forming prayer groups. He would provide most prayer groups with a "mitt," a brown, fingerless glove that Pio wore to cover his stigmata (McArdle 2002; Keane 2008). Today, there is a strong devotion built around the miraculous nature of these mitts, with devotees describing the energy coursing their bodies from the glove when "taking the cure" (see Di Giovine 2012c). Several of those who received such cures would go on to found national centers in Belfast and Dublin, and abroad in Australia, the Philippines, and the United States; the Padre Pio Foundation in Connecticut, the Shrine of Padre Pio in New Jersey, and the National Center for Padre Pio in Pennsylvania were all founded by families whose member had inexplicably been healed through the intercession of Pio. In addition, some shrines developed from prayer groups that had grown in power, such as those in Singapore, Santiago (Chile), and Batangas (Philippines); the shrine in Batangas was started with the help of the National Center for Padre Pio in Pennsylvania, further pointing to the interconnection of this system.

These centers boast statues, relics, prayer centers, and chapels that serve domestic pilgrims who cannot make the trip to Italy. In their liturgies, narratives, and museological exhibitions of relics, they replicate the center in San Giovanni Rotondo. The National Center for Padre Pio takes this quite literally: its architecture reproduces, on a smaller scale, both the skyline of Pietrelcina and the shrine of Santa Maria delle Grazie in San Giovanni Rotondo—down to the artwork inside. It is a simulacra (Baudrillard 1994) of the center. Yet these shrines are also autonomous, particularly if they are not under the aegis of the Capuchin Order or linked to San Giovanni Rotondo (as the Irish ones are): the shrine in Batangas utilizes local Southeast Asian materials and aesthetics, and thus looks quite different from the Pennsylvania shrine; it also publishes its own magazine in Tagalog, which draws from the English version of *Voce di Padre Pio*. However, workers inside the media foundation admit they cannot really control or check the information provided, as they have no workers who read Tagalog. Perhaps more troubling to site managers is that the National Center for Padre Pio also serves as a family shrine that integrates the founders directly into Pio's biography in a manner not found in the hagiographies; it has a museum whose displays juxtapose relics of Pio with artifacts from the founders and hosts an annual "founders' day" celebration honoring the family every summer. While recognizing the good that the family has done for mobilizing devotees, they lament the lack

Figure 1.6 National Center for Padre Pio, Barto, PA. Photograph by the author.

of control they have over the narrative produced. This has not been lost on local religious authorities; the local bishop had shut down regular operations of the Center's church and futilely attempted to take over the shrine (see Figure 1.6).

Finally, a more recent development that disseminates the power of the center outward to the satellite shrines is the authorized circulation of Padre Pio relics to parishes, most notably Pio's heart, which was detached from his body when Pio was exhumed in 2008 and kept in the friary at San Giovanni Rotondo. As pilgrimages began to wane five years later, the friary decided to send the heart to Boston and Vineland, NJ, drawing thousands. It was such a success that the heart has traveled to towns in Italy, Argentina, and the Philippines. Much like the king or royal vassals who pass through the satellites, mobilizing the polities' citizenry, so too does this relic of Pio serve to energize and mobilize devotees and to renew and reinvigorate the connections between the peripheral shrines and the center (see Figure 1.7).

Entropy within the System: Combating Centrifugal Forces

A central dynamic of a galactic political organization is that satellite shrines are relatively autonomous but are connected to the center through a centripetal force of common rituals, worldviews, and practices. The farther away a shrine

Figure 1.7 The faithful venerate Pio's heart in Boston's Cathedral. Photograph by Robert Pennoyer.

is from the center, the more independent it is, and thus the more tenuous is the center's hold on the satellite. In the galactic system of Padre Pio shrines, there are three major "centrifugal" forces that threaten to draw satellites away from the power of the center: (1) the autonomy of its satellites; (2) the rise of entirely new saints' cults that threaten to co-opt or attract these shrines and their devotees; and (3) the exertion of power by the Vatican itself.

The first threat is internal to the galactic organization: What happens when satellites exercise their autonomy outside of the authority of the center? Although the canonization process served as a driver for consolidating San Giovanni Rotondo's power and authorized a particular San Giovanni Rotondo-centric narrative of Pio, it also raised interest in the places associated with Pio's youth prior to his stigmata experience. By the 1990s there was such a crush of visitors to Pietrelcina that one Irish guide, who has led Pio pilgrimages since the 1970s, said, "it was so packed you couldn't breathe" (Di Giovine 2012a: 162). Pietrelcinesi took this opportunity to contest the predominant imaginaries that envisioned San Giovanni Rotondo as the center of the cult: they self-published several Pietrelcina-centric hagiographies that focused on the first thirty years of Pio's life, linking it with their town's history; they also created visual images in the form of stained glass windows, murals, souvenirs, and other artworks to complement these stories (e.g., see Figure 1.1). Finally, thanks to an increased interest in Pietrelcina by tourists during the mid-1990s, as well as the interest in the town by documentary filmmakers, politicians in Pietrelcina were able to secure funds to physically reconstruct the village to conform to tourists' idealized images of a bucolic Italian hill town. Pilgrims who visit Pietrelcina are receptive to Pietrelcina's new look, which prompts them to recall stories of Pio and to exchange accounts of miracles and other supernatural phenomena that the saint has performed in their lives. In my years traveling with Italian, Irish, and American tourists, I have overheard favorable comparisons with San Giovanni Rotondo. And interest in visiting Pietrelcina has certainly grown; at the height of Pio pilgrimages between 1999 and 2009, Pietrelcina saw roughly 600,000 visitors per year—200 times its population size. Yet it is important to note that this is but 10 percent of the total visitors to San Giovani Rotondo during the same period; furthermore, tourists in Pietrelcina typically only stay a few hours and do not frequently spend much money on souvenirs or food: a testament to the continuing power of San Giovanni Rotondo.

The completion of Pietrelcina's restoration effort in 2006 was met with greater iconographic contestation, as San Giovanni Rotondo had just inaugurated a new mega-church designed by internationally renowned architect Renzo Piano and decorated by world-class sculptors such as Mimmo Paladino and Arnoldo Pomodoro. The crowning achievement—other than the 8,300-person Basilica and its beautifully landscaped piazza, envisioned as a "church without walls" that can accommodate 35,000 devotees—is the new crypt for Pio below the Basilica, adorned with scintillating vermillion and golden mosaics by noted Slovenian mosaicist Marko Ivan Rupnik. Juxtaposing scenes from the life of St. Francis (the first stigmatic and the "grandfather" of the Capuchin Order) with similar scenes from Pio's life, Rupnik's mosaic cycle created an avenue to iconographically solidify and consolidate imaginaries of San Giovanni Rotondo as the center of the shrine system, linking Francis with Pio and Assisi with San Giovanni Rotondo. One particular scene is telling: it is a frieze of Pio convalescing in his parents' house in Pietrelcina. The rendering of the one-room home matches the actual home as it appears today, complete with a solitary square window that looks out onto the Piana Romana landscape. But in Rupnik's rendering, the window opens not to Piana Romana but to the shrine in San Giovanni Rotondo, reinforcing the hagiographic narrative that everything, ultimately, happened in San Giovanni Rotondo (see Di Giovine 2014: 159–60).

Recently, site managers have also identified the increase in unauthorized circulation of relics as a particular threat to the authority of the center—by "Padre Pio people who are not genuine," according to one site manager in

San Giovanni (interview, July 2, 2018). Shortly after Pio's heart was brought to Boston in 2016—the result of a deal organized between the Archdiocese of Boston, the Capuchin friary in San Giovanni Rotondo, and its Voce di Padre Pio Foundation, and facilitated on the ground by the Padre Pio Foundation in Cromwell, Connecticut—a new, NY-based organization called the St. Pio Foundation emerged, led by a charismatic young Italian opera singer with "high-up" connections; unlike the earlier North American shrines that were founded by devotees and prayer group members, the foundation's board is filled with investment bankers, CEOs, politicians such as former senator Rick Santorum, even Italian-American actors such as Joe Mantegna and Robert Davi, whose video testimonials are featured on the foundation's homepage (www.saintpiofoundation.org). It seeks to raise money ostensibly for the hospital in San Giovanni and new constructions in Pietrelcina by circulating relics of Pio—vestments, beard hairs, and so on—across the United States. Yet the organization is not endorsed by the shrine or its bishop, and the shrine's managers do not know for certain who provided the relics and laments the lack of control (or knowledge of) the distribution of donations.

A second threat lies external to the galactic system: What happens when a new center is formed that threatens to co-opt satellites that lie farther from the center? After all, this is what occurred between San Giovanni Rotondo and the older pilgrimage sites such as Monte Sant'Angelo or Montevirgine. Even during the height of Pio-focused pilgrimages, it was evident that devotees' interest is fickle and can change on a whim: in 2010, just a few months after a highly publicized exhumation and exhibition of Pio's body in San Giovanni Rotondo, and a hotly contested transfer of his remains from one crypt to another, Italian media attention swiftly shifted from daily reports on Padre Pio to discussions on the extraordinary veneration of the Shroud of Turin that was occurring in the north of Italy, and visitation to San Giovanni Rotondo and Pietrelcina plummeted. Visitation numbers were never the same. Indeed, there is a sentiment among site managers and locals that after 2010, international interest seems to have moved from Padre Pio to newly canonized saints such as Mother Theresa, Pope John XIII (who was vehemently opposed to Padre Pio and sanctioned him), and Pope John Paul II. Italian informants now talk of visiting Krakow, where John Paul II lived, and his hometown of Wadowice; tourist numbers have steadily increased over the past several years in both places, with Italians being the largest demographic of visitors (IAR 2017); Pope Francis also held World Youth Day in Krakow in 2016. To combat this, San Giovanni Rotondo has attempted to co-opt the increasing interest in these saints, publishing books on

Pio's relationship with these popes (its book on John XXIII [Campanella 2011] argues that it was all a gross misunderstanding, though the pontiff was quite clear about his negative thoughts of Padre Pio in his writings [see Luzzatto 2009: 359–84]). Images of John Paul II and Mother Teresa venerating Pio's tomb are frequently featured in publications, and following Pope Francis' recent visit to San Giovanni Rotondo, the shrine has posted large images of the last three popes on its façade, advertising how each have paid their respects to the saint.

While San Giovanni Rotondo has taken measures to shore up its power against these internal and external threats, more complex is the third type of threat to the center: What happens when the Vatican exercises its ultimate control over the shrine? San Giovanni Rotondo and the Vatican have long had a tense relationship. Prior to Pio's canonization, much of this was over the charismatic power of the saint; Pope John XXIII, for example, felt that he was a "straw man" sent by the devil to test the church, which was in the midst of its own reformation in the Second Vatican Council (Luzzatto 2009: 369–70). This is not unusual for popular religious movements, and the act of canonization is often considered the means through which the Vatican can co-opt and "routinize" a popular leader's charisma (Badone 1990: 13–15; see Weber 1958: 297) and assert hagiographic control over the leader's narrative and the rituals that follow. This certainly was the case for Pio; while Pio's message was always one of suffering for others, the official canonization documents constructed by the Vice-Postulator hold him up as an icon of obedience (Holy See 2009)—to God and to the church, even during unfavorable periods. This is one that was constructed and embraced by the Postulator for the Cause of Canonization and the shrine's media outlets.

However, in 2016 Pope Francis extraordinarily changed the narrative: Padre Pio was to be the face of his new Jubilee Year of Mercy. In his official declaration, he pointed out Pio's ministry in the confessional, his exhortation to prayer, and his construction of the Casa Sollievo della Sofferenza that, together, were in line with the Catechism's Corporal Works of Mercy: minister to the less fortunate, the sick, and needy. The *coup de grace*, however, was Francis' extraordinary request to temporarily move Pio's body to the Vatican, where he lay on exhibition in St. Peter's Cathedral along with another Capuchin saint known for his work in the confessional. The Capuchins had already denied requests by Pietrelcina and others to temporarily exhibit Pio's body when they exhumed him in 2008, and they faced lawsuits when they moved Pio's body in 2010 from Santa Maria delle Grazie to the Basilica next door. But the shrine could not refuse the pontiff, though privately there was grumbling; a rumor circulating was that this was a veiled threat by Pope Francis for the shrine to fix certain financial improprieties, lest he permanently remove their income source. The event was certainly extraordinary: Pio's body was paraded throughout the center of Rome, over the Tiber and into St. Peter's Basilica. In addition to being the first time Pio's body left San Giovanni Rotondo since 1918—dead or alive—this was the first time in 800 years that Rome saw a public saint's procession of that scale. The next day, Pope Francis held a papal audience for some 80,000 Padre Pio prayer group members in St. Peter's Square, followed by the veneration of his body inside St. Peter's Basilica. Finally, empowering Pio's hometown, on its way back to San Giovanni Rotondo, Pio's body was ceremonially brought to Pietrelcina for three days; locals unfurled handmade signs, written in dialect, welcoming him home after 100 years. During that time, I traveled to San Giovanni Rotondo; the shrine was nearly completely empty without his body there and restaurants, hotels, and souvenir stands closed. It was an eerie reminder of what could happen should San Giovanni Rotondo lose its power.

Today, San Giovanni Rotondo has continued to innovate new ways of maintaining control over the center of this galactic system. It has welcomed, rather than contested, Francis and his changes—quickly publishing several volumes on Padre Pio and his theology of mercy, and emblazoning the symbol of the jubilee—which was also designed by Rupnik and closely resembles a mosaic at the shrine—on prayer cards and publications. It also has implemented a twice-a-year ritual transfer of Pio's body between the two crypts; managers have told me that this is done for the practical reason that less pilgrims visit in the winter, and the Basilica is costly to heat (and slippery to access in the snow). But they also admitted that since saints' bodies must be transferred through an official liturgical ritual (called the *translatio*), it is also a new event designed to draw tourists to the site to see the body ceremonially paraded between the churches. And whether or not such events stand the test of time, it should be remembered that the Basilica itself was planned to be "the next Assisi," as one informant told me. Nearly 800 years after St. Francis' death, Assisi ranks as one of the top tourist attractions in Italy. "Of the visitors who go to Assisi, 10% go for the saint. The rest go for Giotto," he said, referring to the renaissance painter's iconic frescos, a World Heritage site (Di Giovine 2012: 164). Boasting cutting-edge art and architecture by internationally renowned Italians, St. Pio's Basilica can serve in the future as a draw to tourists visiting not to venerate Pio's body but to see the most representative art and architecture of our era. It is a way to continue to remain sustainable and viable, even if its religious power wanes (see Figure 1.8).

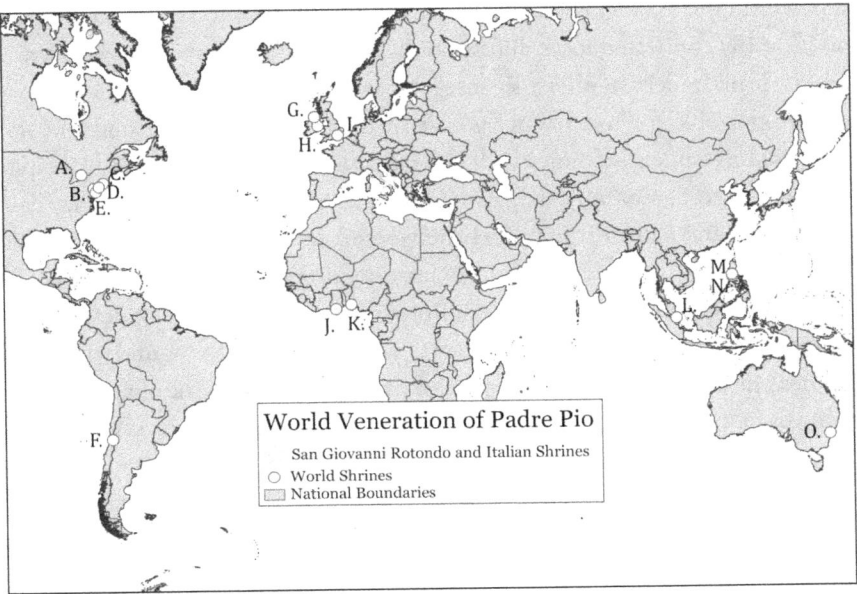

Figure 1.8 Map of the global system of Padre Pio shrines.

Conclusion

Based on over a decade of ethnographic research with pilgrims, site managers, and locals at the major sanctuaries to Padre Pio in Italy and the United States, this chapter adopted Stanley Tambiah's model of the galactic polity to understand the networked landscape of shrines related to St. Padre Pio of Pietrelcina. The arrangement of polities into a galactic structure challenges the Sino-Western understanding of temporal power as established by clearly defined borders and boundaries; rather, such a political organization rests on a core—or political and ceremonial center—around which peripheral satellites revolve. Just like the planets of our solar system, each satellite is itself its own little world, with its own distinctive history and culture, and a certain level of autonomy; however, it is drawn to the center through sociocultural processes: a common worldview cultivated through authorized hagiographic discourses, shared movement of people and goods, and the replication of rituals defined and enforced by the center.

While shrines are not nation-states, they are indeed political entities; they are embedded in broader relationships of power and often struggle with each other to define the value, meaning, and appropriate activities related to a particular saint within the broader context of popular Catholic devotion. The cult of Padre Pio is deeply connected to its diffuse landscape of shrines across the world, and the work of leaders at these shrines—particularly San Giovanni Rotondo—were responsible for the alacrity with which the cult developed and Pio was canonized. Despite sometimes very diverse means of development, and despite sometimes great autonomy, they cannot be seen as fully independent; they gain significance and value through their networked connection with other shrines within a system that is clearly coordinated by a powerful centripetal force of San Giovanni Rotondo. San Giovanni Rotondo defines Padre Pio; it defines how he should be understood and what sorts of activities are to be undertaken by devotees. It is also evidence of not only his work but the work of a century of devotees to the saint—something that all of these shrines evidence as well. This is the true "centripetal force" of the system, the one which each satellite replicates.

Yet we must remember that saints' cults and their shrines, and made by and for people, and charismatic saints such as Pio emerge from the ground up, rather than the top down (see Meltzer and Elsner 2011; Delooz 1983). This provides not only the ultimate power of the central shrine but also the power of other satellites. These satellites are not only brick-and-mortar shrines but rather all sorts of devotional spaces in which Pio is venerated, discussed, and valued. One encounters Pio in church chapels, family homes, hospitals, shopping malls, public buildings—even the Casa Rosada, the Argentine president's home in Buenos Aires. Pio is present at other shrines—from Dublin's Knock Cathedral to Medjugorje in Bosnia-Herzegovina, from the souvenir shops at Fátima and Assisi to churches in Jerusalem in the Holy Land—just as other saints' relics (such as those of Mother Teresa and John Paul II) are present in San Giovanni Rotondo. His image is emblazoned on Italian trucks and mud flaps, on bumper stickers, and, of course, virtually in private websites. These diffuse and often mobile shrines reveal the richness of devotion to the saint, as well as the breadth and depth of this global network. Yet they also present particular threats to the center's control, and while San Giovanni Rotondo has thus far been adept at transforming itself to meet these problems, only time will tell how sustainable these initiatives will be.

Acknowledgments

The author would like to thank his research assistant at West Chester University, Aaron Gallant, for his work in rendering the geographical maps used in this chapter.

2

Sacralizing the Landscape
Water and the Development of a Pilgrimage Shrine

John Eade

Nature and Place Pilgrimage

The subjugation of nature by human institutions to create an ordered, predictable, and "sacred" landscape has a long history. Machu Pichu, Stonehenge, Rome, Jerusalem, Mecca, and Varanasi are just some of the most famous pilgrimage sites where landscapes reveal how the local habitat has been sacralized in the pursuit of religious interests. However, in the Christian tradition "place pilgrimage"—travel to and from a sacred place and participation in rituals there—is not the only form of pilgrimage. Pilgrimage could also involve the retreat from human society to the wilderness, that is, deserts, forests, or mountains, or an internal journey toward God. While place pilgrimage has tended to be a group activity, the two other forms are predominantly individual in character.

While these modes of pilgrimage have been differentiated discursively, in practice they can be linked or morphed into one another. Hence, the places where hermits or monks settled frequently attracted devotees and they lost their isolated character—place pilgrimage triumphed over this attempt by individuals to escape from society. Since pilgrimage has long been entwined with tourism we see the same process at work in the development of tourist destinations. Places "off the beaten track" attract those seeking to escape their everyday routines but over time these destinations are "developed" and the wilderness becomes tamed and "normalized," losing its image as a "paradise" for the pioneers.

Christian pilgrimage has played a key role in the sacralization of the wilderness. Although individual hermits might seek to escape society, the Roman Catholic Church has long sought to bring them together into communities separated from the secular world. Hence, male and female monasteries emerged from the third century CE onwards where members observed a common rule validated by Rome. Yet, the continuing attempt by the Roman Catholic Church to maintain a rigid distinction between the sacred and the secular was limited by the intimate relationship between religious, political, and economic interests. The development of Catholic pilgrimage shrines across Europe places relied heavily on political patronage as well as a growing network of trade routes.

Phenomenological and Relational Approaches toward Pilgrimage and Landscape

In this chapter I will draw on the anthropological investigation of contemporary pilgrimage, which has expanded rapidly since the 1970s. These investigations have focused predominantly on a phenomenological approach where the exploration of the meanings and motivations of pilgrims is paramount (see Turner and Turner 1978; Morinis 1984; Eade and Sallnow 1991; Coleman 2000, 2002; Badone 2007; Reader 2007; Lochtefeld 2010; Albera and Eade 2015, 2017). However, in exploring the sacralization of the landscape, the "material turn" is also very useful since it directs attention toward people's sensuous relationship with the materiality of sacred places and the complexity of "lived religion" (see McDannell 1993; Hall 1997; Tweed 2006; Vasquez 2010; Morgan 2000; Meyer 2012; Hazard 2013; Jansen and Notermans 2011). Robert Orsi's deeply engaged and illuminating studies of Roman Catholicism in the United States (1985/2010, 2013), for example, show the messy, contested, and mobile ways where "lived religion" is expressed through "embodied practice and imagination" (2010: xxxix). He looks away from the phenomenological emphasis on meaning toward understanding how people "exist and move through their built and found environments" where "the material world is not inert background to cult practice" but "its essential medium" (2010: xxxix). With regard to landscape the "material turn" has encouraged researchers to explore the ways in which people engage with space through their bodily, kinetic experience.

People's sensual engagement with the landscape has also been explored in the context of shrines, which have acquired a reputation as centers of healing. The French shrine of Lourdes has attracted particular interest because of its international popularity and the lively debates concerning its reputation for miraculous healing. In an early exploration of "therapeutic landscapes," Wilbert Gesler focuses on Lourdes as a "healing shrine" (Gesler 1992, 1996) and Alana Harris draws on his work to examine Lourdes "as a site for the exploration and negotiation of embodied, communal and holistic aspirations." She detects the growing influence of beliefs and practices concerning "well-being," holistic medicine, and spirituality, and detects the development of "a therapeutic spirituality" at Lourdes, which is informed by "contemporary spirituality (within and outside religious affiliation)" of beliefs and practices that prioritize "self-realisation, connectivity and embodied well-being" (2013; see also Goldingay, Dieppe, and Farias 2014).

Through their focus on meanings concerning health, healing, and the body, these studies point to the advantages of drawing on both the phenomenological tradition and the "material turn." I will also adopt this approach in my analysis of the ways in which landscape was both physically and discursively sacralized. This will lead on to an exploration of the sensuous experience of "Lourdes water," drawing on my role as a helper between 1968 and 1992 and then again from 2013 to the present.

Lourdes: Sacralizing the Local Landscape

In 1858 a young shepherdess, Bernadette Soubirous, experienced a number of visions at a grotto outside the town. During one of the séances she uncovered a spring which soon became popularly associated with claims to miraculous healing. Bernadette reported that the vision identified herself as the "Immaculate Conception," that is, the mother of Jesus or "Our Lady" in popular parlance, and exhorted the people to come and drink the spring water, bathe in it, and pray for sinners, while the clergy should build a chapel and perform ceremonies.

The message concerning the Immaculate Conception was welcomed by those supporting the Vatican's declaration in 1854 that belief in Mary's freedom from original sin was a dogmatic article of faith.[1] However, the shrine's rapid development was largely due to the reports of miraculous curing popularly associated with the spring. These reports became embroiled in lively national disputes concerning physical healing, which involved the fraught relationship between science, medicine, and religion (see Harris 1999; Kaufman 2005).

A bustling pilgrimage town grew between the sanctuary, emerging around the grotto, and the old town, which nestled around the castle standing proudly on its hilly promontory facing southwards to the Pyrenees Mountains and the border with Spain. Hotels, restaurants, cafés, and shops made Lourdes one of France's most important centers for religious and nonreligious pursuits. This development was facilitated initially by the national railway network, and then by an improving road network and a local airport.

The location of the visions was highly significant since the area around the grotto had an ambivalent reputation. Ruth Harris notes that it

> brought together many different elements of Pyrenean life, beliefs and legends in a place of illegality, pleasure and scavenging. . . . From at least the beginning of the seventeenth century the pigs of Lourdes grazed there. . . . The site was, therefore, a marginal and even filthy place. . . . Before Bernadette, people were known to cross themselves when passing by to fend off some "devilish spell." (1999: 53)

The area was also associated with "prophecies of divine visitation" (1999: 54), and once Bernadette's visions were formally accepted, church officials moved quickly to purge the area of its unsavory reputation through a process of physical and discursive sacralization. An altar was built within the inner sanctum of the grotto, which was sealed off from the pilgrims by high gates (see Kaufman 2005: 21), while the spring was channeled into a small hut and then more imposing baths to the north side of the grotto where "sick" pilgrims (*malades*) were ritually bathed. Engineering work behind the face of the cliff overlooking the grotto enabled the spring water to be piped to taps near the baths, where visitors could wash their hands and face as well as collect the water in various receptacles. The sacred character of the landscape was further emphasized physically through the construction of basilicas and chapels on the cliff, thereby visually dominating the grotto and facing out toward a large esplanade and avenue, which was created for the mass blessings of the sick in the afternoon and the nightly torchlight procession. This physical sacralization of the landscape soon extended beyond the sanctuary's boundary through the building of an imposing Stations of the Cross route up the adjoining wooded hill.

The organization of the national pilgrimage in 1874 helped to establish a ritual structure which did not fundamentally change until after the Second World War:

> A fresh set of practices—in which men carried the sick around the shrine, female volunteers bathed them in the pools, doctors examined the cured, and masses of assembled pilgrims participated in spectacular processions—came to define the spiritual life of the shrine. (Kaufman 2005: 107)

These rituals expressed a modern religiosity which was "directed toward and shaped by the idioms of a newly emerging mass culture," bound up with spectacle and visuality (Kaufman 2005: 108), where the invention of photography and, later, film played a key role.[2] The landscape of this liminal area outside the town was transformed into a sacred site where public rituals involving masses of people could demonstrate the power and vigor of the Roman Catholic Church in a threatening secularizing world.

Although the church emphasized the ideological and physical distinction between the sacred and secular, the development of the sanctuary was integrally linked to the rapid expansion of the secular pilgrimage town. Here modern consumerism was vividly expressed through the proliferation of cafés, restaurants, hotels, and shops, while technological innovation and the visual were amply demonstrated by the popularity of postcards celebrating the local landscape (views of the old town and pilgrimage town, the grotto, basilicas, and nearby mountains), as well as events or people representing the shrine, such as the ceremonies, statues, the *malades*, and Bernadette herself.

In a mountainous area where streams were long associated with miraculous healing and spas—another expression of modern consumerism—were sprouting up, the sanctuary's religious leaders "sought to eradicate or at least to domesticate the grassroots devotions that emerged at shrines" (Kaufman 2005: 21). Nature was to be tamed and controlled so that Lourdes could develop as a conventional religious shrine, rather than a spa or a place for "superstitious," magical practices. Visitors were encouraged to focus on the church's teachings concerning Mary, particularly her dogmatic status as the Immaculate Conception. A statue of Our Lady with *Que Soy Era Immaculada Concepciou* (I am the Immaculate Conception) carved on its base was installed in a niche above the grotto, helping to sacralize the site and destroy its reputation as a dangerous, liminal place. Although the religious leaders welcomed the claims to miraculous cures, it moved quickly to establish their "authenticity" through a well-publicized engagement with medical professionals and secular critics such as the French novelist Emile Zola (see Harris 1999; Kaufman 2005). Furthermore, the focus on the spring and the grotto was modified by the introduction of the daily "blessing of the sick" ceremony, which made highly effective use of the new esplanade and avenue in front of the basilicas and where claims to miraculous healing were also made during the late nineteenth and early twentieth centuries.

Lourdes provides, therefore, a vivid illustration of the ways in which traditional Christian "place pilgrimage" can contribute to a reordering of the physical environment through a process of physical and discursive sacralization. While the religious officials sought to eliminate the ambivalence surrounding the grotto area and promote a clear physical and discursive separation between the sacred space around the grotto and the secular world of the expanding town outside the sanctuary's boundary, the boundary between the two was porous. The landscape could never be totally controlled and the increasing constriction of nature—in this case, a lively river close to the mountains—made the risk of nature "biting back" all the more likely and its impact even more costly. A deluge during October 2012, followed by another in June the next year, reminded everyone of nature's dangerous power as the river burst its banks along the pilgrimage town and the sanctuary. The second flood had the greater impact since it occurred during the main pilgrimage season, and hotels, which were recovering from the October 2012 inundation, were hit once more, while the grotto area was briefly put out of action again and the new hospital on the right bank was also affected. In June 2018 the town was again hit by two-day flood, although the structural repairs initiated after 2013 appeared to have prevented similar damage.

Engaging with the Landscape through Water

Two types of water coexisted at this pilgrimage shrine, therefore. The river, which flowed between the sacralized space of the sanctuary and the pilgrimage town, and the spring, which was controlled within the sanctuary through both a physical channeling within the grotto, the nearby taps, and the baths and a discursive ordering which emphasized its symbolic character rather than its miraculous agency. The extensive literature concerning Lourdes has provided a detailed picture of its changing landscape and the rituals performed there but scant attention has been paid to what lies behind the surface of this landscape. I intend to explore behind this imposing façade by focusing on the "back stage" or internal landscape through a study of the men's section of the baths, where people sensually engage with the spring water.

Three enclosed baths were built to the north side of the grotto during the late nineteenth century and catered primarily for the "malades" (sick). Crowds gathered outside and any rumors of a miracle caused great commotion and were celebrated at the public rituals, especially the regular "blessing of the sick" in the afternoon. The rapid increase in visitor numbers after the Second World War led to the construction of a much larger set of male and female baths south of the grotto in 1954. Here "able-bodied" pilgrims could also enter the baths but despite this expansion, bathing did not become very popular—in 1981, for example, less than 10 percent of visitors went to the baths (Billet and Lafourcade 1981: 170, 239) and their popularity does not appear to have increased significantly (see Harris 2013: 34). Visitors continued to be far more attracted by the ceremonies taking place across the external landscape.

In 2012 Nicholas Brouwet, a dynamic, fifty-year-old priest, took over as the local bishop and he has presided over a number of changes to the landscape which seek to reflect and promote the "new evangelization" strategy which emerged during the 1970s. Since the Second World War France and other Western European countries have seen a rapid decline in church attendance and religious vocations. Sex scandals in the United States, Australia, India, and (most recently) Poland have seriously questioned the moral authority of the church and led the current pope, Francis I, to issue both apologies and demands. The Vatican has sought to counter these challenges by encouraging the strategy of "new evangelization." The strategy emerged during the papacy of Paul VI between 1963 and 1978 with the pope declaring in 1973 that

> [t]he conditions of the society in which we live oblige all of us therefore to revise methods, to seek by every means to study how we can bring the Christian message to modern man [*sic*].

Pope John Paul II vigorously pursued the strategy during his reign (1978–2005), focusing not only on "non-believers" but also "non-practicing Christians," particularly in a rapidly secularizing Europe and North America. He saw "new evangelization" as combating the growth of moral relativism, "religious indifference, secularism and atheism," especially in "First World" where affluence and consumerism coexist with "poverty and misery." Pilgrimage was an integral element in the strategy and his deep Marian devotion led him to visit a number of major Marian shrines, including Lourdes. The strategy has continued during the reign of Benedict XV1 (2005–13) and the current papacy of Francis I and has involved in the European region, for example, the development of institutional pilgrimage networks across Europe, and the encouragement of walking pilgrimage, building on the popularity of the *camino* to Santiago de Compostela.

Bishop Brouwet's plans to change key areas of the sanctuary's landscape were immediately challenged by the floods of 2012 and 2013. The cost of repairing the area around the grotto, including the baths, added to the deficit which the sanctuary began to run in 2010. Between 1948 and 2008 the number of visitors had steadily risen despite rises and falls from year to year, reaching a peak of around 9 million during the Holy Year of 2008. Numbers had then rapidly declined after the 2008 global economic crisis and by 2018 were probably down to around 3.5 million. Donations by visitors and private well-wishers helped pay for the repairs, and in April 2019 it was announced that the sanctuary had made a profit of 200,000 euros in 2018. This recovery appeared to have been due, in part, to the appointment of a human resources manager after

2013 which led to "cutting operating costs, increasing the sale of candles, and a slight increase in the contribution asked from organized pilgrimages" (https://www.catholicnewsagency.com/news/pope-francis-names-delegate-to-oversee-pilgrims-at-lourdes-shrine-14830, accessed June 7, 2019).

While the sanctuary's financial health recovered, the bishop and chaplains had to grapple with the changing profile of visitors. As the bishop noted, those coming on organized pilgrimages were no longer the majority:

> We know well that the greater number of pilgrims who come are not in pilgrimages organized by a diocese or association, but make their own arrangements. They are individuals, families, groups of friends. They come to Lourdes or one or several days. Their pilgrimage is included within a wider journey: holidays in the Pyrenees, in France or in Europe. Many already know about the Sanctuary. But many come here for the first time and do not know the message of Lourdes. They include those who are baptized but know little about the Christian faith. Some are not Christian, belong to another religion or do not believe in religion. We have a particular responsibility towards these. We must continue to welcome those who come on organized pilgrimages. But we need to reflect on how to welcome in a fresh way those who are arriving on an individual basis, especially those who do not know what to expect and who stay for only a few hours or several days at the Grotto of Massabielle. . . . How are we going to meet them and welcome them through respecting their rhythms without being afraid to announce Christ?

Between 2013 and 2018, therefore, the landscape of the grotto area was changed in the hope that these more elusive visitors might find the area more inviting. In 2016 the outside of the baths was redesigned to provide more space for the reception of "sick" pilgrims in wheelchairs and stretchers, while wooden benches are provided on either side to cater for the queues of "able-bodied" bathers. Conversation between those waiting to enter the baths was discouraged by the recitation of prayers and hymns through the public address system—visitors were continually reminded of the "spiritual" character of the baths and bathing. However, the interior of the baths remained fundamentally unchanged. The male and female sections were still separated and in the male section two cubicles continued to cater for those on stretchers and wheel chairs, one cubicle was set aside for children while another four were used for able-bodied adults.

The process of male bathing has also remained fundamentally unchanged since the late 1960s when I started working as a helper. Yet, there were some significant changes in practice and discourse. Between the 1960s and 1980s the procedure was highly regimented, with the Hospitality volunteers very much in charge. A leader of each cubicle team was nominated to ensure that the process of bathing ran smoothly. The front area of the cubicle contained four chairs on either side where the bathers undressed and waited for their turn. Two volunteers helped the bathers to undress and lined them up before handing them over to another volunteer to one side of the bath, who wrapped a damp towel round the waist after the bather had put his pants on a rail attached to the wall on either side of the bath itself. Two more helpers on the other side of the bath then guided the bather down the steps into the bath and up to the end where he read a set formula of prayers from large plastic cards in various European languages. He was then asked by the helpers to cross their arms so that they could hold him securely as they lowered him backward into the water where he was usually totally immersed. He was then helped to stand and given a bronze statuette of Our Lady to kiss after saying a short prayer; he then turned round and walked back out of the bath to reclaim his pants while the helper retrieved the wet towel.

When I returned in 2013 the process had already been changed to allow for greater individual choice and privacy. Previously, visitors could see how the process of bathing operated since the curtains on either side of the central bath were only used when the towels were put on and retrieved. Now the curtains are kept closed so that bathing could be a more private event and everyone was asked to sit down once they had stripped down to their pants so the line-up with its conveyor belt associations has been eliminated. The shock of entering the very cold water was minimized to some extent by inviting each person to pray before going down the steps and care was taken to keep the bather's head out of the water so total immersion was dispensed with unless asked for. A jug filled with the bath water was kept ready in case the bather wanted water on his head and a helper poured it carefully over his hand held above the bather's head so that the shock of the cold water was minimized. A cup was at hand in case anyone wanted to drink the water which was again dispensed fresh from a beaker. The statuette of Our Lady was available but again the bather had to ask for it, while the prayer cards had been dispensed with.

These modifications in practice reflected changes in religious discourse since the early 1990s when I stopped going to Lourdes. At the same time there was the same emphasis on the symbolic meaning of water and the rejection of any belief in its magical properties. Hence, the June 2017 Hospitality Newsletter reminded helpers that "[w]e must remember that the water from this spring is a sign, not an object of fetish. It is also a sign of another water: that of Baptism." Although this statement expressed the church's denial of the spring's agency, the great care taken to soften the shock of bathing in the intensely cold water emphasized the danger of coming into contact with the spring. The danger came not just from the short time spent in the bath but also from the shock of having a wet towel tied around one's waist and even the possibility of slipping on the wet floor.

Bathing in the Spring Water—Personal Reflections

A prime feature of pilgrimage across faiths and time has been the official emphasis on its penitential dimension. Pilgrims have long been encouraged to see their journey and stay at the shrine as a sacrifice for others. As travel to Lourdes has become quicker and easier members of my pilgrimage group have debates whether the pilgrimage was becoming "too easy." During the week at Lourdes this debate focused on how demanding the work was. It was generally agreed that all the jobs required endurance, whether it be the boredom of standing for long periods "on guard," the hours waiting at the airport for delayed planes, the preparing of meals in the hospitals, or the intense physical experience of working inside the baths. Since Lourdes, like other pilgrimages, also involved the ludic there were many opportunities for relaxation after work and some of us joked that late nights and heavy drinking added to the penitential experience!! The party atmosphere in the evenings was fueled by the large numbers of young volunteers "off the leash," and veterans like me had the opportunity to meet for a chat over a drink with friends from the other British pilgrimages which regularly arrived in late July.

I have always been fascinated by the intellectual and emotional challenge posed by Lourdes, particularly the apparitions and claims to miraculous healing. I have always believed in the existence of a nonmaterial world and my anthropological career has helped me appreciate how such a belief has been expressed by different religious and spiritual traditions across time and space. Although I was brought up within Protestant traditions and then converted to Roman Catholicism during my twenties, I have become increasingly interested in non-Christian faiths. Furthermore, my involvement in the pilgrimage studies has opened my eyes to the complexity of "lived religion" and its materiality.

During both periods of working at Lourdes during late July I have helped in different areas, such as the station and airport. I have found the baths the most challenging and intense experience of all, so have chosen to volunteer there most often. As noted earlier, even though the baths provide the most intense relationship with "Lourdes water," only a small minority of visitors actually take a bath. Among those who do arrive, many are not sure what to expect and how to behave once inside the baths. During my first period of working at Lourdes, bathers could observe the entire process of bathing but when I returned the closing of the curtain meant that those waiting could only catch a glimpse of what lay behind the curtain when it was briefly opened to let the bather return to his chair. They could also listen to the sounds of the prayers, the splashing in the water, and the occasional gasp as the cold, damp towel was put around the bather's midriff.

The great care taken by helpers in guiding each visitor through the process shows a keen sense of the risks involved with the water, both inside and outside the bath itself. There is the involuntary frisson when the wet towel as it is put round the waist, the shock on entering the bath and the immersion, the danger of slipping and falling over when retrieving pants and returning to the chair. There is also the fear of being lowered backward into the water despite being held securely by the helpers. The volunteers try to help by instructing the bather to sit down but this may be misunderstood, particularly if bather and volunteers do not speak the same language. Sometimes the bather holds on to the sides of the bath and fails to get immersed. Helpers have to be careful not to let the bather slip or launch himself backward and hit the bottom step.

A balance had to be struck, therefore, between helping the bather through the process and allowing them some freedom of expression. With the increasing diversity in visitors' religious involvement the head of the bath (*chef des piscines*) reminded all the volunteers at the beginning of each session to be sensitive to the bather's individual wishes and explained changes which had taken place in bathing practice. He periodically checked inside each bath to see what was happening and might remind the helpers about "correct" procedure. Yet although the bathing process was less mechanical and uniform, the general structure remained the same. Indeed, since bathers usually were coming for the first time and could no longer watch how the bathing process operated, there were moments of ambiguity and confusion.

These moments were particularly evident when someone who identified himself as not a Catholic entered the bath. For example, when I began working in the baths again in 2014 members of a French Tamil pilgrimage group arrived. Since some identified themselves as non-Catholics, there was some confusion among the helpers when the bather stood at the top of the steps before entering the bath. Because the team rotated jobs during the session I took over the role of greeting some of the Tamil bathers and tried to avoid possible confusion by inviting them in French to pray and joined my hands in prayer to make the point. Clearly, I was imposing my own order on the process but the bathers appeared grateful for the guidance.

When the bather entered the bath there was again the possibility of being unsure what to do and I encouraged the bather to "do his own thing." Some non-Catholic Tamil bathers took the opportunity to sit or kneel in the bath and splash themselves all over with the water—a striking contrast to the more restricted immersion performed with most bathers. Ending the ritual could also be a moment of confusion and ambiguity. Unless the bather had something else in mind, such as a final prayer or a request to kiss the statue of Our Lady, I allowed for a short pause and then helped the bather to return up the stairs to retrieve his pants.

Although those visiting Lourdes were reminded in various ways about the importance of penance, I want to discuss here the physical sensation of bathing and the sense of the water's agency drawing on both my own experience. At the end of each session, like many other members of the team I took the opportunity to bathe and this helps to understand what other bathers experience. Hence, the tying of the damp towel around the midriff comes as a shock, even when anticipated and although I then say a private prayer, I find it hard to concentrate and it is easy to get distracted by the physical sensation of the cold wetness seeping into my body and the water trickling down my legs. Walking down to the end of the bath deepens this sensation and then comes a challenge—do I bathe myself or trust my colleagues to lower me back into the water without slipping?

The bath leaves its traces afterwards since everyone is expected to put their clothes back on without using any towel. Many bathers comment on how quickly they dry off, especially when the weather is hot and dry, but on rainy days it is easy to feel the bath's continuing presence in damp shirts and trousers. Many also mention how refreshed they feel and my own experience suggests that this is not only the physical effect of the water but also the pleasure at completing the process.

Risk, Trust, and the Body

The dangers inherent in bathing also seemed to reflect secular considerations. Helpers were reminded of their responsibilities to the bathers—their "duty of care" informed by health and safety legislation and the possibility that any accident might result in litigation. The authorities' sensitivity also reflected the wider scandals concerning sexual abuse which had rocked the church since the 1990s. The Hospitality's declaration of a general Code of Conduct in January 2018 vividly reflected this wider context:

> In the current context in which the Church carries out its ministry of service and compassion, we must all increase our awareness. The standards set by the

Sanctuary and the Hospitalité of Our Lady of Lourdes meet these requirements: first of all to protect children and vulnerable people. At the same time, they also protect the clergy, employees and volunteers as well as the institution.

There were many occasions where helpers were in close physical contact with others so while the following instruction applied to all areas of the sanctuary, it was particularly significant for those working in the baths as the final item in the following list indicates:

Examples of physical contact to be avoided:
- *Signs of affection, usual under other circumstances, are not acceptable inside the Sanctuary. In this way*, it is forbidden to kiss anyone, particularly a child or a vulnerable person, or to force him or her to kiss you.
- Avoid gestures of consolation that might be common elsewhere as customs of other countries, *inter alia*:

  – hug someone, even if the person is very well known to you
  – carry or touch a child or vulnerable person, even in the context of games
  – "tickle" anyone

- It is forbidden to touch someone in a place normally covered by a swimsuit.
- It is forbidden to have someone on your lap (except infants and very young children).
- Exemplary caution must be exercised in the Sanctuary Piscines (Baths). https://www.facebook.com/groups/hndlourdes/search/?query=Code%20of%20Conduct&epa=SEARCH_BOX

Although those coming to the baths expressed a high degree of trust in our role as helpers, I was reminded of some people's suspicions concerning our motives in an admittedly isolated instance. I was standing "on guard" in the empty changing area of the bath during a distinct lull in proceedings. A middle-aged Frenchman entered and brusquely rejected the offer of assistance made by the head of the bath, who retreated behind the curtain. The bather's attitude intrigued me and it was hard not to look at him since we were the only two people now in the changing area. After he had bathed and was putting his clothes back on he summoned me and told me that my gaze had made him uncomfortable. I returned to my post duly chastened. After a brief moment of reflection I thought that I go back to him to explain my duty of care. However, to my surprise he explained that he was concerned about the stories of pederasty.

My immediate reaction was to be shocked by the insinuation that I might have been looking at him "inappropriately" but on reflection I began to see how the scandals around clerical abuse within the church had influenced people's attitudes toward those offering to assist others. Since Lourdes played such an important role in the church's global mission its religious and Hospitality leaders were determined to avoid all scandal. The 2018 Code of Conduct cited earlier was the Hospitality's response to the repeated claims concerning clerical abuse in Europe and the Americas.[3] Significantly, these claims within the church ran in parallel to public debates about sexual harassment and gender inequality more generally, for example, the charges levied against Harvey Weinstein and other Hollywood male luminaries from late 2017 and the #MeToo movement. Indeed, the Code of Conduct showed how the religious and secular arenas were closely connected since it concluded with a section, "French Law and Sexual Abuse," which cited articles 222-3 of the state penal code. All Hospitality members were required to sign up to the code and were made fully aware of the legal implications in doing so.

Conclusion

This chapter has explored the sacralization of the landscape in the context of one of the Roman Catholic Church's most popular pilgrimage centers—Lourdes near the French border with Spain. The spring, uncovered during Bernadette's visions in 1858, became the focal point of both claims to miraculous healing and a highly organized system of bathing, but water, more generally, played a key role in the sacralization of the local landscape. As the grotto and its environs were purged of their association with dangerous spirits through a range of construction works that channeled the spring to specific locations, visitors not only could drink it and wash in it but they could also touch the wet cliff face inside the grotto and gaze at the river over the walls that sought to control its flow.

Yet, the expansion of the shrine led to a more mundane danger. The floods of 2013 and 2014 were vivid reminders of the vulnerability of building so close to a lively mountain river. Admittedly, the inundation was exceptional and the main areas of the shrine were quickly repaired but the financial impact on local businesses was dire. The vulnerability of this reorganized landscape was exposed and added to the unease caused by the decline in visitor numbers evident since the peak of 2008 (see Moore 2014).

The studies by Gesler (1992, 1996, 2003), Harris (2010, 2013), and Goldingay, Dieppe, and Farias (2014) have provided illuminating discussions of changing discourses and practices drawing on such concepts as therapeutic landscapes, holistic spirituality, religious thermalism, and performance, while Jansen and

Notermans (2012) have also shown the importance played by ex-votos in the local landscape. However, besides an early paper I published (Eade 1991) based on my personal involvement, the actual process of bathing has not been examined from a social scientific perspective. Therefore, in the second part of this chapter I sought to shed fresh light on the bathing process by exploring the role played by water in this internally sacralized landscape by drawing on my experience of returning to Lourdes after a twenty-two-year absence.

In the 1991 paper I focused like Andrea Dahlberg, Ruth Harris, and Suzanne Kaufman on the relationship between the sanctuary's officials and bathers in terms of discourse and practice. Drawing on more recent research by Alana Harris and colleagues and insights provided by the "material turn," I have sought to balance the dominant phenomenological approach within pilgrimage studies by focusing on the sensual experience of bathing. The tensions and ambiguities evident during my earlier time at Lourdes have not disappeared but thinking more about my own experience of bathing I see now how these are bound up with bodily sensations. The relationship between bathers and water is crucial here and has led me to ponder this relationship in the context of the material transformation of the landscape. This transformation involved the sacralization of the grotto area and the increasing environmental pressure created by the expansion of the pilgrimage town between the sanctuary and the old town up the hill.

Hence, looking more broadly still, this case study can be seen as contributing to this volume's focus on landscapes of Christianity through an eclectic theoretical approach. Pilgrimage has played a key role in transforming local landscapes through the building of shrines and the development of routes between the shrines and people's homes. While the phenomenological perspective has provided a powerful tool for understanding the meanings and motives involved in pilgrimage, recent publications have opened up new avenues for exploration by drawing on the "material turn" as well as political-economic perspectives (see Reader 2015; Coleman and Eade 2018). Lourdes provides a fine example of how pilgrimage is good to think with and through!

Acknowledgments

I am very grateful for the insights and support provided by Anna Fedele, Evgenia Mesaritou, Amos Ron, Gabriele Shenar, and the anonymous reviewer. Their feedback on the draft of this chapter made me realize that I am only touching the tip of a very large iceberg (another watery metaphor!).

3

Crucifix and Dirt

Catholic and Indigenous Origins of the Holy Earth of the Santuario de Chimayó

Brett Hendrickson

Thousands of people mostly on Good Friday but also throughout the year walk through the high desert of northern New Mexico to arrive at one of the most important pilgrimage sites in North America. They walk toward the Santuario de Chimayó, a picturesque 200-year-old adobe church that is famous for its healing dirt. The landscape they traverse is nothing if not memorable: whimsically named rock formations punctuate the undulating scrubland, all of it in the shadows of the encircling mountain ranges. Lines of archaic cottonwood trees hug the waterways that flow down from the mountains to empty eventually into the Río Grande. In the stretch of New Mexico from Santa Fe to Taos, the scruffy city of Española provides a shopping anchor for dozens of Hispano and Pueblo villages.[1] The Hispano village of Chimayó is just one of these places, but its importance as a center of national and international pilgrimage sets it apart as a particularly luminous point. In large measure, the dirt is what makes the Santuario de Chimayó so attractive. One of the Santuario's side chapels features a hole in the floor, called the *pocito* (little well, or hole), that opens into the sandy soil below. People come to the Santuario to gather up the miraculous dirt from the *pocito* because they believe that it contains healing power. They rub the dirt on their own aches and pains, and they bring it home to share with their loved ones. In this way, the earth of the Chimayó hills has been spread far and wide, a handful at a time.

How did this place, the Santuario de Chimayó, become this place? Why is the dirt holy and miraculous? One answer to these questions would be to suggest that there is something about the natural features of the landscape of the northern Río Grande valley that creates the context for this particular kind of religious place and practice. But, cultural geographers and religious studies theorists have tended to take the opposing view that it is rather human stories and human social structures that make sense out of particular landscapes. In their analyses, even the natural world is enlisted by human cultures to help explain our complex and often conflictual relationships. For instance, Jonathan Z. Smith, in a discussion of sacred places, writes that "place is not best conceived as a particular location with an idiosyncratic physiognomy or as a uniquely individualistic node of sentiment, but rather as a social position within a hierarchical system" (1992: 45). The places in which people find themselves, then, are best understood as contexts in which people experience their social positions vis-à-vis others. Narratives and histories about places are the mechanism by which places become repositories of meaning, and, for Smith, reminders of one's position in social hierarchies. The historian of Christian spirituality Philip Sheldrake argues that remembering the story of a place is an interpretive move that lays claim and implies responsibility. He adds, "Place is also political because the way it is constructed means that it is occupied by some people's stories but not by others" (2001: 20).

In this vein, this chapter demonstrates that the assorted origin stories for the miraculous dirt at the Santuario de Chimayó reveal the overlapping assertions of the Santuario's various stakeholders as to the meaning of the surrounding land. Indeed, religious narratives about Chimayó's landscape and specific geographical points emerge as some of the most salient signifiers of the dirt's miraculous power. A complicating feature of northern New Mexico is the entanglement of Hispano Catholicism with Pueblo understandings of the land and its mythic past. The origin stories for the Santuario's holy dirt, two of which I discuss in detail in the following paragraphs, variously connect the church with Spanish colonial Catholicism and with the earth-based narratives of indigenous people in New Mexico and farther south in the former Spanish empire. I argue that these relatively well-known origin stories for the Santuario's holy dirt have intermingled in the physical space of the church. For some, the Santuario is a latecomer that sits atop ancient indigenous land. For others, the Santuario is a unique extension of the global Catholic Church, and as such, is a place to experience Christ's blessing even if it is in a setting that is locally inflected. The interplay of indigenous and Christian origins at the Santuario provides a dynamic narrative, aesthetic, and geographic site that many visitors find uniquely meaningful and even transcendent.

Contextual Overview

Before entering into an analysis of the Santuario's origin stories, it is helpful to provide a brief description of the immediate area, the Santuario itself, and the pattern of devotion that takes place within and around this unique church. The village of Chimayó lies in a relatively verdant valley along the Santa Cruz River, a stream that flows into the Río Grande. It is approximately 30 miles north of Santa Fe, the capital of New Mexico since 1610, and 35 miles east-northeast of Los Alamos and its famous laboratories. The Santa Cruz River valley, referred to historically as La Cañada, runs west from around Chimayó through the ancient village of Santa Cruz and the newer city of Española. The terrain of the settled areas is flat, though punctuated by hills, and the Sangre de Cristo mountain range rises immediately to the east with the Jemez Mountains to the west and the Tusas to the north. To the south the land is high and dry toward Santa Fe, continuing on to Albuquerque.

No doubt due to the fertility of its land, La Cañada has been the site of nearly constant human habitation for centuries. Various groups of Tewa-speaking Pueblos have lived and farmed in the region since as early as 1000 CE, although there are archeological indications that the Pueblos abandoned the area some 200 years prior to Spanish colonization in the early seventeenth century (Borhegyi 1954b). Spanish farming families settled the area in the early decades of the 1600s, but they, along with the rest of the Spanish population, were forced to leave New Mexico by the short-lived but effective Pueblo Revolt, which returned New Mexico to Pueblo control from 1680 to 1692. During this brief interregnum, some Tano-speaking Pueblos inhabited La Cañada, but they were expelled when the Spanish returned and retook the region. At that point, permanent Spanish settlement was established in Chimayó (Spicer 1962: 164 and Twitchell 1914: 241–57). Nearby Tewa Pueblos include Nambé, Santa Clara, Pojoaque, San Ildefonso, and Ohkey Owingeh (formerly known as San Juan). There is little in the historical record that documents Pueblo and Spanish interaction in Chimayó in the post-revolt period, but the proximity of the Pueblos and the relative isolation of the village make such interaction almost a given.

The Santuario was not built until over a century after permanent Spanish settlement was established in Chimayó. Rather, a church was erected in Santa Cruz in the early eighteenth century to serve the religious needs of the Spanish settlers to the whole Santa Cruz River valley, and this church, despite its 8-mile remove from Chimayó, remained the official site of Catholic worship for village residents. When the Santuario was eventually constructed between the years 1813 and 1816, it joined several other small, family-owned chapels in the Chimayó vicinity, although it immediately differentiated itself as a site of pilgrimage and healing surrounding the holy dirt. Clergy from the Santa Cruz parish would make occasional rounds to the outlying chapels in the region, including the Santuario, to celebrate Masses and administer the rites for life transitions such as baptism, marriage, and death (Usner 1995: 61–6).

Like most of New Mexico's colonial-era churches, the Santuario de Chimayó is a low adobe structure with thick, earthen walls. The nave of the church is lined with *retablos* (painted screens) and *santos* (hand-carved, wooden statuettes of saints). The main altar of the church is backed by a large and colorful *retablo* that features paintings of saints as well as geometric shapes. In the center of the *retablo* hangs a large wooden crucifix carved in the style of typical New Mexico *santos*. Anterior to the nave are two small rooms, now used for storage and office space, but likely used originally to house items for sale to pilgrims.[2] Immediately adjacent to the chancel, and to the left if one is facing the altar, is a low-slung doorway into a long narrow room that is referred to as the sacristy. This room is filled with the memorabilia of pilgrims: cast-off crutches, braces, and thousands of photographs of loved ones. The sacristy also serves as the home to a much-revered statue of the Santo Niño de Atocha, a representation of the Christ-child known for his special care for the sick, the imprisoned, and children. On one end of the sacristy is another low door through a thick adobe wall that opens into a small square room. This room, in some ways the heart of the entire Santuario, has a round hole cut into the stone floor—the *pocito*—that gives access to the holy dirt. Pilgrims and other visitors generally enter the main doors of the church, process through the nave—sometimes stopping for prayer—and then turn into the sacristy. Almost everyone collects dirt from the *pocito* into baggies or other receptacles, and then tourists will often spend time looking at devotees' photos while pilgrims will frequently spend additional moments in prayer at the kneeler in front of the Santo Niño statue.

In recent years, the activities and movements available to visitors have multiplied as the Catholic Church and other interests have developed the area around the Santuario into a veritable campus of devotional and commercial space. It was only in 1980 that the first church-operated gift shop was opened (Roca 2007: 157). Since then, the Catholic Church has introduced three other gift shops in close proximity to the Santuario, one of which forms part of an informational visitors' center and art gallery. In addition to the shops, the church has constructed various centers for prayer and reflection, including a "Madonna Gardens," as well as monuments to the Holy Family, the Santo Niño, and Native Americans. The campus is rounded out by several private operations, including a snack bar, a coffee house, a smattering of art galleries, and another privately owned gift shop, El Potrero Trading Post. To the consternation of the neighbors, a nearby field has been converted into a parking lot to accommodate the ever-growing numbers of visitors.[3] The holy dirt, however, is still the main attraction.

The most common origin story for the *pocito* maintains that a Spanish farmer and village leader named Don Bernardo Abeyta was doing penance in a field near his home in Chimayó on Good Friday, in 1810, when he saw something glowing in the dirt near the Santa Cruz River. He approached the source of the light and discovered a crucifix buried in a hole. Being a pious man, Abeyta immediately took the crucifix to the priest at the closest parish church, 8 miles away in Santa Cruz, where the two men placed the holy object on the altar. The next morning, the crucifix had disappeared only to be rediscovered in the hole in the ground back in Chimayó. Abeyta returned the cross to the church in Santa Cruz, but in vain because the peripatetic Christ went back once more to the original spot in the ground. Understanding that God desired for the crucifix to remain in Chimayó, Abeyta sought permission from the Catholic Church to build a chapel around the site of the crucifix's discovery, a project he began in 1813. Finished in 1816, the chapel was named the Santuario de Nuestro Señor de Esquipulas since Abeyta had identified the Christ as a replica of a famous crucifix of the same name in Esquipulas, Guatemala. Soon, pilgrims were coming from miles around to pray to Our Lord of Esquipulas and to draw the sacred and healing earth that quickly became associated with the hole from which he had emerged. The basic contours of this story are on display at the Santuario today as a testimony to the miraculous presence of the Christian God in this special church.[4]

To be sure, it is easy to notice that this is basically a Catholic story: on a Christian holy day, a faithful local man finds one of the central devotional items of the Catholic Church on his land. After explicit interaction with a priest and the Catholic Church, the man builds a church, the principal physical space of Christianity. Such a story serves the historical and contemporary interests of the Catholic Church. But there is evidence that the association of Chimayó's earth with healing predates Spanish and Catholic arrival to the site.[5]

Tewa Pueblo Origins

The place where the village of Chimayó now sits almost certainly was once inhabited by Tewa Pueblo people, and the landscape still constitutes part of their sacred geography. Alfonso Ortiz, a Tewa anthropologist who was born at San Juan Pueblo, now known as Ohkay Owingeh, has written extensively about Tewa space. According to Ortiz, the Tewa world is comprised of various categories of existence that fall onto a conceptual grid oriented to the four cardinal points.

Marking these cardinal points are several "tetrads," or geographically locatable places, that help set the bounds of Tewa life. At the heart of this world is the "earth navel," which is physically located in the center of the Pueblo village at Ohkay Owingeh (only 20 miles from Chimayó), and serves as a place of eternal emergence and return. Other earth navels are likewise found at the tops of mountains and sacred hills and can also act as places of entrance to a vast, interconnected, and labyrinthine underworld. The outer ring of the Tewa world is marked by a tetrad of high mountains; an intermediate ring is made up of a foursome of lower hills. It is the eastern hill of the inner tetrad, called Tsi Mayoh, that rises directly to the north and east of the Santuario and that gives the village of Chimayó its name. To be sure, while this does not make Chimayó the most sacred spot of the Tewa, it clearly lies in an important place and has narrative significance as a site of activity of the Towa é, both human and supernatural personages who are part of Tewa cosmology (Ortiz 1969: 18–22, 122, 141–2).

Some of the earliest suggestions that the Santuario's healing dirt has Tewa origins come from white explorers in the nineteenth century. For instance, the proto-anthropologist and archeologist Adolph Bandelier mentions in his writings "the gorges of Chimayo" as early as 1892. He understood the place to be something of a lookout for both the Tewa and Hispano villagers against marauders from the plains that lie to the northeast (Lange, Lange, and Riley 1966: 74). The ethnogeographer John Harrington published his study of the Tewa world in 1916, which is mostly comprised of a discussion of place names. He notes that Chimayó, according to the Indians of the region, was once a Tewa Pueblo called Tsimajo'oŋwi, which was situated incredibly "where the church is now." At the site of this Pueblo—that is, where the Santuario currently sits—was a pool called Tsimajopokwi. The pool's mud had healing properties (Harrington 1916: 341–2).

Edgar Hewett was an anthropologist and archeologist of sorts who was fascinated with Native American culture and artifacts. He became involved with preservation as well as educational efforts to study and enshrine New Mexico's native peoples. His 1912 explanation of the healing sanctuary at Chimayó features several factual inaccuracies but is the clearest early exponent of the idea that the Santuario's dirt has Pueblo origins:

> Chimayo was originally an Indian pueblo, a pueblo of blanket weavers. There is a famous old shrine at the place. It was originally an Indian shrine. After the pueblo became Mexicanized a church was built by the shrine and pilgrimages were made to the shrine from all over the Southwest. The church built at the shrine is in the custodianship of purest Indian descent. In a grotto is the curative

earth. Boards in the floor are taken up in order to get at the earth. People used to carry the earth away with them. Articles of silver, brass and glass were deposited at the place. The earth was consecrated.[6]

From Hewett's description, it seems highly unlikely that he ever visited the Santuario, and he unfortunately does not provide his sources about the ancient Indian shrine. Moreover, he mistakenly remarks that the custodians of the shrine, which we know to be the Abeyta and Chavez families, were of "purest Indian descent." Other problems with his picture, of course, include that the dirt is in a grotto under boards, and that by 1912, the people seem to have ceased carrying away the earth, much evidence in other records to the contrary.

Given that Harrington and Hewett likely had little or no personal experience with the Santuario, it is curious that they made such concerted efforts to claim a Pueblo origin for the Santuario's healing dirt. Perhaps the more obvious explanation, examined later in the chapter, is that the Santuario, as a Hispano Catholic Church, expressed at least some form of devotionalism inherited from the Spanish Catholic past. These early Anglophone scholars, however, preferred to argue that the use of dirt for medicinal purposes in the Chimayó area more likely predated the arrival of the Spanish. There are two likely reasons for this "Indian hypothesis." The first is that these explorers were on the lookout for ways they could link the ancient Pueblo past of the land with the new Anglo settlers without acknowledging the centuries of Spanish and Mexican control of the region. In this analysis, the healing mud had always been there but only recently had been "Mexicanized" with the trappings of a Catholic shrine. Conversely, the second plausible reason for the Indian hypothesis is the anthropologists' thinly veiled desire to see the unique and picturesque Catholicism of the Hispanos not as an acceptable counterpart to their own understandings of Christianity but rather as endlessly syncretized with the more creative and ultimately spiritual additions of the Indian. Charles Lummis, a friend of Bandelier and fellow ethnographer and adventurer, provides us with an example of this viewpoint when he wrote, "With the superstitions dwells the simple folk-lore. That of the Mexicans is scant; but that of the Indians infinite and remarkably poetic" (1952: 19).

More recent permutations of the Indian hypothesis generally disregard earlier Anglo interpretations of New Mexico's ancient folklife and instead focus on contemporary Pueblo stories about the origins of Chimayó's healing earth. Photographer and historian Don Usner recounts a Nuevomexicano legend in Chimayó that seems to have originated with the Tewa people of the area. In the story, a cave on the side of Tsi Mayoh—the abovementioned hill that lies behind the Santuario—is an entrance to a warren of subterranean passageways in the Tewa underworld that connect Tsi Mayoh to Black Mesa in San Ildefonso Pueblo, 10 miles away from Chimayó. The passageways, according to the Tewa, serve as homes for dangerous giants and therefore should not be entered except by the ritually initiated (Usner 1995: 16). The Tewa underworld situates the Santuario and its *pocito* of holy dirt onto contemporary Tewa cosmology of an interconnected New Mexican landscape that contains openings between worlds. Moreover, according to folklorist Enrique Lamadrid, Tewa stories confirm the early ethnographic accounts mentioned earlier about Tewa use of healing mud in the Chimayó vicinity. They say that the place was where the twin sons of the Sun killed a dangerous and threatening giant. As a result of this act, fire came out of the ground and dried up what had been a sacred spring. The remaining mud became the source of the healing earth now enclosed inside the Santuario (Howarth and Lamadrid 1999: 10). (see Figure 3.1).

Connections like these, between the Tewa cosmos and the Catholic shrine, suggest that the Spanish Catholics who built the Santuario did so knowingly to capitalize on pre-Hispanic sacred space. In this sense, the Santuario joins other Catholic holy sites in the Americas that sit atop earlier indigenous holy places, the most famous being the Basilica of Our Lady of Guadalupe on Tepeyac hill in Mexico, a place formerly consecrated to a mother goddess called Tonantzin

Figure 3.1 Pilgrims queue to enter the Santuario. Tsi Mayoh Hill rises behind the church. Photograph by the author.

(Brading 2001: 214). Historian Ramón Gutiérrez has studied the Santuario and identifies the *pocito* as a *sipapu* upon which Abeyta built the chapel. A *sipapu* is the Hopi word used to describe the hole in the bottom of a kiva through which the Pueblo peoples emerged into this world. The Tewas do not use the word "*sipapu*," as it is not in their language, but there is a cognate word that is used in a similar origin story. Likewise, the Tewas do speak of "earth navels," one of which, as mentioned, has long been associated with the hill of Tsi Mayoh (Harrington 1916: 568 and Ortiz 1969: 19). Gutiérrez's contention follows on anthropologists Victor and Edith Turner's conclusions that Christian shrines around the world, and perhaps especially in Spanish America, have been built over places once deemed sacred or vital by the pre-existing people. In the Turners' words, the Christians "baptize the local customs" (1978: 33).

The stories that privilege a Pueblo origin for the Santuario's healing earth imagine the land around the church to be imbued with pre-European meaning and mythologies. From this narrative vantage point, the church is an accretion on top of concentric mountain circles of the Pueblo world, which in turn rests above an underworld that occasionally and momentously opens into our reality. The hole in the floor of the church containing the holy dirt, in these stories, suggests that the dirt and the place are ultimately indigenous. This implies, of course, that Hispanos and others who have believed in the power of the holy dirt are, in some measure, participating in Indian knowledge and ritual practice. One effect of this kind of origin story, then, is to push back the starting date for devotional practices at the Chimayó site into the relatively undocumented indigenous past. This interpretive move provides a historical depth to what could otherwise be considered a comparatively young church in northern New Mexico. It also connects the church in a predominantly Hispano village with the more ancient mission structures built specifically for the evangelization of the Indians.[7] Such a connection gives the Santuario a historical patina beyond its 200 years.

But pointing out explicit connections with prior Pueblo traditions and customs has other meaning as well. When Christian practices evince a history of mixing with indigenous non-Christian rituals, the loaded word that scholars have often used to describe the process and its outcomes is "syncretism." For some, syncretism is bemoaned as an adulteration of religious purity or European civilization. If the healing earth in the Santuario has Indian origins, this is proof that the local Hispano devotion to the earth is a sign of cultural declension and religious degradation. We can understand this type of analysis as one example of the *leyenda negra*, the Black Legend that paints the Spanish and their descendants in the Americas as hopelessly backward, medieval, cruel, and superstitious—traits that left them open to the pernicious influences of the natives. On the other extreme are those who have romanticized American Indian cultures as profoundly spiritual, artistic, and natural. In this kind of analysis, syncretism with purported indigenous healing earth in the Santuario can only burnish the shrine's mystical connection to spiritual and miraculous power. Moreover, Native American religions often identify specific places and landscapes as uniquely sacred.[8] If the Santuario is read as an ancient indigenous site, this lends credence to the notion that the church's dirt is sacred because of former and ongoing Pueblo sacralization of the place.

Colonial Catholic Origins

The other major origin story for Chimayó's holy dirt relies not on an ancient Native American past but on the moveable traditions of Spanish American Catholicism. The official and historical name of the Santuario is "El Santuario de Nuestro Señor de Esquipulas" ("The Sanctuary of Our Lord of Esquipulas"), the name ascribed to the Christ on the large crucifix on the main altar screen of the church as well as a smaller statue in the room where the *pocito* is located.[9] The Esquipulas crucifix at the front of the church is the one that Don Bernardo Abeyta ostensibly found in a hole on the ground on his farm, a miraculous detail much emphasized by the Catholic Church's representatives who oversee the site. The Santuario's Lord of Esquipulas, however, is not the first of that name. The Christ of Esquipulas is originally the name of a large crucifix in southeastern Guatemala that was created in the late sixteenth century, over 100 years before the construction of the Santuario at Chimayó. The Catholic origin story thus connects the earth of the Santuario with a Guatemalan Christ almost 2,500 miles away. In this telling, the Santuario is clearly part of a network of Spanish Catholic devotional sites and therefore shares common features from other parts of the wide-ranging empire.

At the time of the Spanish conquest of the eastern portion of Guatemala in the early years of the sixteenth century, the area was inhabited by Chorti Indians, a subgroup of the Maya who still reside in Guatemala, Honduras, and El Salvador. To avoid their own massacre, the Chortis, under the guidance of their leader named Esquipulas, agreed to turn over custodianship of their territory to the Spaniards.[10] By the 1560s, they were resettled into a new town called Santiago de Esquipulas in present-day southeastern Guatemala; the town was felicitously located on a popular trade and pilgrimage route between points in Guatemala and the vaunted Maya religious center at Copán in Honduras. A small Christian church was built at Esquipulas in 1578, and the villagers commissioned and paid for a noted colonial artist, Quirio Cataño, to craft a large crucifix to adorn the altar. Significantly, the crucifix was made in such a way that the typical white skin of Spanish Christ images was replaced with a lustrous black such that the image has long been known as the "Cristo Negro de Esquipulas" (Borhegyi 1954a: 389).

Despite this last detail, one might assume from the story that the Spanish had pacified and evangelized the Chortis with unusual dispatch, settling them in a well-administered village centered on a Catholic Church. However, reminiscent to the later Pueblo stories associated with Chimayó, the Esquipulas shrine was built on top of an older indigenous sacred place known for its health-giving springs and curing earth. By the opening years of the seventeenth century, a pilgrimage to Esquipulas for the purpose of seeking healing was underway, and the indigenous roots of the place had already become entangled irreversibly with the image of the Black Christ. Pilgrims found relief as a result of venerating the crucifix, and they also purchased and ingested tablets called "*benditos*" made from local earth. Furthermore, such geophagy, or earth-eating, was common from the central valley of Mexico and south throughout the Maya region. Eventually, due to the prominence of the Black Christ, whose image is often impressed on the earthen tablets, the practice of ingesting or using earth for healing became associated with the Lord of Esquipulas. The health-seeking pilgrims to Esquipulas were blessed and sanctioned by the Catholic Church in 1737.[11]

In addition to the common feature of the presence of healing earth, the artistic rendering of the Guatemalan "Cristo Negro" also relates to the Esquipulas crucifix in Chimayó. First, the dark aspect of the skin of the earlier image may signify a further indigenous connection to the Maya and other Mesoamerican peoples. Remaining art and codices, as well as colonial-era episcopal reports, suggest that several groups of Maya ranging from the Yucatan and throughout Guatemala venerated black-tinted deities, "the lord of black ones," and "the tall black lord" (Borhegyi 1954a: 390). Second, Quirio Cataño, the artist who crafted the crucifix, situated the Christ on a dark green cross carved with leaves and growing vines. Trees of life, or world trees, are a common motif in Maya art and may represent a graphic depiction of Maya cosmology. Whether or not the Esquipulas crucifix's green, leafy cross was intentionally carved to make this connection, it has been made by both academic and ecclesiastical observers.[12] One conclusion that can be drawn is that the speedy rise of the healing pilgrimage in Esquipulas relied on not-so-subtle connections to Maya religious aesthetics and ideas that can be discerned in the crucifix's appearance. In this analysis, the

Santuario does not only boast deep-seated ties to an ancient Pueblo past, it also is rooted in Mesoamerican cosmology.

While the Guatemalan and New Mexican crucifixes are not identical, they share enough similarities that Catholic officials in New Mexico have made an effort to explain the more explicitly indigenous aspects of the image, particularly the green, leafy cross upon which the New Mexican Christ figure is mounted. The interpretive materials regarding this fact are displayed prominently in the church-operated visitor center adjacent to the Santuario:

> The most distinguishing characteristic of the crucifix is the green color of the wood on which Jesus has been crucified. Truncated stems on the cross signify that the wood is alive. For that reason, it is green and not brown.
>
> Tradition calls the cross *"the Tree of Life."* The Indians from Santiago de Esquipulas (Guatemala) revered the *"Tree of Life"* before the arrival of the Christian missionaries. This tree has the form of a cross and when the Indians saw the cross of Jesus for the first time, it was easy for them to accept that this was the God that they should worship ...
>
> The Tree of Life or the Tree of the Knowledge of Good and Evil is also found in the Bible. Trees are often used as images of the strength and weakness of the human being.[13]

In this version of the arboreal cross, the leaves and tree motif facilitated the Indians' evangelization to "the God they should worship." The Maya world tree that stretches up and down the axis mundi becomes a symbol shared across religious traditions that can and is replaced with the cross of Jesus Christ, the mediator par excellence between the heavens and the earth.[14]

Although the Esquipulas crucifix in Chimayó is easily the most important replica of Esquipulas in New Mexico, there are other images of Esquipulas in the state. The noted contemporary *santero* (saint carver) and researcher Charles Carrillo has found that, by the 1830s, an image of the Lord of Esquipulas was part of the typical repertoire of most *santeros* in New Mexico. "In New Mexico, the principal key in the identification of the colonial images of Our Lord of Esquipulas is not the color of his flesh; rather it is the identification of a Latin cross from which seven living branches emanate." Carrillo argues that the green, leafy crosses metaphorically suggest life and curing to the devotee, and possibly even the more specific idea of medicine (Carrillo 1999: 51–3). In this reading of the Esquipulas devotion, the emphasis is again on healing. And while the Santuario and its healing dirt lead the pack among healing devotions in New Mexico, the fact that there are other Lords of Esquipulas around the state suggests that healing and recovery have been attractive themes in New Mexico Hispano Catholicism even outside the precincts of Chimayó.

If artists were supplying statues and images of Our Lord of Esquipulas to the New Mexican faithful in the early decades of the nineteenth century, then there must have been a demand for this image. The earliest specific mention of it occurred in 1803 when the vicar of the Santa Cruz parish wrote a letter to his friend, Fr. Mariano Sanches Bergara (spelled elsewhere as Sánchez Vergara), and asked him to remember him in prayer with the "Sr. de Esquipula."[15]

The connection to Bernardo Abeyta, the Santuario's builder, can be established shortly thereafter. In 1805, Abeyta's nephew was born, baptized, and christened as Juan de Esquipulas. One of Abeyta's own children was born and given the name Tomás de Jesús de Esquipulas in 1813, and it was later in that same year that Abeyta, speaking on behalf of all the families in El Potrero—the area of Chimayó where the Santuario is now located—solicited approval from the priest in Santa Cruz to begin construction of a chapel named for the increasingly popular image of Christ.

> I declare [illegible] myself desirous of [illegible] tribute to our God and Redeemer [illegible] the corresponding worship in his form as Esquipulas, to be allowed to be built in the said place a chapel where people can congregate with the objective of [illegible] his mercies in all their needs.[16]

Fray Sebastián Álvarez, the priest in Santa Cruz who received this letter, was in full support and sent the request on to the diocesan authorities in Durango. Álvarez's explanation of the devotion to Esquipulas demonstrates the extent of its popularity by 1813.

> I affirm that the miraculous image of the Lord of Esquipulas, which for three years has been venerated in the shrine that is contiguous to his [Abeyta's] house and dwelling, and supported at his own expense. . . . This place is frequented by many people and in pilgrimage they come from even twenty and more leagues away to give their intercessions (*votos*) to the Sovereign Redeemer, and to experience relief and healing of their ailments. From the constant fame of these portents has originated the laudable desire that comes from the faithful and other devotees of the Lord of Esquipulas to build him a chapel in the most decent and well-proportioned place that has been chosen in the same Plaza or Rancho of El Potrero, that they already have named the Santuario de Esquipulas, wherein they hope to offer to the Lord their reverent worship.[17]

It is clear, therefore, that not only was Abeyta devoted to Esquipulas but that the devotion had spread by this point to many in the region. It is also evident that some sort of story about the "miraculous image" and its "portents" had already become sufficiently well known to attract an extensive pilgrimage.

How the New Mexicans, including Abeyta, came to know of the Señor de Esquipulas in faraway Guatemala is not precisely known, although historians have ventured two reasonable hypotheses. The first is that Abeyta, as a relatively successful citizen and leader in his community may have had business connections that led him to travel down the Camino Real and into southern reaches of New Spain. There is no reason to suppose this is not the case, as commerce up and down the empire was common.[18] The other supposition is that, rather than a New Mexican visiting the south, the natural movement of goods, people, and ideas inevitably brought the Esquipulas devotion north all the way to Chimayó, and indeed, the veneration of Esquipulas had spread throughout several other more northerly precincts of Mexico. Shrines to Esquipulas were established, often along with the practice of geophagy, or earth-eating, in places as diverse as Oaxaca, Veracruz, and Guadalajara, as well as points south of Guatemala in many of the lands that would eventually become independent Central American nations[19] (see Figure 3.2).

Another purported connection between Chimayó and Esquipulas, Guatemala, draws on popular legend, one that has been promoted relatively recently in

Figure 3.2 Señor de Esquipulas crucifix on the main altar of the Santuario. Photograph by the author.

a publication produced by the Archdiocese of Santa Fe. The story goes that a Guatemalan priest accompanied the first Spanish settlers to the Chimayó area; no date is given—this may refer to the poorly documented settlement of the area that occurred before the Pueblo Revolt or the later settlement in the 1690s. In any case, Indians killed the Guatemalan padre, and he was buried along with a crucifix in Chimayó. When the Santa Cruz River flooded its banks in 1810, the legend tells that both the body of the priest and the crucifix were uncovered by the surging waters. According to the tale, there were still older people alive at the time of the flood who recognized the priest, and they shouted, "Miren, el Padre de Esquipulas" ("Look, the Father from Esquipulas"). The locals soon began referring to the crucifix that emerged from the ground as Our Lord of Esquipulas not after the namesake crucifix in Guatemala but due to its association with the Esquipulan priest.[20] This version of the Esquipulas connection (which perhaps invites skepticism given the detail that personal familiarity with the alleged priest spans more than a century for some Chimayó residents) has the virtue of explaining both the Guatemalan connection and the persistent notion that the original Chimayó crucifix emerged from the ground. It also emphasizes the role of heroic Catholic clergy in spreading the faith and specific devotion to a powerful, healing image of Christ, which unsurprisingly has meant that this particular origin story has been lifted up by Catholic Church authorities.

To summarize, the origin stories that focus on the Esquipulas crucifix tend to highlight associations with two interrelated historical forces. The first, of course, is the colonial Catholic Church and the complex reconfigurations of Christian symbols and narratives that emerged from the crucible of evangelization and colonization of Indian peoples. These stories exalt Christian motifs, none more central than Christ himself, even though they are often entangled with pre-existing Indian devotions and sacred places. Thus, the Lord of Esquipulas, the Black Christ of Guatemala on his budding tree of a cross, connotes the miraculous suffering and caregiving of Jesus *and* the long-standing geophagy in Mesoamerica *and* the black-skinned deities of the Maya as well as other indigenous groups in the region who situate themselves in relationship to a great Tree of Life. Related to this intricate web of signifiers is the massive entwining of the Viceroyalty of New Spain that allowed commercial goods, members of the clergy, and popular devotions to communicate and spread from the Isthmus of Panama to the upper Río Grande valley.

The second interrelated force is the historical and ongoing interpretation of Esquipulas by official Catholic voices. Fray Álvarez of Santa Cruz approved of Abeyta's petition to build the Santuario because he understood the place as one where Catholic devotion to Christ could flourish. He insisted in 1813 that the Christ image, experienced by faithful pilgrims, brought upon the miraculous healing and excited faithful devotion among his flock. Contemporary Catholic interpretations have echoed this original sentiment by reminding visitors to the Santuario that the Esquipulas crucifix, no matter its indigenous features and heritage, is ultimately an image of Jesus.

Conclusion

The Santuario de Chimayó and its *pocito* full of miraculous dirt remains one of the most remarkable features of northern New Mexico's landscape. It is an adobe Catholic Church building, akin to so many others in the American Southwest, but the soil of its walls extends down, seemingly deeper than that of other, similar churches. The hole in the floor punches through the surface of the land and connects at least two stories and two worlds together. There is little reason to doubt that the Santuario rests where it does because of pre-Hispanic narratives about the land. Pueblo stories about the mud of healing springs as well as Pueblo cosmologies of openings between this world and a vast underworld speak eloquently of an indigenous origin for the healing dirt of Chimayó. But, the legend of Bernardo Abeyta and the discovery of the Señor de Esquipulas in the ground also persists as another origin, one that begins with the appearance of the crucified Christ in New Mexico's sandy soil. The Santuario is ultimately a Catholic place of worship, and, as such, is a place where people go to worship the Christian God, to pray for his healing intercession in their lives. The interplay of these two basic origin stories for the place and the dirt (which are only the most prominent among even more origin legends) helps explain why the Santuario is such a special place for so many thousands of people.

The interpretive concern for the observer as well as for participants is that the Santuario—as a special place—has multiple origin stories and therefore layers of signification. Or, to put this another way, the place is not the essence of one story *or* another, it is an accretion that exceeds its constituent parts. The historian Philip Sheldrake explains this phenomenon. He writes that such places have

> an excess of meaning beyond what can be seen or understood at any one time. This excess persistently overflows any attempt at a final definition. A place can never be subordinated to a single valuation, one person's prejudices, or the assumptions of a single group. The hermeneutic of place progressively reveals

new meanings in a kind of topography, memory and the presence of a particular people at any given moment (Sheldrake 2001: 17).

Visitors to the Santuario de Chimayó, whether or not they are familiar with its competing origin stories, perhaps sense this excess of meaning, this imbrication of memory. They move quietly through its rooms, rub its dirt on their aching joints, and gather earth in containers to take home. In so doing, they participate in the ongoing stories of healing, power, and blessing that belong to this place on the earth.

4

Captivating Landscapes

Gender and Religion in Mormon Captivity Narratives

Sara M. Patterson

She was walking down the street holding her mother's hand when she first saw him, the man who would hold her captive for months. They had been shopping in downtown Salt Lake City, the skyline shaped by high-rise buildings and the Mormon temple. The city was abuzz with preparations for the Olympics. "I don't remember a lot about him," she recalled, "but . . . he was clean-cut and well groomed. No beard. No robes. No singing or talking about prophets or visions or being the Chosen One. All of that would come later. For now, he appeared to be nothing more than a normal guy who had hit a rough patch in his life," one who needed a little work or money to make ends meet. That normal guy looked at her briefly, disguising the fact that he had been observing her for some time, waiting for the moment when he would be able to take her from her home, from her community, from her church. He was waiting to take her captive (Smart 2013: 1–2).

Not long after, in the middle of the night, David Brian Mitchell broke into Elizabeth Smart's home, into the bedroom where she slept with her younger sister, and kidnapped her at knife point. He kept her quiet by threatening to murder her family if she made a noise. Smart described herself before the kidnapping as an innocent girl: "Some people say I'm pretty. Blond hair. Blue eyes. But I promise, I've never thought of myself that way. . . . Some of the girls I knew were boy-crazy, but I never thought about those kinds of things. I didn't wear makeup. I had never had a boyfriend." Setting up her narrative of innocence lost, Smart described her Sunday school class meeting prior to her kidnapping as a very significant one in which she learned a key lesson from her teacher: "If you will pray to do what God wants you to do, He will change your life" (Smart 2013: 8–9).

In Smart's account this description of her identity and her faith before captivity is juxtaposed against her description of the lascivious, lustful Mitchell who "began his journey to [Smart's] bed many years before he actually found himself standing beside [her] bed in the middle of the night." What Mitchell sought that night was a captive, someone he could take to his camp and force to become his second wife. In her narrative, Mitchell's identity was the opposite of Smart's: he was evil and savage. On the one hand, Mitchell represented bad religion, bad masculinity, bad family, and bad marriage. Smart, on the other hand, represented all that was good, feminine, faithful, and civilized.

Over 100 years earlier, another woman wrote a captivity narrative in which she described her captor in ways similar to Smart's description of Mitchell. Her captor admired her for some time from afar, desiring her youth and her beauty. He wanted to marry her and was willing to go to great lengths to achieve that marriage. He was so persistent that Ann Eliza Webb decided to marry another man, James Dee, just to avoid his pursuit. It was a major mistake, because Dee physically and emotionally abused her; she eventually stood up to Dee and chose to divorce him. Her earlier admirer, Brigham Young, president and prophet of the Church of Jesus Christ of Latter-day Saints (LDS), was still interested. He "looked often" at Ann Eliza Webb in church. "He was so confident of his success with the women he chose to woo, that he had no idea of meeting any settled opposition," she recalled. She "fought against [her] fate in every possible way." Young was "equally persistent" and tried "in every way to win [her], a willing bride, before he attempted to coerce [her]" (Young 2014: 264–72).

What do these two stories, written more than a century apart, have to do with one another? Both stand in the long tradition of American captivity narratives that captured American readers' attention. As part of that tradition, both texts play with the border between the civilized and savage, a border that was affirmed and troubled in texts of the American West, the space where Americans negotiated their identities by explaining who they were and *who they were not*. Captivity narratives played a critical role in these negotiations; they delineated the border between "civilized" and "savage," as the lead character was captured and taken to a savage, unfamiliar world. In so doing, the narratives affirmed the readership's civility while also defining the boundary between cultures and worlds. Although Native Americans were most likely to be the "other" in these narratives of a racialized, unfamiliar world, this was not always the case. Latter-day Saints, too, played a part in captivity narratives. Whereas in the nineteenth century, they played the role of the savage, as they did in Ann Eliza Young's story, by the beginning of the twenty-first century, the Saints had become the civilized characters, as they are in Smart's narrative the innocent world from which she was ripped. This transition indicates the new status of Mormons on the cusp of the twenty-first century—as an accepted religious minority rather than a scary racial and religious other.

Both Young and Smart juxtaposed the religious, sexual, and gender expectations of their captors' world with the expectations of the larger culture. In Young's nineteenth-century narrative, it was the monogamous Protestant culture that was reinforced as the morally appropriate model when compared to the Mormon captor's culture and religious worldview. By the twenty-first century, Elizabeth Smart could write a captivity narrative that portrayed Mormonism as the morally appropriate model of religion, gender, and sexuality and defined it against a fundamentalist worldview. In each narrative, what we will see is that these expectations about what *appropriate* religion, gender, and sexuality look like were written onto the landscapes of the American West. Thus, the dichotomies of civilized and savage, orthodoxy and heresy, acceptable and unacceptable gender roles were all mapped onto the physical world. In Smart's twenty-first-century captivity narrative, we will see that these dichotomies are less clearly defined, messier, yet the remnants remain, imagined as manifesting in the dramatic landscapes themselves.

Captivity Narratives

From the beginning, captivity narratives told by Europeans in the "New World" celebrated a European hero or heroine who was captured by Native Americans and forced to live in what was characterized as a racial and religious otherworld. Those narratives ended with the return of the captive to his or her own culture, having changed and not changed in several fundamental ways. Why were and are captivity narratives so popular? What about them has captured the American imagination for hundreds of years? From the mid-seventeenth century to the mid-nineteenth century European and American readers, interested in reading such stories, grabbed captivity narratives off the shelves. Over the course of those 200 years, somewhere between 450 and 500 captivity narratives were published in more than 1,200 editions. The popularity of the genre continued after the mid-nineteenth century and takes many forms to this day (Srikanth 2002: 85; Ebersole 1995).

In part, the popularity of the genre has to do with curiosity about and fear of the captor culture, depicted as the racial and religious other in the narrative.

In the story, the captive is yanked from "home" and taken to a new culture where her identity is stripped away and she must make her way in an unfamiliar world. The loss of relationship leads to a crisis of identity—who that person was, who that person mothered, or sistered, or befriended, who that person had community with is torn from her. Thus, as they told the stories, the authors often structured the narratives as a series of removes; as the captives moved from one location to another, they felt farther from home at each step. As the captive transitioned from freedom into captivity, she lost her identity, her social status, and the cultural markers that made her who she was. The captive then endured physical hardship as well as psychological obstacles. Her body was the site on which these removes were marked: "[T]he body is a painful register of the shattered or porous boundaries of inside and outside, self and other, past and present. The body is seen and experienced as a boundary whose integrity is ever in danger of being violated" (Ebersole 1995, 6–8; Samyn 1999: xi).

Perhaps the best-known captivity narrative is Mary Rowlandson's *The Sovereignty and Goodness of God: Being a Narrative of the Captivity and Restoration of Mrs. Mary Rowlandson*. First published in 1682, Rowlandson's book went through multiple editions and has been called "the first distinctly American best-seller" (Castiglia 1996: 1–2). The narrative focuses on Rowlandson, depicted as an innocent white Christian woman who is captured by dark-skinned savages, who steal her from her community and steal her identity in the process. Her story was marked by her distance from home and all that was familiar. One particularly popular passage in the story recounts Rowlandson taking on the traits of the "savage" in order to survive (Bross 2011: 314).

One of the functions of the captivity narrative was to justify the imperialistic and racist worldview of Europeans and later European Americans. The narratives did so precisely by "othering" indigenous cultures, portraying them as dark, savage, and bloodthirsty. The absence of any counter-narratives, the absence of questions about the ethics of the violence brought by civilizers is also a noted trait of captivity narratives (Bross 2011: 310). In fact, the narratives served as evidence for the need to use violence to "tame" the savage. The popularity of the narratives continued even after the United States had taken Native American land and resources because they offered an explanation or justification for that history.

These narratives also followed several biblical tropes that were drawn from the book of Exodus, the story where a divinely ordained leader, Moses, is sent to lead God's people out of captivity and to their promised land. In so doing, the narratives affirmed the Christianity of the captive and denigrated the religion of the captor. Perhaps unsurprisingly, white Christian audiences embraced these stories at precisely the same time as they were upholding a racial and religious hierarchy that enslaved, dislocated, and disinherited large groups of people. In the narratives, the captor was depicted as both a racial and religious other, acting as he did precisely because of his savagery, his less-than-human status on the social hierarchy embraced by the home culture.

In Mary Rowlandson's account, God became the sole focus of her attention during her captivity, a divine sustainer, and thus the narrative confirmed a particular relationship with God that her home community had. In Rowlandson's case, the story was also meant to warn the community that a displeased God had allowed these things to happen precisely because the community had turned away from God. Though this message was not the moral to all captivity narratives, a reaffirmation of Christian principles and divine generosity and sustenance often was (Bross 2011: 310–12).

At the same time, captivity narratives appealed to readers because they metaphorically spoke to other types of gendered "captivity" that occurred in European and European American cultures. Scholars have suggested that women readers in particular might have been drawn to the stories precisely because they troubled the notions of gender and home that some readers may have experienced as its own type of captivity (Castiglia 1996: 2–4; and Srikanth 2002: 85). Many captivity narratives explored gender norms and roles in their culture as well as in the "other" culture about which they wrote. The narratives about women captives tended to be about women passing from the custody of one group of men (her husband and/or her father) to another group of men and then back again. In this transaction of women, gender roles and expectations on both sides of the cultural frontier could be explored and challenged (Castiglia 1996: 8, 1–2).

The narrative structure—from civilization, to the savage world, and back to civilization—allowed authors and audiences to imaginatively cross boundaries. In so doing, some of those boundaries and expectations about identity could be troubled and challenged, while others were confirmed. Each story explored the porosity of boundaries and the individual and collective identity in different ways. Once returned to the home culture, the captive often felt emboldened to express the knowledge gained to the rest of the world. Female authors of captivity narratives in particular often used the narratives to create platforms to speak publicly about the cultures they had visited, often portraying themselves as saviors wanting to help others held "captive" in the world they had just left.

Nineteenth Century: Captured in Her Own Culture

Writing at a time when Mormonism served as a racial and religious other for many white, Protestant Americans, Ann Eliza Webb Young seized the imagination of the nation when she wrote her 1876 book *Wife No. 19: The Story of a Life in Bondage, Being a Complete Exposé of Mormonism, and Revealing the Sorrows, Sacrifices and Sufferings of Women in Polygamy*. That she had escaped polygamous Utah to return to "civilization" and that she had been married to Brigham Young, the central, most powerful figure in Utah Mormonism, authenticated her story in the minds of many Americans. Her description of polygamous marriage reinforced what many stereotypes of polygamy claimed: that it kept women in abject poverty, that they would leave it if they could, that they wished for the love of their husbands and never received it, and that they would be better off in a monogamous Christian (read Protestant) culture.

Ann Eliza's story justified the actions that were already being taken against Latter-day Saints by deeming Mormonism the radical other and suggesting that LDS women needed to be saved from their men's savage ways. Americans in the east could not get enough of Ann Eliza, who, in the words of Brigham Young biographer John Turner, "packed lecture halls, earned generous fees, and became an overnight celebrity and newspaper darling" (Turner 2012: 386). Her tour of the East Coast included a trip to Washington, where she met with members of Congress. Even President Ulysses S. Grant came to hear her story of captivity (Dowling 2012: 40). Ann Eliza and her captivity narrative seemed to confirm every fear and rumor about the Mormon community. In her book, politicians found evidence for all of the legislation they wanted to pursue against the church in order to stop the "savage" practice of polygamy (or plural wifery, as insiders called it).

In 1852, Brigham Young had publicly announced that God had revealed to Joseph Smith the importance of plural wifery in the spiritual lives of Mormons. After that announcement, church members in Utah had taken it up as a central and public religious practice that was commanded by divine revelation. The practice of polygamy contrasted sharply with middle-class Protestant values. For this reason, Protestant church leaders, political leaders, and reformers sought to rid America of what they defined as polygamy's evil presence. Doing so on social, legal, and economic fronts allowed government officials and the Protestant hierarchy to reinforce the middle-class Protestant values they sought to protect. For many of these individuals, Mormons served as an important point of contrast in defining what "American" was (Firmage and Mangrum 1988).

Prior to the publication of Ann Eliza's book, Congress had passed the Morrill Act in 1862, an act that outlawed bigamy in US territories, limited the power of Utah's territorial legislature, and denied religious institutions the right to own property worth more than $50,000 (Van Wagoner 1989: 107–8; Gordon 2002: 81; Firmage and Mangrum 1988: 129–36). Though the Morrill Act attempted to place severe restrictions on the LDS Church, it had little actual impact on the lives of church members in Utah. Distracted by far more immediate concerns in the 1860s, US government officials were unable to uphold the act's restrictions in a territory so far from the center of government power. However, as reconstruction efforts in the post–Civil War South began to take less energy, the LDS Church in Utah territory began to receive more (Gordon 2002: 120). When the LDS Church tried to get the Morrill Act stricken from the law, Congress refocused its energies on outlawing the church and the practice of polygamy (Van Wagoner 1989: 108; Gordon 2002: 82–3). The first step in this process was the Poland Act of 1874, which put Utah's courts under federal control (Flake 2004: 28; Firmage and Mangrum 1988: 148–9).

Though numerous acts and court decisions supported attempts to define Mormons as un-American and un-Christian, their central intent can be seen most clearly in the 1879 Supreme Court decision *Reynolds v. the United States* that came on the heels of the publication of Ann Eliza's story. Reynolds, a Latter-day Saint with two wives, sought protection under the First Amendment; he argued that his right to religious freedom protected him from persecution for his marital practices (Gordon 2002: 122–30). In the *Reynolds* decision, the Supreme Court voiced a unanimous decision that reflected the feelings of many Americans about religious freedom: "Laws are made for the government of actions, and while they cannot interfere with mere religious belief and opinions, they may with practices" (*Reynolds v. U.S.* 1878). That is, American citizens could *believe* what they chose, but *practices* fell under the purview of the government and could therefore be restricted. And practices that lay outside the bounds of what the American mainstream considered proper conduct would be punished.

By the 1880s, the government sought to *enforce* and put teeth into the laws it had created in previous years. In 1882, the Edmunds Act defined the legal classification of "unlawful cohabitation," which made it easier for the government to prosecute those who practiced polygamy. The act also declared that anyone who had been convicted of the crime of polygamy could not serve on a jury in such cases (Flake 2004: 28, 64; Firmage and Mangrum 1988: 193). The Edmunds-Tucker Act of 1887 permitted plural wives to testify against their husbands in court, disinherited children of plural marriages, and ramped up the charges against those found cohabitating. All of these laws sought to control marriage in Utah and make Mormons conform to middle-class Protestant values. They sought to take the "savage" out of American civilization.

This disdain for Latter-day Saints in some ways mirrored the treatment of other American minority groups. And yet, Mormons were a distinct challenge for white Protestant America. The Mormons, too, were largely white Americans claiming to be Christian and so were in some ways part of the "we" of the white Christian majority. In response to this particular problem, many Americans claimed that Mormonism was a false religion and that it had, precisely because of polygamy, begun to form a new degraded race of people. That new race was savage and depicted as standing in the way of American manifest destiny. Because of this sentiment, stories about polygamy would describe Utah territory as "a kind of mythic space, a mysterious region of darkness and secrecy" (Givens 1997: 123–30; Reeve 2015; Fluhman 2012). In fact, the "Introductory Note" to Ann Eliza's book, provided by Mary A. Livermore, an abolitionist and suffrage leader of the time, suggests that Utah itself has a foundation that is "laid in the degradation of woman" (Young 2014: viii). The book suggests that the landscape itself was corrupted by the people who brought a false and savage religion to its territory. The frontier that it describes, then, was imagined as the boundary that separated American advancement from the uncivilized, savage Mormon territory.

Ann Eliza Webb grew up while anti-Mormon governmental activity increased. Ann Eliza was born in Nauvoo, Illinois, on September 13, 1844, the youngest child of her Mormon parents. In her narrative Ann Eliza traces the movement of Mormons westward as they were forced to leave the Midwest and journey to Utah territory. She provides a very sympathetic reading of the Mormons and their journey west and recognizes this journey as the exodus event that cemented the Mormons as a people (Young 2014: 18–19; see also Shipps 1987). In so doing, she separates lay Mormons, whom she describes as innocent, faithful followers, from the church leadership, whom she blames for the evils of polygamy. She explains that it was only after Mormon converts left their homelands in other nations and traveled to the United States and then ultimately journeyed westward "outside the pale of civilization" that they found themselves under the thumb of the church. Once they "had gone so far that retreat was impossible, then [the church] would tell them the truth [about polygamy], knowing that they could not choose but listen" (Young 2014: 199). In this way, she argues the leadership promulgated polygamy to a largely unwilling audience. They used the isolation of the landscape to hold people captive.

Ann Eliza grew up in a loving home that she felt was injured by her father's entry into plural wifery. When her father took a second wife, Ann's mother changed and "grew indifferent on the subject [of polygamy], and declared that a few wives, more or less, would make little difference to her now, and she would be as well satisfied with one fourth of a husband as with one half." Ann Eliza believed that women were given a theological justification for a practice that they knew intuitively was wrong: "You will stand at the head of your husband's kingdom as a queen; no one can ever take your place from you, but you will be honored to stand by his side through the endless ages of eternity." She argued that "It was by such nonsensical talk and absurd promises as these that the Mormon elders tried to make polygamy attractive to the women." Not only were women taught that their eternal salvation relied on a man, but they were also taught that "floating through space were thousands of infant spirits, who were waiting for bodies . . . but if they had no bodies given them, their wails of despair would ring through all eternity; and that it was in order to insure their future happiness, necessary that as many of them as possible should be given bodies by Mormon parents" (Young 2014: 177, 55, 186). Thus, Ann Eliza believed that women were defined solely as wives and mothers and that they were held captive in those roles by a theology that taught them their eternal lives depended on it.

Ann Eliza Webb saw Brigham Young standing at the top of the hierarchy teaching things that she believed had injured her family; this is why she tried to escape his initial interest in her as a potential wife by marrying James Dee. Ann described Brigham Young in critical ways throughout her narrative: if it was the elders who duped people, Young was at their helm. If it was the leaders who practiced polygamy, it was Young whom she thought benefited most from that system. In fact, Young married at least fifty-five women over the course of fifty years, though not all of those marriages were consummated (Turner 2012: 377). Each wife seemed to be another piece of evidence for Ann Eliza that Brigham was a false prophet. He was simply power hungry, not genuinely religious (Young 2014: 15, 27, 269). Religion was a tool he used to draw power to himself. He was "supremely selfish, caring for . . . personal aggrandizement, disloyal to the government under which [he] live[d], treacherous to . . . friends, revengeful to . . . foes."

In Ann Eliza's narrative, Brigham Young represented all of the evils of the Mormon faith and its practice of polygamy. From her perspective, he was "not above positive vulgarity and profanity, both in language and manner, often making himself very offensive to the more refined portion of his audience" (Young 2014: 74). Not only was he an uncivilized character, but the polygamy he promoted taught all men to be desensitized to the status that should be afforded to women, thus rendering them savages: "all the finer feelings and sensibilities of man's nature were killed by this horrible system. [Brigham] regarded women's suffering with utter indifference; he did not care for their affection; their tears bored him and angered rather than touched him. He lost all the respect and chivalrous regard which he once had for the sex." And, in turn, Ann claimed that men came to call their wives "my women" or "my heifers" or even "my cows" (Young 2014: 175). Thus, Brigham promoted a system that taught *bad* masculinity. In fact, she noted that Mormon men in Utah shamed monogamous men; thus, men operated in a culture that pressured them to do what went against their true and best nature.

Ann Eliza was adamant that polygamy also and especially went against women's nature. While it inflamed men's baser passions, it crushed women's true spirit (Young 2014: 169, 177). Because of this, what she saw as the natural family structure, a monogamous family, could not survive. She claimed that polygamy caused wounds for families "and its hurts are deeper and more poisonous than any other wounds can be. They never heal, but grow constantly more painful, until it makes life unendurable" (Young 2014: 85). In monogamy, mothers could properly take on the nurturing role, unlike in Utah where "weary-hearted mothers" experienced maternity as bringing "no such joy, and added love, and tender care" (Young 2014: 49). They were simply stripped of all of their naturally feminine traits. "True women" knew that polygamy was wrong, even as they were taught that it was heaven sent.

Ann Eliza portrayed Brigham as a terrible husband, unable to fulfill even the most basic manly duties. She wrote: "We lived very sparely, even poorly, as did most of the wives, except the favorite, and one or two others, who asserted their rights to things, and got them after a great deal of insisting" (Young 2014: 278–83). Brigham rarely visited her, Ann recounted, but spent much time with Amelia Folsom, whom she claimed was his "favorite wife." But even Amelia had been reluctant to marry him, Ann wrote, and so he had used his "last resort" argument: "You must be my wife; God has revealed it to me. You cannot be saved by anyone else. If you marry me, I will save you, and exalt you to be a queen in the celestial world; but if you refuse, you will be destroyed, both soul and body" (Young 2014: 304–5). And so, every woman consented, her wishes trumped by what Brigham Young labeled divine revelation. Ann Eliza believed there was no avenue of escape unless she fled Utah. The place itself held people captive. And so she created a plan.

After suing Brigham Young for divorce in July 1873 on the grounds of neglect, poor treatment, and desertion, Ann Eliza was effectively divorced, though she could not receive alimony because her marriage had never been a legal one. Brigham Young was only legally married to Mary Ann Angel (Derounian-Sotodola 2009: 151–2). It was to a new and broader cause that she then turned.

Ann Eliza claimed to speak for the Mormon wives still held captive in Utah. She believed that her work, her cause, was their freedom. To that end she dedicated her book to them:

> As long as God gives me life I shall pray and plead for your deliverance from the worse than Egyptian bondage in which you are held. Despised, maligned, and wronged; kept in gross ignorance of the great world, its pure creeds, its high aims, its generous motives, you have been made to believe that the noblest nation of the earth was truly represented by the horde of miscreants who drove you from State to State.

Drawing on the mid-nineteenth-century exodus of Mormons to Utah, Ann Eliza acknowledged that the history of Mormon oppression by other Americans lead Mormon women to believe that the United States was a less-than-kind, even savage, place. Yet she promised that it was something else. It was a different landscape: "This Christian realm is not 'Babylon,' but The Promised Land!" (Young 2014: 3). Continuing with this trope from the biblical story of Exodus, Ann Eliza focused specifically on the wives of Brigham, suggesting she had a sisterhood with them made up of "the warmest and tenderest feelings." In her narrative, and in a great reversal of LDS story-telling, Ann Eliza positioned herself as a Moses figure and Brigham as the Pharaoh. In addition, Utah became the enslaving Egypt rather than the Saints' Promised Land. In her narrative, the East was the site of virtue, civilization, and godly living.

Portraying herself as a bridge person, explaining a savage, unfamiliar culture to another one, Ann Eliza also affirmed that her new culture was more civilized and its expectations preferable to where she had been. In the chapter titled "Breaking the Yoke—I Leave Home," she played with the genre and narrative structure of captivity narratives. One would think that leaving "home" would not also be described as "breaking the yoke," but indeed it was for a woman who saw herself as enslaved. Her mother later apostatized, but at the time of Ann Eliza's divorce, she wished her daughter were dead, rather than leaving the church and Utah. Shunned by her home culture, Ann Eliza was happy to expose that culture to others.

In following a public lecture circuit and telling her story to packed houses, Young affirmed the sexual and gender expectations of the larger culture. Utah was an unruly territory where "women [were] neglected, or, worse than that, cruelly wronged, every attribute of womanhood outraged and insulted." Young juxtaposed this degradation against the culture she now lectured to. She saw women there "cherished, protected, loved, and honored." And she portrayed the theological and social messages of her new culture as radically different: "I found, to my surprise, that woman was made the companion and not the subject of man. Motherhood took on a new sacredness, and the fatherly care and tenderness, brooding over a family, strengthening and defending it, seemed sadly sweet to me, used as I was to see children ignored by their fathers" (Young 2014: 362). Here, Young made a theological set of assertions about family and civilization. In the right place, the East Coast, traditional heterosexual monogamous families were understood as sacred. In the wrong place, Utah territory, heresy abounded, justifying a savage family structure. A bad place equaled a bad religion. At the end of her narrative, Ann Eliza reminded her readers that a good, true God valued the gender and familial norms of the East: the culture she deemed civilized. She believed that as a false prophet Brigham called upon God's name to justify his own baseless, immoral system. Yet she maintained that the true God was good and knew "how much I could bear" (Young 2014: 219). In so doing, Ann Eliza affirmed a God who had a divine plan and who had a broader sense of the good that could come out of her own experiences of captivity.

Twenty-first Century: Abducted from Her Own Culture

When Elizabeth Smart saw David Brian Mitchell as she walked down the street with her mother, she felt sorry for him and was glad that her mother handed him a few dollars. Little did she know that he had been observing her with the plan to make her his second wife. Smart's narrative juxtaposes her child-like innocence with the loss of innocence upon meeting Mitchell. Everything changed with her captivity, and everything burned in her sensory memory: "It's as if I can still smell the air, hear the mountain leaves rustle above me, feel the fabric of the veil that Brian David Mitchell stretched across my face. I can picture every detail of my surroundings; the tent, the washbasin, the oppressive dugout full of spiders and mice" (Smart 2013: 3). Mitchell kept Smart captive, fixed by a steel cable wrapped around her ankle and tied to a tree outside of their dugout in the mountains outside Salt Lake City.

When Smart recounts her narrative, the landscape plays an important role in communicating the differences between her previous freedom and her captive existence. She describes her neighborhood on Kristianna Street, a wealthy neighborhood in Salt Lake City, as "beautiful homes, some new, some older" that "looked down on the University of Utah, the capital and downtown buildings, and the Mormon temple." The view from her home was of the valley that spread south and west in "neat rows of street-lights that line up in an almost perfect grid" (Smart 2013: 20–1). Ordered, neat, civilized. These recollections of order tied to safety and security are juxtaposed with Mitchell's view of Salt Lake City, which he called Babylon, conjuring up the biblical culture that was described as full of sin, discontent, and chaos. In her story, Smart and Mitchell see the landscape differently.

These different views of the landscape extend to how Mitchell and Smart viewed the camp where he took her the night of her kidnapping and where they lived, along with Barzee, Mitchell's "first wife." Although Mitchell viewed the camp as a place of safety and security, away from the evils of Babylon and from prying eyes, Smart saw it as a natural world filled with bugs, dirt, danger, and privation. Several times she mentions how the trees provided a screen, making it difficult to see the camp. This hiddenness was especially significant when helicopters flew directly over the area, searching for Smart; even with the winds kicked up by the helicopter blades, the trees prevented the searchers from seeing the camp (Smart 2013: 19, 89, 94). Smart's views on the landscape laid out in her 2013 *New York Times* best-selling autobiography, *My Story*, were reinforced in the 2017 A&E television show called *Elizabeth Smart: Autobiography*. Smart's description of her youth in a safe environment, a "bubble" as she calls it, is juxtaposed with shots of the wilderness and the camp. The camera shakes as it shows the woods, emphasizing the overwhelming sensations brought about by the vastness of the natural world and offering a claustrophobic sense of the wilderness to which Smart was taken.

As did countless captivity narratives before, Smart recalls that her initial feelings upon her captivity were of terror and fear tied to the disorientation of the wilderness and not knowing where she was. Then she felt "embarrassment and shame so deep, I felt as if my very *worth* had been tossed upon the ground." After several days of captivity, which included being raped repeatedly, Smart's perspective shifted and she found a determination that she would survive what had happened to her, even if she could only achieve that by simply outliving Mitchell.

Smart contrasts her own innocence with Mitchell's savage ways. In her narrative, he fails at being a man, a husband, and a figure who understands God. Mitchell's failed masculinity is tied to his abuse of power, his assumptions that both Barzee and Smart are there to do his bidding. Smart also characterizes

Mitchell as a failed provider: his responsibility to ensure that they all have enough to eat is rarely filled because his laziness and selfishness get in the way. His failed masculinity is also tied to his views on sexuality, which allow him to think that he deserves more wives than one and to believe that he can have sex with Barzee and Smart without their consent. By portraying Mitchell in this way, over and against men like her father, she creates a portrait of what savage masculinity looks like.

Smart suggests that early on in his life Mitchell learned that religion could be used as a tool of manipulation and therefore had "an evil that grew inside him." As he grew older, he saw prophetic activity as the easiest form of manipulation but adjusted whatever he was doing for his audience. If necessary, he would turn the switch of prophetic activity on in much the same way Webb described Brigham Young. Similarly, "when he really needed something—knowing that prophets were difficult to take seriously—he could turn the switch off and act very rational. When the situation required it, he could act very sane."[1]

In her captivity narrative, Smart navigates a fine line in her discussion of Mitchell's claim that he was a prophet of God. Because she is a Latter-day Saint, she affirms the Mormon claim that there is a living prophet on earth who guides the church and can have direct revelations from God. While Ann Eliza Young could assert to a largely Protestant audience that anyone claiming to be a modern-day prophet was a false prophet, Smart had to make a distinction between a true and a false prophet of God. She refers to Mitchell as a "caricature of a prophet" and as "manipulative, antisocial, and narcissistic" (Smart 2013: 16). And in other small ways, she notes that Mitchell could not possibly be a prophet, rather he was someone who put the prophet act on. For example, she sarcastically recalls that before heading down to Salt Lake City he changed from hiking boots to sandals because "Prophets didn't wander around in hiking boots, don't you know. They had to wear sandals to match their robes" (Smart 2013: 166).

Mitchell was not the only one who held his religious perspective; he seemed to always have at least one willing practitioner, a woman named Barzee, Mitchell's wife (whom he referred to as his first wife). When Smart first saw Barzee in the camp, she hoped that the woman would feel pity for her and at least take her under her wing, as a nurturing mother figure. She quickly found that that wasn't the case. Barzee failed her standards of feminity: "Her hard stance and cold eyes told me she was anything but a friend," Smart recalled. "She had a wild look about her, emotional and tense, like a strand of wire that was being pulled too tight. . . . Her eyes were dull. . . . She had rough hands and a rough manner that was all-business and curt" (Smart 2013: 40). Barzee believed that Mitchell was a prophet and so allowed him to kidnap and rape Smart, claiming that Smart was his second wife. Barzee believed he was a prophet to the extent that she wrote down his revelations and followed what he said faithfully, no matter what his vision of their next step was. Smart discusses how Mitchell was able to soften Barzee anytime that she disagreed with his choices: he would "put his hands on her head and . . . pray. Using his authority as a prophet, he reminded her that he was God's servant. He had been called by God" (Smart 2013: 101). Soon thereafter, Smart writes, Barzee would acquiesce, accepting Mitchell's vision of what they should do.

Smart recalls that Mitchell would use the fact that she was a faithful Mormon against her. Knowing that she would be innocent in certain ways, Mitchell played upon that innocence: "[He] knew what he was doing. He understood my upbringing, my family, my religious and personal beliefs" and so "he targeted me ... because I was LDS ... he knew what the Mormon beliefs were and so he knew how I would feel about them" (Smart 2013: 79 and A&E Autobiography). This happened in two ways: first, in forcing her to view pornography and "instructing" her in sexual activities. He "knew I had been taught about modesty (a quaint word, I know, old-fashioned and out-dated, but that was who I was then and I still hold such values dear)." And, second, in forcing her to drink alcohol. He knew she would not want to drink for religious reasons, sure that the Word of Wisdom, an instruction by the first prophet of Mormonism, Joseph Smith, Jr., now considered an important revelation, would shape her beliefs. She viewed her body as a temple. When he required her to drink alcohol, she wrote, "He was asking me to betray everything that I held dear" (Smart 2013: 115).

In this "family" of three, Smart decided that she had to rely on her own perception of God. She suggests that throughout the trials of her captivity she might easily have lost faith, but instead clung to the idea that a just and loving God was present with her. In a particularly important scene in the book, Smart tells the story of a Mormon girl traveling west on the nineteenth-century trek to Utah. The young woman did not have shoes during the winter and other trekkers were dying all around her. One day she woke up and there was a miraculous pair of shoes next to her. Smart likened her own journey to this young girl's; she was faced with a series of obstacles and God was with her. One day when they were starving and dehydrated Smart woke up with a cup full of water beside her. She wondered where the water came from and believed it was from God. "This experience reminded me once again that God had not deserted me," she recalled. "He was aware of my suffering and loneliness" (Smart 2013: 131–2).

Drawing on stories of the Mormon pioneers heading to Utah, Smart tapped into the narratives long promoted and valued in her religious community. They were stories that were meant to encourage modern-day Mormons to imagine themselves as pioneers of their own sorts, facing new obstacles with perseverance and courage (Eliason 1998: 96–108; Eliason 2013). Retelling the stories of biblical exodus, Smart wished for her own type of deliverance from slavery to freedom (Smart 2013: 30).

Smart also works out theological questions of theodicy in her autobiography. In the midst of suffering, one might reasonably ask why a good and powerful God would allow such suffering to happen. Smart repeatedly assures her reader that what happened was not "something that God intended. He surely would not have wished the anguish and torment that I was about to go through upon anyone." Instead, she argues that it was Mitchell's free will and his association with evil that caused what happened (Smart 2013: 10, 75). When she told the story of the miraculous cup of water, Smart explained that

> [God] wanted me to know that He was still near. He wanted me to know that He controlled the Earth and all the heavens, that all things were in His hands. And if He could move the mountains, then he could do this thing for me. To Him it was a small thing—a terribly easy thing to do—but for me it was as powerful as if He had parted the sea. (Smart 2013: 132)

Thus, Smart was able to affirm God's goodness and power, while also explaining away God's seeming inactivity. For her, the glass of water served as a reminder of divine power and goodness.

Latter-day Saints reading Smart's autobiography might also recognize aspects of their own faith in the narrative that other readers might pass over. Smart notes that throughout her suffering, she was not alone, that there were others, like her ancestors, who were present, "unseen but not unfelt" (Smart 2013: 5). The theological idea that the veil between the living and the dead is thin, at times thinner than others, sustained her through her time of trial. Later, she feels and hears the voice of the Spirit reassuring her *"Stay strong. I haven't left you . . . I will provide a way"* (Smart 2013: 178). While others may read this as a simple heavenly assurance, Mormons would understand it as the spirit working on and speaking to Smart, providing her with her own personal, revelatory experience.

After months in their camp in Utah, Mitchell decided they had to move on. Too many people in Salt Lake City had seen them walking around with Barzee and Smart wearing veils on their faces. When they were traveling around Salt Lake City, Smart noted that even though she went to places she had gone by or visited before, "it still didn't feel like it was my world" (A&E Autobiography). Her disorientation made familiar places strange. In Salt Lake City, the trio encountered many people who found the story Mitchell told about Barzee being his wife and Smart his daughter suspicious. Smart never spoke up to these people they encountered, feeling worn down after months of manipulation and physical threat. As winter approached, Mitchell decided that California was the place to be; they could escape prying, concerned eyes and flee Utah's cold winter. Smart describes their camps in California as isolating, lonely, and boring wilderness. She had to get back to Utah, where she knew people would still be looking for her. She wanted to go home to familiar landscapes and convinced Mitchell Utah was the place to be.

When they arrived south of Provo, Smart saw Mount Timpanogos, which affirmed that she was somewhere near home. The landscape re-affirmed the identity that she thought she had lost and brought a sense of hope: "I thought I recognized the distinctive peaks of Mount Timpanogos. . . . Looking at my surroundings, I felt a rush of joy" (Smart 2013: 267). In identifying Mount Timpanogos, fondly called Mt. Timp by locals, Smart tied her identity to place in the way many Mormons and Utahans did and do. In the words of historian Jared Farmer, Mt. Timp is "by far the most-loved, most-hiked, most-photographed, most-talked-about mountain in contemporary Utah." Describing Mt. Timp as a landmark, Farmer explains that "Landmarks are these fastening-points. We use them for orientation. They are the icons of our mental maps" (Farmer 2008: 2, 6). And Mt. Timp played precisely this role for Smart. It oriented her after experiencing landscapes that had disoriented her, making her life feel out of her control.

In a moving chapter titled "I am Elizabeth," Smart recounts her rescue. As the group took a bus toward the Salt Lake Valley, she continued to be oriented by the landscape: "I looked at the mountains on the east, recognizing their features. . . . It felt so good to be so close to home." As they stopped to get something to eat, several people stared at them. When they left the restaurant, the police arrived. Moving her away from Mitchell and Barzee, an officer continued to ask what her name was for forty-five minutes. She hesitated, "Was it Esther? Was it Shearjashub? I hadn't been called Elizabeth for so long." Finally, she declared "I am Elizabeth," thus starting her own path home. She had "gone from being a hopeless prisoner to being someone who would soon be free" (Smart 2013: 278). In this instant, Smart's strength comes through—she brought about her own freedom, she escaped to home. She escaped from a savage captivity. She moved from disorientation to reorientation, returning to an understanding of who she was. As television host of *America's Most Wanted*, John Walsh, declares at the end of the second episode of the A&E series, "We got one back to her loving family." The words linger as the screen shows sunshine on the mountains with fluffy white clouds floating through the sky. The natural world—the land—confirmed that she was in the right place.

* * *

Despite the fact that 150 years separated the two authors, they both deployed the strategies of traditional captivity narratives, setting a clear boundary between civilized and savage, good and bad. These concepts were intimately tied to theological claims. Both authors sought to undermine the prophetic authority of the men who had held them captive. At the same time, they also supported the theological worldview of their presumed readership. God had not designed what had happened to them, had not granted their captors authority. Instead they protected a model of an all-powerful, all-good God who was angered by what had happened. The wrongness of their captivity was associated instead with sexuality and family structures gone awry. Their captors were portrayed as failed masculinity which was intimately tied to their corrupt religious worldview.

Both Young and Smart juxtaposed the sexual and gender expectations of their captors' world with the expectations of the larger culture. In Ann Eliza's nineteenth-century narrative, it was the Protestant, monogamous culture that was reinforced as the morally appropriate model when compared to the Mormon captor's culture. Her narrative affirmed the theological worldview of a Protestant culture while also moralizing its way of addressing gender. Framed as an "authentic" exposé with firsthand knowledge most readers would not have, her narrative easily became a tool for the governmental forces that sought to stop the practice of polygamy in Utah. It served as evidence that the savage still existed within American borders.

By the twenty-first century, Elizabeth Smart could write a captivity narrative that portrayed Mormons as the morally appropriate model of gender, family, and sexuality and define that model against Mitchell's fundamentalist worldview. Mormonism's embrace of a complementary gender model and a monogamous family structure in the late nineteenth and early twentieth centuries enabled both Mormon and non-Mormon readers to see themselves as a part of the larger civilized and orderly culture Elizabeth described as "home."

Each author shored up her own innocence by claiming to work for a voiceless innocent victim who could not speak out against the "savage" culture that held her in bondage. For Young, that innocent other was the women bound by Mormon polygamy; for Smart, it was abducted children. By giving the projects that emerged after their captivity an altruistic cast, these authors turned their captivity narratives into a platform from which they could speak, enlarging their areas of influence and promoting and critiquing the value systems of their own cultures, particularly their cultures' gender and sexual values.

In a telling passage of *My Story*, Smart recalls a time in California when Mitchell decided their camp was unsafe and that they ought to find a new one. They arrived at the new camp after struggling across boulders and rugged terrain. When they finally arrived, they slept. In the morning, "Mitchell figured it was a great time to do some exploring," and they spent the morning hiking around the new camp. Mitchell found a crevice under a boulder that formed a cave. Mitchell told Elizabeth to crawl in. As she did, she thought "I must be the first human who has ever been underneath this rock." Moving further, she realized that she was wrong. She found a magazine and looked at its cover. When she saw it, she "let out a quick gasp and dropped it as if it were a spider." The magazine was a copy of *Hustler*. "It was horrible ... the horrible image was seared into my mind." Mitchell quickly entered the cave, saw the magazine, and said "We have made the right decision. This place has been sanctified of the Lord. The Lord has seen fit to bless His servant with this sign" (Smart 2013: 237). After they left the cave, Mitchell forced Smart to look at the magazine and then raped her.

The passage itself is indicative of a theme running throughout Smart's narrative. All that is wrong and bad is hidden in and by the natural world, away from what most people see. Over and over, no one could see their camps. The pornography was hidden in a cave. In the midst of affirming the gender complementarity and the monogamous larger culture, Smart also uses her platform to critique what is hidden within the larger culture. Because she affirms so much in the broader culture, she is able to also raise questions about its morality.

This is also true about how she positions herself in relationship to her church. Smart affirms LDS theology throughout her narrative and at the same time celebrates its notions of family, particularly by juxtaposing her own biological family with the "family of three" that is formed with Barzee and Mitchell when she is kidnapped. Yet in her narrative, and especially in her later adult life as she used her book to expand her public platform, Smart critiques LDS teachings about the importance of purity and chastity. In an early chapter of her autobiography titled "Broken," Smart remembers that after Mitchell first raped her, she wondered about her family: "Would they still love me? Would they want me? Or would they feel like, 'We don't want her anymore?'" (Smart 2013: 47).

These feelings that her family and her community might reject her because she was now "broken" are tied to the teachings she learned at church on Sundays. They had placed so much emphasis on "sexual purity [and] waiting until you're married for those kinds of relationships" that she feared she had been ruined and could never have a family life again (Smart 2013: 47–8). She had been taught to tie her virginity to her sense of self-worth. In an interview, Smart told the story of a particular lesson she had learned when she was young: "You're like this stick of gum, and if you have sex before you're married, it's like someone chews up that piece of gum, and then when you're done, who wants a piece of gum that's already chewed up? No one" (LDSliving.com). Another time she was told that "You're like this beautiful fence . . . and you hammer these nails in, and then every time you have sex with someone else, it's like you're hammering in another nail. And you can take them out, you can repent of them, but the holes are still there" (Thecut.com). These were the theological teachings that left Smart wondering if her family and her religious community would want her back after she was raped. And so Smart chose to use her platform to speak for children who have been sexually assaulted and abused. She worked to bring to light what had been hidden.

A key difference between Ann Eliza's nineteenth-century narrative and Smart's twenty-first-century one is tied to the contexts in which they wrote, both historical and spatial. Ann Eliza wrote in a period when European Americans imagined a frontier space, a clear line between savage and civilization. Because of this she could deploy frontier tropes that were popular in her day: the savage, in this case Mormonism, embodied bad masculinity, bad sexual relations, and bad religion. Civilization represented good gender, good sexual relationships, and good religion. Ann Eliza could readily tie these cultural concepts to the landscape itself. Her readership expected it. Utah territory and its relative isolation from the centers of government and culture could be portrayed as giving rise to a dictator-like theocracy where masculinity ran amuck, supported by false prophets and played out in family structures.

Elizabeth Smart, in the twenty-first century, had more complex concepts to communicate. While her readership would still be familiar with and interested in all that captivity narratives had promised in the past, she had to navigate more intricate systems in order to achieve the same ends as Young: to tell a captivating story that would confirm her culture's assumptions about gender, sex, and family enough to satisfy readers while critiquing that culture enough to effect culture and policy change for the group for whom she claimed to speak. As a member of the LDS Church, Smart's project was further complicated by her need to make a distinction between true and false prophets, a distinction that she rooted in her portrayal of good and bad masculinity and good and bad sexuality. Smart, too, rooted these dualistic concepts in the landscape. While in her narrative Salt Lake City was both captivity and freedom, she used the characteristics of the natural world to communicate the difference between order and chaos, between proper gender, sexuality and family and improper. The improper was hidden in the wildness of caves and dense foliage, symbolizing what was still bad in the broader, orderly civilization which she affirmed. By deploying lingering cultural assumptions about wilderness and civilization, Smart could suggest that landscapes could harbor bad religion, bad gender, and bad sexuality, that they could hold people—and cultures—captive.

Part Two

Temporalities

5

From the Messiah's Glade to the Gods' Mountains

Christian Landscapes of Africa and Asia

Jonathan Miles-Watson and Sitna Quiroz

As social anthropologists working with Christian communities in distinct areas, we not only share a common frame (that draws from both the anthropology of Christianity and the wider anthropology of religion) but also are shaped by our engagement with the distinct regional literatures of postcolonial engagement in these regions. We consider that these distinct literatures have tended to skew our research and writing in different directions and seem to draw an apparent distinction and distance between both of our field sites: one in the former rainforests of West Africa[1] and the other in the mountains of India. However, when we look at these regions through the methodological frame of landscape, we notice important similarities, as well as informative differences, in how Christian communities shape and are shaped by their interactions with the ecology of the places that they inhabit and through which they circulate. Building from this analysis, we will advance a twofold model centered on the concepts of the "node" and the "bridge" for the comparative analysis of two seemingly distinct Christian communities in postcolonial contexts.

To approach this comparison, we therefore operationalize the term "landscape" as a verb, drawing from its etymological route to work the land. In so doing, we follow what has become the accepted convention in anthropology (Ingold 2000), geography (Wylie 2007), and allied disciplines (Gibson 2007). However, we move beyond the common discussions of landscape in relation to Heideggerian (1971) notions of dwelling and engage the concept of landscape with dynamic concepts of pilgrimage, change, and social transformation. A focus on Christian landscapes allows us to also complicate the discussion of human/nonhuman interactions, beyond the purely material. In choosing to focus on the sacred and numinous elements of landscape, we are not, however, seeking to reinforce a Durkheimian/Eliadeian division of the sacred and profane. Rather, following the work of Gregory Bateson, we shift in emphasis away from division and toward integration. Especially, we focus on the way that an ecology of relations exists within the landscapes that allow them to become sites of grace, awe, and enthusiasm.

The abovementioned concepts are operationalized in this chapter to help us understand the processes of postcolonial Christianity in landscapes within radically different contexts. To achieve this, we will place in conversation two sites of Christian "pilgrimage" and the communities that shape/inhabit them: Christchurch Cathedral, located in the Indian Himalayas, and Canaanland, located in southwestern Nigeria (West Africa). Through this conversation, we will develop an understanding of how both landscapes are powerful sites of becoming that maintain their relevance precisely because of the traumas of history. This will lead us into an understanding of the anthropology of Christianity that operates from a phenomenological, inductive, basis and in so doing opens new avenues for the comparative study of Christianity in both regions.

A Journey to "Shiloh"

December 2009: A group of five Pentecostal pastors and Sitna are traveling from Pobe in Benin Republic to Ota, Ogun state in Nigeria. They are on their way to an event called "Shiloh," an international Pentecostal convention that takes place every year at Canaanland, the headquarters of David Oyedepo's international ministry, also known as Winner's Chapel. Oyedepo is one of the key representatives of the Prosperity Gospel in Africa, and his influence has spanned over sixty-five countries around the world. Pentecostal conventions, such as Shiloh, are events that gather large numbers of people, who often travel long distances to reach a "religious destination." Shiloh attracts thousands of people from countries in Africa, and Africans in the diaspora, where there exist branches of Oyedepo's church. The shared experience of travel to these conventions creates a sense of interrupting the flow of everyday life to meet with people from different geographical locations. It enables the exchanging of news and sharing of meals and conversations that contribute to creating a sense of "communitas" (cf. Coleman 2002a; Ebron 1999; Turner 1969), and belonging to a Pentecostal global community.

The pastors traveling with Sitna decided to rent a taxi to travel directly from Pobe, a small city located in southeast Benin, to Canaanland. On the day of their journey, their departure was delayed because two pastors were trying to complete their budget for the trip, asking relatives and friends to lend them money. Renting a taxi resulted in higher expenses for the pastors, however, they all concurred that it was the best way to guarantee Sitna's safety. Although dwellers in southeastern Benin share a historical and cultural past with people in southwestern Nigeria, most Beninese people distrust Nigerians. Pobe is located only few kilometers away from the border with Nigeria. They took a shortcut, a dirt road that goes through the palm oil[2] plantations (that have existed since the colonial period) between Pobe and the Nigerian border. They reached a makeshift border control where two men sitting behind an old desk checked and stamped Sitna's passport. Shortly after they entered Nigeria, they were stopped at a military checkpoint, where army officials asked for Sitna's passport. The pastors intervened on her behalf to explain that they were on their way to a religious convention. The officials checked her documents and allowed them to continue. Although the whole journey to Ota is only 110 km, they were stopped at military checkpoints two more times.[3] The pastors explained to Sitna that if they had not intervened on her behalf, the officials would most likely have asked for a bribe. They also feared that if they had traveled on public transport, someone would have tried to mug her.

The areas of southeastern Benin and southwestern Nigeria belong to what has been historically known as Western Yorubaland. This is an area with predominantly ethnic Yoruba population under the control of the major Yoruba kingdom, Oyo (Adediran 1994: 1). During the nineteenth century, before the colonial period, this area became the battleground of rivalries among the Yoruba and between the kingdoms of Oyo and Dahomey (Fon), each of which sought to establish their dominance over the slave trade. The French and the British took advantage of the existing rivalries to gradually consolidate their power (Asiwaju 1976: 9). In 1889, after the Berlin Conference, this area was partitioned between the French and British governments. Most of Yorubaland remained under British control, leaving its western portion together with the kingdom of Dahomey under French control (Asiwaju 1976: 45–53). This arbitrary division fractured towns and families that today live on each side of the border. Their subjection to different colonial regimes contributed to shaping different political and economic trajectories. It also shaped people's mutual perceptions of difference, including linguistic, religious, and economic. Throughout the years, and after the independences of Dahomey—today's Benin Republic—and Nigeria, the border has remained porous (Flynn 1997). People have continuously engaged with each other, mainly through the commercial activity that has shaped an important corridor of trade between Lagos and Cotonou.[4] Relatives visit each other and participate in each other's funerals or ceremonies. With the flow of people across the borders there is a constant exchange of ideas, of tangible and intangible cultural objects, such as music, fashion, films, and, nowadays, of Pentecostal churches and preachers (cf. Mayrargue 2001, 2005; Noret 2010b), where politics has sought to divide, and commerce and, latterly, religion have forged connections.

The pastors and Sitna journeyed from the green plains of inland Benin and Nigeria to the urban asphalt, noise, and traffic of Ota, a township at the outskirts of the city of Lagos. The relative freshness provided by the green vegetation gradually disappeared into the dry dusty air of the urban landscape. The hot temperatures of the West African coastal areas get dryer in December with sandy winds coming from the Sahara. The taxi dropped them in front of the gates of Canaanland, an area that covers over 5,000 acres of land, which houses a complex of buildings, including Faith Tabernacle, a temple with capacity of 50,400 people, a university campus called Covenant University, several schools, businesses, and banks that belong to the church. Canaanland appears as an oasis of green and well-manicured gardens, with well-traced wide paved roads, and modern urban architecture. It stands out in contrast to the overcrowded and precarious dwellings, lack of urban planning, noise and traffic that characterize many African cities, such as Lagos. Canaanland thus offers visitors the promise of rest inside the icy air-conditioned environment of its buildings and a bit of greenness in the midst of dusty urban air. An aerial view of Covenant University reveals a complex of carefully designed geometrical buildings among which one can see two stars of David from above. Canaanland is a place that inspires a sense of awe to the visitor. It therefore generates a sense of spatial separation at the same time as opening the door to interpersonal unity, through a shared religious experience (see Figure 5.1).

For the occasion, near the main temple, a series of large white tarpaulins were installed to host stalls selling Oyedepo's books and videos. Several areas within the complex had temporary food stalls and recreational spaces for the visitors. During the five days of the convention, people from different social and economic backgrounds from all over Africa gathered to listen to a series of talks and seminars on the conference's theme, attend prayers, worship, healing, and deliverance sessions. Most people were lodged onsite at the student dormitories of Covenant University, others slept in tents placed within reserved areas of

Figure 5.1 Canaanland. Photograph by Sitna Quiroz.

the green open gardens. There was a festive and communal environment. The worship sessions were particularly emotive, with thousands of people singing and dancing to gospel music played to African and modern rhythms.

Oyedepo's Prosperity Gospel ministry is part of the global "Word of Faith" movement that first originated in the United States. The crux of his messages preached during Shiloh, and delivered through video and publications, is that God's purpose for his people is to provide wealth and prosperity. In the Old Testament, God established a "covenant" of prosperity with Abraham. Thus, any born-again can access this covenant and receive God's blessings as long as they become "covenant practitioners" (cf. Gifford 2015). This means that a person must "step into" this covenant by putting in practice biblical principles, such as "sowing and reaping" (giving and receiving). In many ways, it follows practices common to the "Word of Faith" movement, especially in relation to monetary offerings (cf. Coleman 2000, 2006; van Wyk 2015).[5]

Oyedepo has adapted the American origins of the Prosperity Gospel to his African audience. Aside from engaging with the well-documented practices of deliverance from an African "tradition" characteristic of Neo-Pentecostal churches in Africa (cf. Marshall 2009; Maxwell 2008; Meyer 1998, 2004; van Wyk 2015), a central aspect of Oyedepo's ministry concerns his message of personal, in particular, Black or African empowerment. He presents himself as a prophet who received the divine command to "rewrite" the history of the African people. In August 1987, Oyedepo narrates, while being a young migrant in the United States, God spoke to him and said: "Get down home [sic] and make my people rich!" (Oyedepo 2005: 14). While being in the United States, he preached at Shiloh and realized that many Black people and Africans are poor and looked down upon because they do not have a "prosperity mentality." He condemned many Africans' dependence on foreign aid because it does not help them to develop their full potential. Thus, a key part of his ministry is to "equip" people with "knowledge"[6] and education, and by promoting an ethics of arduous work and entrepreneurialism. Covenant University was founded as part of his ministry to inspire a "new generation of African leaders." Throughout the university campus, motivational messages and Bible passages encourage young people to believe in themselves, to feel worthy, and to step into "their destiny." The architecture and aesthetics of the buildings reinforce these messages to the students who inhabit these spaces and the visitors who circulate through them. They contribute to creating an embodied experience where prosperity becomes a tangible reality that can be inhabited. In front of the building where Sitna stayed, there was a statue of a bald eagle about to take off, which evoked quite evidently the American symbol. It was accompanied with a biblical passage that read: "And you shall remember the LORD your God: for it is he who gives you power to get wealth" (Deut. 8:18). Inside her dormitory, one of the students who normally inhabit this space during the academic year had glued on the wall a paper with a list of "positive affirmations" and Bible passages (see Figure 5.2).

Oyedepo's message of personal empowerment had great appeal to the pastors with whom Sitna traveled, and to lesser extent that of prosperity. They belonged to the association of independent evangelical churches in Pobe and occupied a rather marginal position compared to religious leaders from better-established churches in Benin. Many had become born-again while being migrant workers in Nigeria and, upon their return to Benin, had felt called to the ministry and founded their own independent churches. Their congregations hardly reached forty members. They struggled to maintain significant numbers and the necessary income to sustain themselves in a full-time ministry. The majority of the pastors had only a low-level schooling and they had not received any official training in ministry. Their lack of biblical training contributed to their lower status compared to Catholic priests or pastors from larger Pentecostal churches, such as the Assemblies of God, or other Christian denominations, who receive several years of biblical training. Attending events such as Shiloh gave them an opportunity to

Figure 5.2 The Eagle of Shiloh. Photograph by Sitna Quiroz.

follow informal training. They diligently took notes during sermons and teaching sessions and bought Oyedepo's books on sale during the event.

One day, during a lunch break, one of the pastors started to calculate the potential amount of money gathered after each service during Shiloh. Even if each attendee gave only a few cents, he said, the amount became significant when multiplied by the number of attendees and sessions held during the day. It was his first time at Shiloh and he was astonished by the way that the landscape draws together expensive materials: with its modern buildings covered with glass, its roads paved with asphalt, and well-kept gardens. He concluded that Oyedepo did not really need all that money from the offerings. In fact, Sitna noticed that this pastor did not give "seed offerings" after each session. Another pastor said that they could never possibly achieve the same wealth as Oyedepo in Benin. They further explained to Sitna that Oyedepo's wealth was only possible in Nigeria because of the revenues from oil available in this area of the country. Many of Oyedepo's "patrons," they said, were rich and surely gave him large donations that covered most of his expenses including his private jet. Thus, despite finding the prosperity message appealing, these pastors were aware of their limitations. Nonetheless, they did not lose hope that one day they would also find a "rich patron" that would sponsor their mission abroad.

By the end of the convention, all the pastors were encouraged and inspired. On their way back in the taxi, they animatedly talked and expressed how inspired they felt by the messages and prophecies that Oyedepo had declared at the closing ceremony. Oyedepo had proclaimed that God was rising in Africa a new generation of "Abrahams." They felt proud of being part of this new generation. The collective conversation gradually faded out. Sitna continued talking to the pastor sitting next to her, who had organized the trip. He attends Shiloh every year. He expressed his admiration for Oyedepo, a Black man like him who has been able to achieve "great things" with God's help. For these pastors, Oyedepo constitutes a role model; he represents an example of an African man with similar cultural background, who was able to achieve greatness.

Oyedepo's message and the tangible lived experience of visiting Canaanland opened for them a world of possibility, a sense of entitlement, even if it fails to materialize concretely to the same degree. Transformed by the journey, as they traveled across the border back into Benin, these pastors were building a bridge between Benin and Nigeria and overcoming the differences left by the colonial past; they were redrawing a fragment of the postcolonial landscape and contributing to shaping the face of global Christianity in late capitalism.

Silent Belfries and Whispering Deodars

May 2009, the Indian Himalayas: tourists from the plains have begun to flood the region in search of cooler weather, but the winter days, where the sun was an ally, have long since passed and the mercury stretches into the 30s. Jonathan is stood with Arjun, a local church elder, in the shade of the large bell tower of Christchurch Cathedral (see Figure 5.3). They are positioned on the edge of the ridge where the church hides them from the sun's glare and a warm breeze rustles through the surrounding deodars. Arjun, who has lived in the church's hinterland for decades, is in the middle of a familiar lament about declining standards when a man, whose loose-fitting clothes contrast so greatly with the tailored suites that we have chosen to wear, draws our gaze. His steps are accompanied by the tapping of a large, rough cut, pilgrim's stick; his forehead adorned with the vermillion blessing of a Goddess temple. From this we can discern both that he has come from Kali Bari and is going to Hanuman (at Jakhoo), a journey that requires a staff to pacify the simian guardians of the threshold. The pilgrim does not, however, turn to the forest path but instead walks directly toward the church. Conversation pauses, both now watching the

Figure 5.3 The House of Ancestors. Photograph by Jonathan Miles-Watson.

stranger approach the four-cornered portico. At the entrance to the church, he lays down his stick and genuflects, before standing again and moving on, following a path that tracks behind the Cathedral, where it winds through the monkey-filled forest to the temple of Hanuman at the mountain's summit.

In the wake of the seemingly syncretic actions of this pilgrim, talk turns to the majority Hindu population's engagement with the Cathedral:

> "This place is popular with tourists, but it can be a problem, if they don't know how to behave," Arjun asserts, before adding "we have tried different things to accommodate them, but it can be confusing."

Arjun's statement captures both the certainty and confusion that surround discussion of this sacred landscape. For, this Himalayan Cathedral's landscape is, when presented as a snapshot, certainly confusing, as seemingly discordant elements lend a collage effect to the anticipated pastoral. At the same time, the sure-footed way that Christians and non-Christians navigate these complex landscapes presents a contrasting certainty that inspires a desire for understanding. This impulse draws from the way that a tangle of historical and contemporary actors (both human and nonhuman) create a balanced ecology of relations in this region. For, while Christchurch Cathedral is suggestive of the type of building that you would expect to find at the heart of an English village, it stands in relation to peaks and groves that are foregrounded by discordant (oriental and orientalist) narratives.

Christchurch is the sacred heart of Shimla, once known as Simla, the former British summer capital of India, which was always understood as more than simply a place from which to govern (Miles-Watson 2013). Set high in the Himalayas, it was cast from the beginning as a Mount Olympus from which the elite could govern the plains below while remaining distinct from it (Pubby 1996: 36). Perhaps more importantly, the site was chosen not because of existing trade links, or transport connections, but rather because the comparatively colder climate and heavily forested mountainside reminded some Europeans of various parts of Europe (Gorden-Cumming 1884: 288).

The often-overlooked importance of the "weather-world" (Ingold 2010) of sacred landscapes emerges colorfully in colonial descriptions of the Himalayas (Kennedy 1996: 51), at the same time as the binary categorizational scheme that lies behind these descriptions diminishes the quality of their insight. What is, however, important to note here is that something in the weather-world of these mountains connected with the imagined weather-world of the colonists homeland. For, although the rain of the monsoon and the chill of the mountains are readily distinguished from whatever we may imagine an English weather-world to be, this connection was enough for the British to attempt to build on what they viewed (incorrectly) as *tabula rasa*, a "little England" in the hills. The core of Shimla can therefore be seen as a deliberately crafted landscape that combines local and imported materials to create a space of ancestral memory (Miles-Watson 2015). Local deodar and stone blended with imported materials, as it was worked by local artisans to interpret the drawings of Gothic and Tudor buildings. Alongside the native deodars and Himalayan wildflowers, imported trees and flowers were planted. Pedigree European dogs crossed the ocean to join the local monkeys, leopards, and langurs; Christian saints, icons, and crosses came to join the local *murtis*. European dress of the time joined with local dress customs and the distinct landscape of Simla began to come into focus.

At the center of the city, on the highest tier of construction, Christchurch Cathedral slowly emerged between 1844 and 1857 through the efforts of far more craftsmen and laborers than are today remembered (Buck 1904: 118). The church used to be filled with women in ball gowns and men in tailored suits who charged the air with renditions of Victorian hymns accompanied by the sound of the pipe organ. When their voices could sing no more, they were woven into the fabric of the walls, through commemorative plaques that gradually came to cover every part of the interior surface. The building continued to shift and be marked by those whose lives it so greatly impacted on during the colonial years as successive patrons commissioned adornments to the church that had both a personal and a theological resonance (Buck 1904: 81). The landscape began to dramatically draw attention to the traces of the past actions of its constituents at the same time pointing to a greater belonging, and this allowed the formation of a rooted feeling among those who dwelt in a transitory, transnational community.

The colonial period, however, came to a dramatic end, a little over fifty years ago, but Shimla lives on as a thriving postcolonial state capital. The Europeans and the ball gowns have almost all gone, and the church bells no longer chime, but the pipe organ, the memorials and the dogs remain, creating a tangle of relations that defies expectations. This appears at first as a dramatic rupture in the ecology of the landscape: however, this is not the case, for new people joined with the landscape binding their lives with the ancestors of the place (Miles-Watson 2015). Christchurch remains an active place of worship, led by a small number of Indian Christians whose faith clearly connects them with the cosmological elements of the landscape, but it also remained of central personal importance to not only Christians but also to the wider Hindu population, who live in and around it. As the sign at the entry to the city proudly proclaims, "Our Built Heritage Is Our Identity," which (whatever we think about the problematic terms) is clearly an indication of the importance of this landscape to people of all faiths and none. This is crucial because the self-identifying, postcolonial, Christian population, of both the region and the nation, is an extreme minority (0.62 percent and 2.3 percent, respectively—2011 census). The significance of the Christian landscapes would be lost if they were restricted to just this population. The majority of the population at both local and national levels is Hindu (93.5 percent and 79.8 percent, respectively). Therefore, what we may want to call a colonial, "Christian" landscape is overwhelmingly constituted by postcolonial Hindus. As in Shiloh, politics divides whereas sacred space presents the possibility for unity.

European Weather in the Land of the Gods

Shimla is something of a migrant city still. It attracts people to it, from both the wider region and across the nation, to work at its various institutions and to visit it as pilgrims, or tourists. These latter constituents of the landscape are not only significant but also seasonal. For, just as Simla of old was marked by extreme seasonal flows of people today the population of the city can double during the peak summer periods. These modern-day flaneurs mix and meld with the landscape dramatically changing its tone and feel, just as the seasonal changes from rain, to sun to snow markedly impact upon it. Conversations over the years have revealed an important range of intersecting reasons that people from the plains give for being drawn to Shimla, that range from viewing it as the land of the gods to a European weather-world.

Shimla is a gateway city to the western Himalayan range; as such it stands in a border zone that is geographically peripheral but cosmologically central to millions of Hindus. These mountains are known as "the land of the Gods"; they are the places where mythic events unfolded and crossing points between the eternal and the time-bound (Eck 2012: 7–12). Countless shrines act as local nodes housing local manifestations of divinity that to the synthesizing mind appear as variants of a grand scheme of divine revelation. At the same time, Shimla offers people a chance to travel to a little piece of "England," or "Switzerland," and promises to provide an entry into the world of the myths of Colonial India and its Christian Cathedrals. Uniting both these sacred geographies is Shimla's promise of weather that is distinct to that of the plains, offering both relief from heat and a magical encounter with snow.

Shimla's weather tends to disappoint, for sure it is colder than the plains, but at the main point of tourism it is far too hot for the fabled snow, which tends to fall only a handful of days a year. However, the connection with sacred landscapes is generally (although not universally) judged to deliver on all fronts. The city is surrounded by well-established temples, set in the sort of striking environment that readily generates a sense of "grace" (Miles-Watson 2016). None more so than the Hanuman temple that lies behind Christchurch, hidden within the famous, sacred deodars that the monkeys call home. To walk to this temple is to enter the Hindu epic the Ramayana, the events of which gave rise to the spontaneous generation of the current Hanuman. This is the journey of the pilgrim who we began this section with and yet he also stopped to pay obeisance to Christchurch, a striking and yet (as Arjun stated) frequent occurrence.

Entangled Christian Landscapes

Christchurch is clearly an important marker to all who travel the Shimla hills, a selfie with it in the background is the equivalent of collecting a shell (Frey

1998). There are also those who dwell a little longer, often entering inside the building and even engaging in worship. Two months after the conversation with Arjun, Jonathan was eating snacks and drinking coffee in a café five-minute walk from the cathedral when Jaswant, a practicing Sikh in his early thirties, visiting from the plains with his family, asked to join him. Over tea Jaswant related that he was taking a break while his family did some shopping, having just visited Christchurch Cathedral.

"That place" he said, "It's really something . . . it's so beautiful . . . I felt peace."

Like our unnamed pilgrim, Jaswant entered the landscape of the Cathedral, thickening its contemporary significance by his presence and at the same time feeling within it a sense of connection to other places and times that he describes as a sort of transcendent peace. This is a common theme repeated in many coffeehouse discussions, on internet chatrooms and recorded in the church's visitor's book (Miles-Watson 2019). Alongside peace a sense of awe, hinted at through the employment of the term "awesome," is constantly repeated in the comments of non-Christian pilgrims from the plains. Awe, beauty, and peace then emerge as the key themes and yet by his presence in the landscape was our turbaned friend, like the Goddess pilgrim, also transforming it? This is certainly what Arjun was hinting at when he said that "it can be confusing," but confusing to who? Certainly not to the travelers themselves who do not seem to register any confusion in their comments.

As the summer days of 2009 lengthened it was possible to see more people entering the Cathedral and with them increasing flash points in the otherwise peaceful landscape. These all occurred during the standard, weekly, English-language service, which involves traditional hymns, supported by both a choir and pipe organ. The problems came with people talking over the prayers, or the sermon and constantly wanting to record the service by means of photograph. On one occasion, a man was wrestled out of the doors while fighting to get one last snap in. This is in part a commodification of the landscape of worship and in part a cultural mislabeling, for the very striking peace of the Cathedral is at odds with much Hindu temple worship. The latter is characterized precisely by its soundscape (Prasad 2015) and that soundscape is so powerful that during less-essential ritual moments silence is not demanded. However, when this soundscape ethic is transposed to the cathedral then it risks destabilizing its fragile ecology of relations.

This is only part of the story, Hinduism itself has a tradition of silent retreat and in Jonathan's experience these flash points of tension characterize only a small minority of Hindu/Christian entanglements in this landscape. Many middle-class Hindus, throughout India, have a strong affinity with Christian spaces of worship that draws from childhood formation in church schools (Lobo 2002: 186). These Hindu elements of the landscape are not only highly familiar with convention but also skilled interpreters of the landscape, able to meaningfully engage the trans-communal religious symbolic elements within it. Perhaps more importantly they have personal memories connected with places that are similar enough in appearance as to give an associated sense of personal belonging within the space (Miles-Watson 2015).

Jonathan lived in Shimla imbedded in Hindu familiar networks and found throughout his time there that the local Hindus viewed themselves to be authentically part of that Christian landscape. Many of these would attend the church at key rituals and others simply drop in between ritual events, lending the landscape vitality at times of quiet. One local Hindu resident captured this sense wonderfully when she reported that Christchurch is "an oasis, [where] when my soul is tired and dry I come for refreshment."

Local Hindu residents are able to engage with the landscape as wayfarers, who carefully move around the landscape, blending sympathetically with it, moving with a developed awareness of the trace that will be left by their own actions and how this connects with the trace of historic actors both living and dead (cf. Ingold 2000: 237–40). At any given time, they constitute an important part of the landscape and no more so than during the previously mentioned service, for here, a substantial proportion of the assembled schoolgirls (whose hymnal voices are said to resonate angelically) self-identified as Hindu. If these girls return to the church when they are older (as many have done before them) and they will return to a place that is not only of global historic experience (through the symbolic revelation of Christ), or even national significance (through its colonial roots), but also personal historic significance (through its connection to their own childhood). In such ways, a seemingly alien, colonial landscape is revealed to be a vibrant, postcolonial landscape that is intimately bound up with the identity of contemporary Christians and non-Christians in this modern migrant city.

Ruptured Landscapes and Balanced Ecologies

Both Sitna's and Jonathan's ethnographic accounts reveal striking similarities in areas that are seldom placed in dialog, at the same time, they point to significant differences that are also a key source of revelation. Using Bateson as an inspirational point of departure, we will now turn to explore how these similarities and differences shine a light on the way different ecologies operate in distinct Christian landscapes to achieve balanced systems of operation. That is to say, we use Bateson's "systems theory" (1972, 1979, 1987) to think with as we critically explore the processes of rupture and healing that lie at the heart of both our Christian landscapes. Through such an exploration, we aim to demonstrate the ways postcolonial Christian landscapes can operate as either bridges or nodes of entangled relations, paving the way for future comparative explorations along these lines.[7]

The accounts of both the Christian landscapes of Canaanland and Shimla open with a journey, highlighting the importance of movement for these seemingly static landscapes. The journey in Jonathan's account is told from the perspective of engagement with movement into a place of long-term dwelling. In contrast, Sitna's ethnography operates from the perspective of movement from a place of dwelling. However, in both we have a common theme of movement, yet while one focuses on movement to, the other emphasizes movement from. This is no simple coincidence; both of the landscapes' systems powerfully combine movement and transformation with stability and continuation. The ethnographic material that we have presented, therefore, demands that we address, from two distinct perspectives, the same central issues of both life lived *in* Christian landscapes and life enriched by movement *to/through* Christian landscapes. This suggests a key feature for a potentially wider exploration of sacred landscapes. In Canaanland, we see quite clearly the importance of collectively undertaking a potentially perilous journey, coupled with the site operating as a place of coming together to attend Shiloh, "a gathering," of distinct threads in the overall weave of this region. In Shimla, the journey is less perilous and stressed and yet there remains a sense that here too we have a landscape that gathers together distinct elements, even if these elements are not so much joined through processes of bridging as winding (around a node of remarkable significance).

The dynamism of the movement that the ethnographic accounts present contrasts with the implicit static bias of "dwelling" associations, which take off from Heidegger (1971) and move through Ingold (2000) into the anthropology of Christianity. In particular, Ingold's influential discussion of a church landscape painting has been important for highlighting the way that Christian landscapes might operate to ground a traditional community in its environment (Ingold 2000: 202). This has many resonances with Jonathan's account of the way the landscape operated during the colonial period. However, both ethnographies dramatically break the cozy presentation of dwelling that Ingold's painting allows, by engaging with real-life messy entanglements of postcolonial societies and (crucially) by adding the dynamics of "movement to" and "movement from" to that of "movement within." These movements not only evoke a conceptualization of rupture (cf. Robbins 2007; Meyer 1998, 2004) but also highlight the importance of the systems of continuities and realignments (cf. Engelke 2010; Chua 2012) that different forms of Christianity facilitate in these different geographical locations.

It is of course possible to address this journeying through the more familiar tropes of pilgrimage and/or tourism, which have a strong tradition of discussion in both contexts as well as within the wider anthropology of religion (cf. Sax 1991; Graburn 1983; Coleman and Eade 2004). At times, especially in Shimla, we found people deploying the terms "pilgrim" or "tourist" to describe the actions of those within their environments. It is interesting to note that in the context of Shimla the term "tourist" is often operationalized by the Christian community to talk about someone who is commodifying the landscape. Yet, just as the Turners argued that a pilgrim is half a tourist if a tourist is half a pilgrim, so too in both regions, it is common to refer to pilgrims and tourists as simply travelers.

We do not wish to simply add another discussion to the ongoing pilgrim/tourism debate or to reduce the message of the ethnographies to a discussion of these terms. Instead we will now turn to consider how thinking about these as landscapes, all-be-it, more varied and dynamic ones than those frequently discussed, can both do justice to the material under discussion and push it in new directions. The concept of journeying, walking, and movement has of course featured in both Ingoldian writing (Verngust and Ingold 2016) and in Ingold's own turn to lines (2011, 2015). However, there is still work to be done to integrate these movement-based metaphors with the landscape perspective, as well as to draw out the significance of this for sites that are both complex (i.e., postcolonial) and sacred (Christian).

Truly Awesome Landscapes

The Christian landscapes of Canaanland and Shimla integrate issues of movement and dwelling in distinct ways that draw from the varied ecologies of relations that emerged from each region's distinct colonial experiences. However, there are also striking similarities that offer possibilities for the formulation of more general rules about postcolonial Christian landscapes. The journey to Canaanland involves crossing a national border to enter a landscape that is both cartographically and ideologically separate from the usual world of the pastors. Although the journey to Shimla is more easily undertaken and does not involve the crossing of national boundaries it is clearly also a movement to a place that is readily separated due to its distinct (mountainous) geography and its association with spectacular ways of being (be it those of the Raj, or the gods). Despite the ideological separateness of these regions, the reality is far more entangled with each landscape being in part constituted by the very people who view it as distinct, as well as material goods (commodities) that constantly flow across and draw together these ideologically divided realms.

They are also landscapes that are at first glance radically distinct not only from the everyday but also from each other (one ultra-modern and the other clearly traditional). Yet, they are united by the fact that both actualize a sense of difference, of being misplaced, to create a sense order and peace. They awake a sense of reverence and awe that draws individuals together and sacralizes processes that are commonly cast as profane (such as economics). In this, they resonate well with Sheldrake's general conception of the way that sacred landscapes function in the contemporary city as truly awesome places (cf. Sheldrake 2007: 252). Sheldrake argues for a reclaiming of the word "awesome" as something capable of generating reverential wonder rather than just a description of something vaguely pleasing (2007: 244). Sheldrake links this sense of awe to Otto and Eliade: however, the idea of awe also has a useful link to Bateson's concept of grace (1972). For awe contains within its etymology the suggestion of that uplifting and yet, disquieting, loss of self that can occur when say we become conscious of our connection to weather. This sense of awe links to Bateson's idea of grace as a loss of the self that occurs during moments of heightened awareness of the ecology of relations and our integration within it (Bateson 1972).

In Jonathan's account, we hear of people who frequently and literally describe the landscape as awesome and who pair this with descriptions that suggest that awesome is indeed being used in more than simply a colloquial sense. Interestingly, "awe" here is often associated with peace rather than the common association with fear (Keltner and Haidt 2003), and this highlights the way that Bateson's notion of grace can bring a sense of relief that comes from the momentary reintegration of our sense of self and its wider ecology of being. In Sitna's account, we hear of a sort of loss of the self in the collective that links to familiar pilgrim theories of communitas. This is especially the case in moments of massive communal worship and prayer, for example, or in the seeming blurring of socioeconomic differences of people gathering together. However, it also draws us beyond the often narrowly defined employment of this concept into a realm where communitas extends beyond the human to take us into the realms of the ecology of constitutive relations, where materials are drawn to the fore (cf. Keane 2008). Canaanland is strikingly constructed in an ordered way that is perhaps only fully appreciated when viewed from above, just as Shimla is from below, although both in reality are moved through. This extremely ordered and organized nature of the place is itself awe inspiring, especially when paired with the sacred message of the Prosperity Gospel that invites the "pilgrim" to understand how Bible passages and buildings bring sermons and messages of prosperity into existence. Shiloh also means "place of peace" and it evokes a biblical place where miracles happen, where the power of God is made manifest. Through the landscape, prosperity, miracles, and "greatness" become a lived reality that has the power to transcend the inconvenient constraints of history.

These landscapes are clearly awesome, at least in part because of the theological significance of both their symbolic and material natures. They are spaces that embody Christian myths and visions of what it means to be holy or blessed. In Sitna's ethnography we see how the use of Old Testament terms and sacred places, such as "Canaan," "Shiloh," "Tabernacle," and "Covenant," seek to reinscribe a biblical historical narrative into the African landscape. Moreover, this biblical narrative is actualized by infusing it with contemporary symbols of power and prosperity, such as the American bald eagle, which together congeal into a lived promise of blessings in the Abrahamic covenant. In Jonathan's account the landscape draws upon established European conventions for invoking the divine. A theology of light (Bony 1983: 117–95) is employed, which suggests that light is a way that the divine draws us toward itself (Merton 2008: 137). Inside Christchurch the striking mountain light both pervades and defines the space, as it filters through brightly colored representations of biblical scenes. Each scene is not only symbolical resonant of these trans-Christian motifs but also phenomenologically resonant with its European heritage, both implicitly through its style and explicitly through the inscriptions and mythologies that connect these windows to particular colonial actors (Miles-Watson 2012).

These are also landscapes of social status and wealth. It would be easy to associate the awesome nature of both with worldlier economic fortunes; yet to simply dismiss the power of these landscapes in this way would be to ignore both the message of the people and the lessons of the landscape. For sure, both employ costly materials and construction methods that speak to other places (the

United States and Europe) and the political-economic relations through which these materials were extracted, and architectural forms achieved (colonialism and globalization). Yet, both entwine these architectural forms with more local materials, movement, and craftsmanship to work landscapes that are of deeply localized significance. This echoes Sheldrake's understanding that for a landscape to be truly awesome it is not enough for it to simply be a symbol of oppression (2007: 252). Awesome landscapes speak to the collective about possibilities and aspirations; they must lift people's ideas toward something greater and must be embraced by the people.

Both contemporary Christchurch and Canaanland gather people to them, allowing people to be transformed by the very landscapes that their presence also transforms. Both ascending and bridging through worshipful presence. What is more, the very message of prosperity is key to Canaanland's theology and, as such, it would be misleading to simply subjugate the later to the former. The concepts of awe and enthusiasm demand that we consider these landscapes as being as much about sacralizing the economy as reducing the sacred to an economic analysis. In Shimla, the situation is less clear-cut and yet a sense of status, if not necessarily wealth, is clearly implied in membership in the body of the church. Crucially, both use prosperity as markers of distinction (Bourdieu 1984) that lead to more substantial connections. In the case of Christchurch, the landscape connects through its appeal to the status of heritage to the past and, in the case of Canaanland, through its promise of prosperity to the future. Both, of course, are united in being landscapes of the Eternal.

Time and Space

In both Shimla and Canaanland it is possible to see how the material trace of past action is crucial to the present landscape and some of these traces evoke a sense of rupture (Miles-Watson, Reinert, and Sooväli-Sepping 2015). Both sites were subject to European colonialism in the nineteenth century. In both cases, Christianity left a tangible presence in the buildings and identities of the people, which has given rise to different iterations that point toward different appropriations. Sitna's ethnography presents a scenario where colonialism left its mark with a border that divided towns and families. It established differences of language, culture, and wealth disparity between Nigeria and Benin. Different colonial regimes (French and British) supported officially different types of Christian missionary projects, which in Benin were mainly Catholic and in Nigeria Anglican. Nonetheless, Christianity in its postcolonial iteration manifests itself in a Neo-Pentecostal narrative and practice that unifies broken/ruptured pasts.

In Jonathan's ethnographic account we saw that Christchurch (and Shimla) can be easily understood as a physical rupture in the wider Indian Himalayan landscape. A cathedral and city intended to invoke their European counterparts could easily be understood as reminders of colonial domination. Moreover, an overtly Christian landscape, nested in a region of sacred Hindu significance could easily be viewed as problematic to the majority Hindu population. Yet, this is not the case, instead, the landscape continues to operate as a site of awe and peace for travelers and residents, Christians and Hindus. It has become a site not only of awe but also of enthusiasm, which fires the work of postcolonial Hindu artists, poets, and authors—a place that feeds the soul. This is because of the inclusive way that participation in the landscape draws people together with not only contemporary actors but also historical ones (both colonial and biblical). The ecology has reset itself and the landscape has become a site of reintegration rather than rupture.

In both accounts, the historical ruptures of colonialism are overcome by the circulation of postcolonial people who are woven into the landscape as they continue to reweave the threads of the past. In Canaanland we see how the landscape operates as a bridge that brings different and distant places in a "single" Christian gathering (Shiloh) that unifies. In Shimla, the distinct ecology has led to the landscape functioning as a sacred node, around which diverse past, present, and mythological actors become entangled in deeply meaningful landscapes of awe and inspiration. It is clear that this comparative exercise suggests that unifying biblical narratives and colonial experiences take root in distinct ways in the varied ecologies where they are positioned. Yet, through spatially enacted and temporally significant practices, unifying elements of reintegration are common to these often-held apart Christian landscapes. Despite clear differences in ethnological details, both of our experiences find common ground at the processual level where they bring *eris* and *harmonia* together into a *concordia discors*.

6

Geography as Eschatology
Moral Freedom and Prophecy Fulfillment on Land and at Sea

Joseph Webster

Introduction

By reflecting upon fieldwork among Brethren deep sea fishermen in Gamrie, NE Scotland, this chapter explores how two sources of authority—biblical apocalyptic prophecy and the agentive acts of individual Christians—came to be located within and constituted by their experience of geography. More specifically, by using the term "eschatological agency," this chapter considers how local Christian fishermen placed themselves at the center of "end-times" events by first reading and then fulfilling such prophecy within the materiality of different landscapes and seascapes. How, in this context, are we to understand what it means to be a moral actor or a free agent? These questions are made more complex still by attending to the ways in which Gamrie's Christian fisher-families obfuscated their own agency by attributing all human actions to either God or the devil, while at the same time working tirelessly to identify and enact various "signs of the times" that collectively evidenced the nearness of the end of the world. Here, "self-fulfilling prophecy" is given a new double meaning; not only does it create the semiotic conditions necessary for its own apocalyptic realization, but it also creates the geographical conditions necessary for the apocalyptic realization of the Brethren self and community, for example, in stormy seas, or in religiously inspired construction projects. This chapter offers an ethnographic sketch of that self and community in relation to material place and space, and, in so doing, attempts to query anthropological pairings of freedom and morality through a re-examination of the notion of authorship.

What precisely do we mean by a self-fulfilling prophecy? Most of the time the phrase is used to refer to how a predicted state of affairs will come to pass simply by virtue of the fact that those who are the object of its prediction *believe* that it will come to pass. While to some in anthropology, this definition might feel strikingly similar to popular notions of destiny, a more usual interpretation of the phrase holds it to be the result of some kind of cognitive observational bias. The logic runs as follows. If I am labeled an imbecile at a young age, and am also frequently reminded of my imbecility by parents and teachers, I will, in all likelihood, believe it to be true and act accordingly. In acting accordingly, I produce fruits in keeping with my imbecility and thereby "become" an imbecile. Thus:

Prediction + belief = behavior + fulfilled prediction + reinforced belief

The question this leaves us with—not one usually addressed by the motivational speakers most dependent on the circular and dubiously individuated logic outlined—is one I have asked elsewhere about agency, namely, "who is acting, and for whom" (Webster 2013a: 81)? *Who*, then, is acting? Am I the cause of my imbecility, or are my parents and teachers to blame? But note how this framing eschews wider questions of structure and influence by avoiding the *"for whom?"* part of the question. Addressing these two parts in tandem is really what this chapter is about. Where previously I had attempted this enquiry as an end point in my analysis, I want to attempt it here also, but this time as my starting point. By shifting my focus from earlier work on the specificities of religious rhetoric about global warming to much more diffuse religious practices of prophecy fulfillment—what I want to call "eschatological agency"—my intention here is to critically engage with Laidlaw's (2010, 2014) writing on responsibility. So, who *is* acting, and for *whom*? In order to help me phrase (and hopefully answer) the question in a more intelligible way, I want to present two brief fragments of ethnography—one taken from land, and the other from the sea. But first, a word of context.

Context

I conducted my fieldwork in Gamrie, a fishing village in Aberdeenshire, NE Scotland, for fifteen months, between 2008 and 2010. Gamrie is very small, very religious, and, in parts, very wealthy. Its population is fewer than 700, but the village is home to 6 churches, and several millionaires—reputedly the highest in Scotland, per head of population, for both factors. Gamrie's "statistical outlier" status is shaped by historical and contemporary happenings. Founded as a Presbyterian fishing village in 1721, Gamrie came to be dominated by a millenarian sect called the Plymouth Brethren with their arrival in the village in the 1850s. Today Gamrie has an independent evangelical church, a Free Presbyterian Church of Ulster, and four Brethren Assemblies. The most distinctive contribution made to Gamrie religion by the Brethren has been their eschatology, a pre-tribulational pre-millennial dispensationalism that posits the utter imminence of the Rapture by glossing the present as "the *last* of the *last* days."

Connected to this were strong Christian Zionist convictions, particularly that the end of the world would not occur until all the Jewish peoples of the world immigrated to Israel and miraculously converted en masse to Christianity. In this political temporality, the mission of Gamrie's Christians was to remain faithful to God and resist the devil by, among other things, separating themselves from the world, praying for and sending missionaries to the State of Israel, and watching for "signs" of the soon to arrive apocalypse. The everyday experience of this eschatology was made more distinctive still by the fact that, in Gamrie, religion and fishing could not easily be separated. Indeed, both God and the devil were held to be intimately involved in the Scottish fishing industry at both a macro-policy and micro-interactive level. The EU, for example, was believed locally to be the anti-Christ, and its Common Fisheries Policy quota system a diabolical conspiracy to impose upon humanity a global world ending famine. The blessing and providence God, conversely, was held to be ultimately responsible for putting every fish in the nets of fishermen. God provided and the devil destroyed, but both were undeniably active. To better understand this last point, some ethnography seems needful.

Prophecy Fulfillment at Sea

Consider first how Gamrie fishermen experience their time at sea as framed by the EU anti-Christ. From the perspective of fishermen, Common Fisheries Policy (CFP) legislation dictates almost every aspect of their practice—where they can fish, which species they can catch, the amount they can catch, the number of days they can be at sea, the type of fishing gear they can use, how catches are to be recorded, and the minimum prices they can accept at the market. Additionally, boats are required to facilitate the monitoring of fish stocks by allowing EU scientists to survey the live catch as it is processed. Fishermen also told me that EU enforcement officers could board any vessel to conduct spot checks by scrutinizing log books and comparing these to the contents of the hold, with discrepancies punished by hefty fines and possibly by revoking a boat's license. Activities around the harbor and fish market were also tightly controlled, with inventory lists submitted and checked against boxes being unloaded, and then, at market, individually labeled and coded boxes auctioned off in line with minimum pricing, or withdrawn from sale where minimum prices were not met. Such was the bureaucracy of fisheries management.

It is within this context that local Christians came to experience the EU as a demonic-political entity (literally) hell-bent on destroying humanity by offering it a soul-ruining false salvation disguised as genuine virtue. I first came to realize what a predicament this placed my informants in during a small Brethren Bible study meeting. Gregor, Carol, and Mitchell were discussing the books of Daniel and Revelation, and how their prophecies were presently being fulfilled as a direct result of the CFP. It was Mitchell's comment that really stuck with me, when he said: "You're nae allowed to buy or sell fish without the Mark of the Beast. It's the Mark of the Beast at the end of days." In referring to the way in which fisheries is managed through coding, quotas, logbooks, barcodes, and others forms of top-down bureaucratic management, Mitchell was not alone in drawing straight lines between work in the fishing industry and being implicated within the devil's end-times schemes. The implications here for the way in which Gamrie's Christian fishermen understood their own actions were serious and complex, and extended beyond the specificities of EU bureaucracy into the seascapes of commercial trawling more generally.

A common observation among Gamrie's Christian fishermen was that patterns of weather out at sea frequently had the effect of disincentivizing Sabbath-keeping. The particular pattern these informants had in mind was one whereby seas would be stormy and treacherous during the Monday to Saturday working week, becoming mysteriously calm on Sundays. The result was that skippers and crews losing income from being stuck on shore during bad weather found themselves under significant financial pressure to break the fourth commandment by going to sea on "the Lord's Day." One informant, describing to me this pattern in particular detail, explained how such weather patterns, and the moral compromises they encouraged, were the work of the devil, who sought to attack God's people by tempting them to stray from his laws. Other fishermen agreed, with one skipper confessing to me how, having succumbed to this temptation on only one occasion, his disobedience was punished by God transforming the calm seas into a severe storm as soon as he dropped his gear to begin trawling. Still others told similar stories of divine judgment, involving fellow fishermen obtaining ruinously poor catches on Sundays, or losing gear and sustaining other damage to their boats as a result of their willful desecration of the Sabbath.

Such happenings provoked little surprise for Gamrie's Christian fisher-families. Indeed, the expectation of the soon arrival of the eschaton gave these spiritual happenings a quality of obviousness, since, according to their dispensationalist reading of biblical end-times prophecies, "these things must happen." Prophecy was simply being fulfilled in their day and generation, according to God's divine appointment. As such, biblical apocalyptic texts which described an increase in godlessness in the last days gave my (mostly elderly) Christian informants a semiotic schema with which to come to terms with wider changes to how many *younger* Gamrie fishermen choose to interact with this same seascape in *their* day and generation. For these men, in their teens to their forties, Sabbatarianism was largely dead tradition—an outdated mode of production which modern trawling could not be reasonably expected to conform to, especially given fishing vessels were now larger and operated further off the coast, making short six-day trips nearly impossible.

Yet, these "fallen" logics and "worldly" excuses were also things that my older Christian informants found prophesized in scripture, and shared among themselves in critical conversations about how Gamrie's youth idolized money. Woe unto them who call evil good, and good evil (Isa. 5:20) was one such commonly quoted verse—a verse which was understood to prophetically speak to contemporary changes to popular moral standards. The eschatological implications were clear, my informants would tell me: "For the time will come when they will not endure sound doctrine. . . . And they shall turn away their ears from the truth, and shall be turned unto fables" (2 Tim. 4:3-4). It was thus with sadness and self-assurance that Gamrie's elderly Christians looked out on the seascape which surrounded them, and, reading verses such as these, concluded not that these times *will* come, but that they *had* come, arriving into Gamrie's present day with a prophetic clarity which befitted their divinely inspired certainty. The final irony, according to these older informants of mine, was heavy, namely that EU bureaucratic mismanagement of Scottish fisheries emerged as a direct consequence of the actions of these young Sabbath-breakers: "there would be no quotas if people didn't go to sea on a Sunday," one retired fishermen told me, with a shake of his head.

Yet, seascapes were said to be used by God to bring about more than eschatological judgment, with both storms and calm waters described as being instrumental in bringing about born-again salvation in these "last of the last days." Beyond vivid discussions during local Bible studies of Jesus miraculously calming the seas, more personal conversion narratives—referred to as "testimonies" in Gamrie's Christian lexicon—were also shared with me during my fieldwork. Some of these stories contained real drama, with one retired fisherman detailing to me how he had been "saved" during a terrible storm. The fishing boat he was working on ran aground, and his father and three other crews tragically lost their lives. As he clung to the rocks, being battered by the waves, he prayed to God that if he survived, he would dedicate what remained of his life to Him. His prayer was answered, and he was rescued—physically and spiritually—becoming a born-again Christian in that moment of ultimate peril. On a different occasion, another retired fisherman shared with me his testimony, but seemed embarrassed by what he deemed to be its unexciting nature. Alone in the wheelhouse during a night watch, he explained how the sea, which was unusually calm, was suddenly bathed in orange and yellow light, as the sun rose over the horizon. Its beauty was so immense, he told me, that he came to an undeniable ("born-again") realization that God—the creator of all things—was not only real but demanded and deserved his worship before his soon return to judge the world at the point of his Second Coming.

Prophecy Fulfillment on Land

Storms were also a prominent feature of the eschatological imaginings of my informants on land, including highly localized (and seemingly mundane) eschatological signs such as increasingly harsh winters. More dramatically, one informant described to me how he had once experienced such a severe thunderstorm that he went outside to look into the skies, expecting to see that the Rapture was occurring. Importantly, weather conditions were held to be a source of signs that the apocalypse was near because physical and climatic changes (although not climate change per se [see Webster 2013a]) were thought to mirror wider declines in the moral state of the world. A stark example of how this mirroring was seen to take on prophetic resonances came during a Christian Zionist conference I attended in Perth as part of my fieldwork. In between long prayers for Benjamin Netanyahu and the Likud Party, one of the conference speakers told the audience how God had personally warned him about the future danger Islam posed to the

State of Israel, and thus to the eschatological fortunes of the world. The prophetic warning came in the form of a crescent-shaped storm cloud, which the speaker described as looming over the entire sky, darkening the land beneath as it spread. "I feel that pain is coming to Israel" one delegate offered in agreement.

Crucially, while this cloud was understood to be a real material sign of eschatological suffering to come, so too was the danger it pointed to, with much of the rest of the conference focusing on the real-world threats posed by Islam in the Middle East and globally. As a result, the message about the crescent storm cloud prompted a wider discussion about what action might be taken to meet this threat head-on. Several delegates agreed that what was required was a mobile tract library stocked with Zionist and other Christian literature, to be distributed across Scotland's towns and cities as a way of combating what they regarded to be the anti-Israel stance of the British media. Yet, while this call to action was undoubtedly an assertion of eschatological agency, it also carried with it very deliberate claims about the agentive limitations of "saved" and "unsaved" persons. "It's not about winning the argument; it's about being a letter from Christ. What we know about Israel we got by revelation not by education," suggested one man. The speaker agreed: "There needs to be a fire and purification. Everybody is affected by a media that is not telling the truth, and we have the truth through scripture. We are just instruments."

Other terrestrial signs of eschatological immanence and imminence were more directly linked to prophetic biblical texts—texts which were frequently quoted by preachers, and then recirculated in everyday Christian conversations about the end times. One of the most frequently cited examples was a passage from Matthew, which speaks in apocalyptic terms about war, famine, disease, and earthquakes:

> And ye shall hear of wars and rumours of wars: see that ye be not troubled: for all these things must come to pass, but the end is not yet. For nation shall rise against nation, and kingdom against kingdom: and there shall be famines, and pestilences, and earthquakes, in divers places. All these are the beginning of sorrows. (24:6-8)

Such was the importance of this text, that Brethren preachers frequently turned to it (and to similar passages in Mark 13 and Luke 21) when pleading with their listeners to "come to Jesus," as seen in the following two quotes, from gospel sermons. The first develops the image of earthquakes and spiritual deliverance, while the second refers to wars and famines. Importantly, both do so with reference to the nearness of the eschaton and the fulfillment of prophecy:

God has lengthened out the day of grace. God is waiting tonight. Is there one tonight who is without Christ? My friend the call of the gospel is to come out of this world and into God's world to settle the sin question. Come to Jesus! God loves you! But he hates the sin! Tomorrow may be too late! It's urgent! God speaks! God speaks in visions! God speaks in dreams! God speaks in earthquakes! That's what conversion does: it takes you and transports you out of this world. Will you be ready when Jesus comes? If he comes tonight where will you spend eternity? You'll not get a tract in hell!

* * *

When you hear of wars and tumults: these things must take place. There are still wars today, famines. We are in such days. Why? It is a sign. These things must happen. Apostasy is rife today: you won't cure it; you have to withdraw from it. Where there is evil, there is only one remedy; you have to withdraw from it. We aren't living in First Timothy days; we are living in Second Timothy days.

This final comment, that the present—understood as an acute time of eschatological crisis—exists as a prophetic fulfillment of the "perilous times" of 2 Timothy (see also Webster 2013b: 184) significantly influenced how my informants experienced the landscapes and seascapes of these "last of the last days." Storms were not just inclement weather, but were messages from God—"God speaks!"—which did more than communicate a divine timetable for earthly transformation. Indeed, storms, wars, famines, earthquakes, and diseases actually *constituted* this divine timetable, and did so in such a way so as to allow the Christians of Gamrie to be part of the action. During my fieldwork, as well as localized storm events experienced by fishermen, major global events—such as the 2009 swine flu pandemic—came to be incorporated into the wider eschatological speculations of my informants. While the spiritual discipline of prayer was an often practiced form of engagement with these imaginations about the unfolding of biblical prophecy, other avenues for this-worldly engagement with end-times happenings were developed by my informants.

As discussed earlier, much of these terrestrial engagements focused on Israel, with eschatological agency taking diverse forms. These acts ranged from supporting afforestation programs in the Negev desert to fulfill an end-times prophecy in Isaiah 35 that "the desert shall rejoice, and blossom" (see Webster 2013b: 188–90), to funding historically Christian Zionist organizations such as Prophetic Witness Movement International. Importantly, these agentive acts also involved personally traversing certain eschatologically important landscapes. Many of Gamrie's Christians, for example, undertook regular "Holy Land" pilgrimages to Israel, explaining to me that doing so was a way to offer not just spiritual but also political and financial support to Israel and Israeli Jews. Several of those who became my closest informants during my research had returned from one such pilgrimage shortly before I arrived in the field. Those on the trip made a film of their travels to share with those back home, much of which consisted of close-up shots of an open Bible which filled almost the entire screen, meaning the person reading could be heard but not seen. This footage initially struck me as odd, given how little it showed of the pilgrimage sites and surrounding countryside. It was only after being told that the readers were standing in the geographical locations which the passages being read described that I realized the importance of the (largely unseen) landscape, and its textual representation as part of the DVD.

Of course, the cinematography made complete sense to my informants from the outset, for it was only the *reading* of the biblical text *in Israel* which would bring about the mass conversion of the Jewish peoples, thereby triggering the final events of the Second Coming—a conviction also held to by the Christian Zionists Harding (2000: 229) describes as having buried Bibles in the caves of Petra in anticipation of their end-times discovery by Jews seeking refuge from the anti-Christ. Such was the literalness of this terrestrial eschatology that some of informants came to regard the work of the Temple Institute—an organization seeking to physically "rebuild the Holy Temple on Mount Moriah in Jerusalem," as well as all its sacred vessels and vestments (templeinstitute.org 2018)—as yet another fulfillment of prophecy. Here too the spatial immanence and temporal imminence of the apocalypse was further assured by those who donated money to the "special temple building fund," with supporters candidly informed that "your generosity can make the difference between dream and reality" (templeinstitute.org 2018).

Such observations about the terrestrial nature of eschatology are not new to the ethnographic record, which is littered with infamous examples. Thousands of Native North Americans danced the Ghost Dance in anticipation of the return of the bison, both in 1870 and 1890 (Mooney 1896). "Cargo Cultists" build thatch airplanes and clear runways in the forests of Melanesia to allow for the soon arrival of "cargo" (Burridge 1960). As I sat surrounded by Brethren young people during a home Bible study, listening to the group leader explain the prophetic importance of the work of the Temple Institute, the excitement in the room was palpable. The Ark of the Covenant and the Temple were being (literally, materially) remade ahead of a totalizing *Aliyah*, understood to be the precursor to Judaism's sublimation into born-again Christianity, at the point of the Second Coming. Prophecy *was* being fulfilled in their day and generation, of that my informants were sure. Different Brethren informants, speaking to me in different contexts agreed. "God has chosen this piece of land," one informant told me, speaking of Israel. "We're living in a world where people are trying to take that land away from Israel. Look at the extent of land God promised Abraham; they have never yet possessed it, *but they will when the Lord comes back!*" said another.

Agency, Responsibility, and Ethic

What are we to make of this? While I do not want to claim any full explanation for these ethnographic encounters, I do want to suggest that they may be able to teach us some interesting things about agency, and thus about the anthropology of ethics. In attempting to show how, I want to start by considering Laidlaw's (2010, 2014) writing on agency and responsibility.

Laidlaw identifies what he sees as two dominant formulations of agency within anthropology, namely "practice theories" and Actor Network Theory (ANT). Practice theories, according to Laidlaw, tend to emphasize "empowerment, liberation, and equality . . . [which are] assumed to be always and everywhere advanced by the authentic expression of individual subjectivity" (2010: 144). In this school of thought, it is The Individual (capital T, capital I) who acts, both *by* and *for* themselves. ANT, on the other hand, takes a rather different view of things Laidlaw suggests, insofar as:

> The efficacy, and hence the responsibility, of an individual may be extended by the agency of his or her body or body parts, properties, dependents, or works, and this happens either because these entities are intrinsically connected to or are a part of him or her. (2010: 152)

Laidlaw then moves to suggest that such an observation is hardly new within anthropology, drawing on Gluckman's (1972) rereading of Evans-Pritchard's (1937) analysis of witchcraft, where

> mechanisms for the allocation of responsibility . . . create their own distinctive kinds of interconnectedness. People can be held accountable for actions that are simply not conceivable as actions without the practices, such as divination and accusation, through which culprits are identified. Witch finding, as a practice of allocating responsibility, turns what might otherwise be an accident or random

misfortune into an action. It therefore creates agency, so to speak retrospectively [whereby] the attribution of responsibility . . . involves postulating unseen entities . . . not all located "inside" an individual and not necessarily simply psychological. (Laidlaw 2010: 157–8)

This is important because it highlights profoundly different ways of treating human agency and responsibility, as based either on individual subjectivity or on the connectedness of persons, practices, and things—just as visible in statistical analysis and UK audit culture, we are told (Laidlaw 2010: 160–1), as within Zande witch finding. For Laidlaw:

The point is simply that institutions and practices can work so as to proliferate the kinds of connections that sustain attributions of responsibility or they can tend to constrain them. They may expand and distribute agency, or they may contract it. (Laidlaw 2010: 159)

I find this analysis hugely insightful, especially when interpreting the everyday experiences of Gamrie eschatology, and how these relate to wider ideas about agency and responsibility. Gamrie's Christians find themselves caught between, on the one hand, a conviction about the reality and ultimacy of divine/demonic activity, and, on the other hand, a recognition that human action not only happens but matters greatly. The EU, then, is the anti-Christ, and the devil is its puppet-master who seeks to deceive and enslave humanity. God, in contrast, protects during storms and provides by drawing fish into the nets. Christian fishermen, however, are neither still nor silent, but must live lives and catch fish in a way that glorifies God and shuns the devil. Their occupation, while fulfilling their Protestant calling to (literally) "have dominion over the fish of the sea," was also the very thing which threatened to imperil their salvation. Not only was their dominion secondary to that of the EU, but the devil himself sought to force Christian fishermen to take the Mark of the Beast in the form of total compliance to the CFP and its diabolical apocalyptic agenda.

This same complexity resided on land, seen through my informants support for Israel. Their Christian Zionism called them to pray for the conversion of Jewish people globally, but especially in the Middle East. Supporting the work of Prophetic Witness Movement International, publicly reading the Bible in situ during Holy Land tours, and donating money to the Temple Institute extended and accelerated these efforts to see "God's Chosen People" return to God's chosen land—a return which would bring about both their born-again salvation and (thereby) the beginning of the end of the eschaton. Yet, as in fishing, my informants' actions were not entirely their own, for they were fulfilling not their own words but "The Word of the Lord." Agency, and thus responsibility, was shared out, not in neat portions with clear boundaries, but with a degree of messiness, with boundaries that bled into one another.

Thus, while my informants did take great care in studying their Bibles and identifying "signs of the end times," this did not represent the totality of their millennial Christian activity. Indeed, in addition to learning about and locating eschatological prophecy in their everyday lives, Gamrie's Christians also actively sought to *fulfill* that prophecy, for example, by going on pilgrimage to—and publicly reading the Bible within—the Holy Land. In this sense, the claim that Israel has "never yet possessed" the "land God promised Abraham" needs to be read as a challenge which Gamrie's Christians are leveling at themselves—a call to action which seeks to transform the "never *yet*" into a soon-to-occur *now* of prophetic fulfillment. The full extent of this intent can be seen in the follow-up statement, "But they will, when the Lord comes back!"—a state of affairs which my informants felt significant responsibility for, as they sought to foster the conditions necessary for the Second Coming, through prayer, Bible reading, missionary work, and, in some case, by financially supporting tree planting and temple rebuilding projects which sought to transform the world eschatologically by first transforming in geographically.

In other instances, my informants found themselves overtaken by events, for example, through changes in CFP legislation. Some reacted by lobbying the Scottish Fishermen's Federation, while others took the more drastic step of leaving the industry altogether, rejecting their increasing entanglement in EU politics as spiritually unbearable. Most recently, some Aberdeenshire fishermen campaigned for the UK to leave the EU, most notably by taking part in the "Brexit Flotilla" led by Nigel Farage, which, in June 2016, traveled down the Thames to the Houses of Parliament. Yet, whatever decision my informants took involved both the "seen entities" of fishermen and bureaucrats and the "unseen entities" of God and the devil, with both being attributed real agency and thus genuine ethical (or, in local terms, *moral*) responsibility.

Who, then, was acting, and for *whom*? At risk of stating the obvious, it seems that multiple agents are at work here, undertaking actions for themselves *and* on behalf of others. What, in this context, are we to make of Laidlaw's suggestion

> that institutions and practices can work so as to proliferate the kinds of connections that sustain attributions of responsibility *or* they can tend to constrain them. They may expand and distribute agency, *or* they may contract it. (Laidlaw 2010: 159; emphasis added)

It seems that, when considering my informant's eschatological agency, we encounter not an "either/or" but a "both/and" situation. This agency, directed toward the reading, locating and fulfillment of prophecy, involves both a proliferation and constraint of the kinds of connectedness and responsibility that Laidlaw holds to be central to a properly anthropological understanding of ethics. The agency of Gamrie's Christians, then, was indeed constrained by the attribution of certain "unseen" agentive forces. This agency was layered *on top of* their own, in the case of God, and *below* their own, in the case of the devil, contracting the authority and responsibility they experienced in daily life. Thus, while my informants would often impress upon me the fact that "God works through us," they would also seek to remind me that we "live in a fallen world" and are often "controlled by sin." Here we may come to regard agency as cut in half, or into thirds, with local Christians imagining that this-worldly human activity is itself subject to the activity of divine and demonic forces. Indeed, as the speaker as the Zionist conference told his audience, "We are just instruments"—instruments which my informants hope and pray were used by God, but were also liable (i.e., predisposed and accountable) to the machinations of "The Tempter," that is, the devil himself.

Yet, even as their agency contracted, it seemed also, paradoxically, to expand. As well as *God* working through them, my informants would also speak with real excitement about how *they* were "doing God's work," by praying, catching fish, traveling to Israel, publicly reading scripture, planting trees, and rebuilding the Temple. So too in their interactions with demonic forces; while still being partially enslaved to "the world, the flesh, and the devil," my informants also sought to fight against this "Evil One" by engaging in what many Christians call "spiritual warfare" (Elisha 2017, McAlister 2016) or "spiritual battle" (Smiderle and Mesquita 2016; cf. Bialecki 2011; van Wyk 2014). Here, preaching, praying, and bearing testimony combined with more bespoke efforts such as organizing a mobile tract library to combat the spread of Islam. Equally, resisting the temptations of the devil to fish on a Sunday—no matter how much a pattern of weather conditions seemed to require it—came to be understood as a form of spiritual warfare, just as the decision taken by many younger Gamrie fishermen to abandon Sabbatarianism was by their older Christian critics as an act of spiritual surrender, or, worse still, an act of spiritual betrayal. Here, human agency was not only divided into halves or thirds, but simultaneously found itself doubled or tripled, for not only were human actions attributable to God and the devil but so too were divine and demonic actions attributable to saved and unsaved persons. Such was the simultaneous expansion and contraction of eschatological agency.

Conclusion

I am reminded of Edwin Ardener's famous essay "The Voice of Prophecy," which begins by suggesting that "prophecy . . . is a kind of condition both of individuals and structures" (2007: 135). Ardener's real contribution is not simply that prophecy and prediction are not the same thing (for prophecy, according to Ardener concerns not the future but the present [see also Jenkins 2013]), but that the distinction between individuals and structures is "a tautology" (Ardener 2007: 135). For Ardener, "the paradox of individual freedom" (Ardener 2007: 152) can be most clearly seen in the fact that "prophecy may well exhibit paradoxical features" (Ardener 2007: 153). This paradox is what I have been describing here, which, in Ardener's terms, is encapsulated by the fact that "individuals are in constant contrast to their worlds, from which they never entirely free themselves" (Ardener 2007: 154).

In Gamrie, this paradox means being both the master of one's own spiritual destiny and a slave to both God and the devil; it means being responsible for what goes on in the North Sea and on Mount Moriah, while also being subject to the unimaginably powerful eschatological forces that are being unleashed during these "last of the last days." Perhaps most poignantly and painfully for my Christian informants, this paradox also means being ethically and morally responsible—through their life of faith and witness—for the salvific status of one's own soul, and the soul of their unconverted neighbor, be they in Gamrie or Jerusalem, while also recognizing that salvation and damnation are ultimately acts of God and the devil. Here we a find basic tenet of classical logic—the law of non-contradiction—broken by the seemingly competing local logic of eschatological agency, where one is both *the author* and *not the author* of one's actions, *at the same time*. Extending this seeming contradiction, the previous ethnography also suggests that, for the Christians of Gamrie, one is simultaneously *the author* and *more than the author* of one's actions, with the actions of other (divine and demonic) forces also laid claim to. Such is the paradox of the individual freedom and structures of prophecy—a paradox which, if more fully recognized and engaged with, might help anthropology develop "a better understanding of the ethical dimension of social life" (Laidlaw 2014b: 497).

In order to gain this better understanding, it is important to realize that this paradox is not just a theological puzzle but also a material one. This is because the multi-authored nature of eschatological agency concerns not only how Gamrie's Christians treated the Bible as a millenarian intellectual project (see also Keller 2004) but, in so doing, also concerns how that intellectual project came to shape—and be shaped by—different seascapes and landscapes. The geography of eschatology is thus not illustrative, but coconstitutive of the religious life of Gamrie's fishers. Indeed, calm and violent seas jointly instantiate the temporal nearness of the end of the world through the physical nearness of God's salvation and the devil's temptations—in beautiful maritime sunrises, in fatal storms, and in humanity's fate being tied to the demonic-bureaucratic (mis)management of fish and other world food supplies. So too on land, where a mobile tract library, a crescent-shaped storm cloud, the Ark of the Covenant, earthquakes, and public Bible readings on location in Israel not only demonstrate but also instantiate a this-worldly apocalypse-to-come.

By taking this terrestrial focus, self-fulfilling prophecy—that is, a prophecy which gives fulfillment to both to the self and the religious community—can be seen to raise sociality from the sea and the land just as literally as Adam was said to have been raised from and returned to the dust. "Cursed be the ground on thy account. For dust thou art; and unto dust shalt thou return" (Gen. 3:17b, 19b). Yet, contrary to Sahlins' (1996) own penetrating analysis of the curse of the Fall, for the Christians of Gamrie, the pain of unattained pleasure (i.e., "the sadness of sweetness") did not have the final word. Within their millennial expectancy resided one final terrestrial prophecy about the reestablishment of Eden within an eschatologically (and eternally) conjoined New Heaven and New Earth. Normally stern-faced Brethren preachers would, on this topic, break out in warm, broad smiles when describing how the Bible began and concluded with a perfect garden—the latter of which would be enjoyed by His saved people forever, free from the devil and his agents, exactly as was prophesized. Commenting on the certainty and security of such a promise, one of my closest Brethren informants explained the matter by reflecting not on landscapes of Christianity per se but on the (literal) creation of *all* land. On the third day, he said, God created the land, which lay a "secure foundation" for the world and all which was later built upon it. Millennia later, God raised Jesus from the dead on the third day—"another secure foundation! This book dovetails in!" he said, with that characteristic smile. Such was the terrestrial certainty of biblical prophecy—a certainty built upon (and by) the geography of eschatology, both on land and at sea.

7

Imagining an Ethnic Ecumene

Evangelical Landscapes as Gentile, Jewish, and Native in the American South

Rebekka King

On one Wednesday afternoon, a few months into my fieldwork at Shield of Faith, a non-denominational, charismatic church in rural Tennessee, Pastor Ronnie, Pastor Jim, and I sat in the church's boardroom. We were engaged in a method of conversation, which I now understand as a form of Christian gossip: one-part torrid details of people's lives and one-part prayer request. It is a communicative act that resembles the more prevalent Southern practice of declaring "bless your heart," a double-speak phrase that I have come to revere since moving from Canada to the American South.

My intention for this casual meeting had been to ask some questions about the Rapture. In church on Sunday, Pastor Ronnie had surprised his congregants by preaching that the Rapture would not occur any time soon and that Christians should "unpack their bags." An argument that he withdrew a few months later as a partially incomplete revelation.

That day, as on many occasions, the conversation naturally found its way to Lily, Pastor Ronnie's much-beloved granddaughter, the first-born child of his daughter Charlene, a youth pastor at a Methodist Church in Memphis. While Lily is a regular fixture at the church both in sermons and on her weekend visits with her grandparents, I had not yet met Charlene. I was acquainted with Ronnie's other daughter, Samantha, a social worker who lives close by. I asked if Samantha was planning to have children, knowing that she and her husband appeared to be settling down in the area.

"I don't know," Ronnie said, his usual expressiveness notably absent. "Her husband . . ." Ronnie trailed off momentarily and then went on to explain that Samantha's marriage was in flux. Her husband was not working at the time and his struggle to find employment was taking a toll on their marriage. Ronnie and his wife Kathy found themselves at odds with Samantha's husband's approach to work and family life.

"Me and Kathy, we like him a lot. We really do, but he's kind of hard to get in with." Jim nodded stoically.

"It's not that he's a bad person," Ronnie repeated. "We like him a lot, but he's a Northerner. They have a different way of doing things up there. We have a common understanding of what folks are like. You can trust Southerners by looking them in the eyes. But up North? They're different."

Jim nodded again. I smiled. "So, what do you think of me?" I asked. "Canada is much closer to the North than to the South."

Ronnie leaned back in his chair. I could tell he was choosing his words carefully. I had asked the question as a joke, but he had taken it seriously. As a good Southerner, he was working hard to come up with a response that would be genuine. I could tell that Ronnie had not intended to equate me with his son-in-law and was concerned that the comparison would hurt me. Over the previous months, Ronnie has made clear his affection for me. His commitment to my research at the church and my spiritual health resonated through many of our interactions. I immediately felt guilty about putting him in a position where he might think that he had offended me. I started to tell him that I had only been joking when his eyes lit up and he smiled widely.

"Well, you're from the south of your country," he pointed out, referring to the fact that I had grown up in a town directly on the Canadian border with New York state. "So, you're also a Southerner." Ronnie looked at Jim, who was also leaning forward. Emphasizing the cadence of his deep Tennessee accent, he exclaimed: "*We's* all Southern folks round here!" Jim hit the table with the palm of his hands and I burst out laughing.

Ronnie's willingness to incorporate me into the larger category of Southerner was primarily humorous. However, it also reflects the greater practices of reimagining kinship and religious creativity at the heart of the congregational dynamics at Shield of Faith. The church is part of a larger movement known as "Jewish Affinity Christianity," an off-shoot of Messianic Judaism that adopts Jewish practices and categories into American evangelicalism, conferring on Christians within this movement the identity of "first fruit Gentiles." It differs from Messianic Judaism in that it does not presuppose any Jewish lineage or heritage. Nor do adherents posit themselves, as many Messianics do, within contemporary Judaism as "completed" by virtue of belief in Jesus' messiahship (Imhoff and Kaell 2017: 95). Instead, Jewish Affinity Christianity encompasses a broader spectrum of evangelical absorption of Jewish practices, artifacts, and categories. Their incorporation of Jewish rituals and holidays follows a model that Hillary Kaell sees as a form of mimesis of both Jesus specifically and Jews more broadly (Kaell 2016; cf. Dulin 2015).

Within the anthropology of Christianity, much discussion has been devoted to how Christian conversion engenders a break or rupture from previous cultural practices (Robbins 2007; Daswani 2013). Judaism, in particular, has historically signified a "parting of ways" from Christianity and served as a proximate other (Boyarin 2009; Smith 2004). Recent work on Jewish Affinity Christianity has explored how adopting a Jewish identity or Jewish markers enables new religious ontologies comprised of a conflation of multiple identities (e.g., Dulin 2015; Kaell 2016). While certainly from a scholarly perspective, one might discern an overt form of hybridity or religious syncretism at work, I am interested in the ways that affinity between different religious traditions are imagined across temporal and geographical regions (cf. Handman 2011). In the case of Shield of Faith, such affinity enables novel Christian subjectivities to be reified through a dichotomous focus on absence and presence, distance and proximity, and foreign and familiar.

This chapter examines the case study of the relationship between an evangelical congregation in rural Tennessee and a Messianic rabbi, Larry Mallet, from Oklahoma who promotes a new Christian selfhood that is simultaneously Jewish and Gentile while also incorporating Native American identity into what Mallet refers to as a "triple-bound cord."[1] In Mallet's view, Jewish and Native American identities are privileged for their perceived cultural antiquity, uncontaminated spirituality, and respective claims to being original inhabitants of Israel and North America. In contrast, Gentile Christians in North America are disparaged because they are conceptualized as interlopers in Jewish temporality and Indigenous territories. Mallet teaches that in order to overcome this interloper status, Gentile Christians are required to tithe directly to his organization, Covenant Ministries. As a Jewish believer in Christianity whose property is located on Native American land, he embodies this tripartite religio-ethnic identity.

At work is a form of deterritorialization in which Christian American spaces gain authenticity by virtue of their failure to resemble Jewish and Indigenous ones (cf. Hovland 2016). Based on ethnographic fieldwork in both Tennessee and Oklahoma, this chapter outlines the ways that Jewish and Indigenous religio-ethnic landscapes are extrapolated into an evangelical Christian imaginary and made accessible through a focus on their absence and in contrast to other religio-ethnic identities deemed undesirable. Lending authority to these imagined and otherwise inaccessible identities and locations enables the Jewish Affinity Christians featured in this study to make sense of recent demographic, political, and socioeconomic shifts within the setting of rural, conservative Christian America.

Temporality and Promise: The Context of Jewish Affinity Christianity

> Two are better than one; because they have a good reward for their labor. For if they fall, the one will lift up his fellow: but woe to him that is alone when he falleth; for he hath not another to help him up. Again, if two lie together, then they have heat: but how can one be warm alone? And if one prevail against him, two shall withstand him; and a threefold cord is not quickly broken. (Eccl. 4:9)

The recent Pew Survey on American Jewish Life revealed a surprising cohort of individuals who claim to be Jewish, or partially Jewish, despite having no religious, cultural, or ethnic ties to Judaism and no family members whom they considered ethnically, culturally, or religiously Jewish. When pressed, many asserted that their Jewish identity stemmed from the fact that Jesus was Jewish (see Lugo et al. 2013). These results point to a growing subset of evangelical and charismatic Christians, whose interest in Judaism has emerged through involvement in movements such as Messianic Judaism or Jews for Jesus, though a significant portion attend run-of-the-mill evangelical and charismatic Christian churches (Kaell 2013; Dulin 2013; 2015; cf. Kollontai 2004).[2]

While Jewish Affinity Christianity is linked to Messianic Judaism, it is distinct because its adherents cannot claim any concrete connection to what we might consider "traditional" Jewish identity markers, such as ancestry, marriage, religion, or other kinship and family resemblance models. Instead, their relationship to Judaism is mediated through their relationship with Jesus and certain conceptions of biblical promises perceived to have been made to the ancient Israelites. Jewish Affinity Christianity is mostly comprised of Gentiles who were raised in evangelical Christian traditions. A few have or claim Jewish ancestry, but in most instances, their interest in Judaism emerged vis-à-vis participation in evangelical forms of Christianity, a desire to learn about the religious practices of Jesus and early Christians, and concern for the modern State of Israel, which plays an important role in contemporary Christian dispensationalist theology (Goldman 2010; Merkley 2001; Spector 2009; Weber 2005). For many, their interests were sparked by learning about certain Jewish holidays and practices, especially Passover Seders, which have become increasingly popular within evangelical Christianity in the late twentieth and early twenty-first centuries (Sandmel 2010).

An important component of Jewish Affinity Christianity is tied to a subtle shift in evangelical thinking about eschatological temporality. According to the logic of many forms of evangelical Christianity, the "Church Age," that is, the temporal period following the death of Jesus until his return at the end of time, was an afterthought. The Jewish rejection of Jesus as the Messiah in the first century ushered in an unscripted period of time in which the Christian church was established and salvation was extended to Gentiles in place of Jews (Boyer 1992; Weber 1979). Adherents of both Messianic Judaism and Jewish Affinity Christianity refer to this temporal framework as "replacement theology" and criticize its presumption that a new covenant based on the figure of Jesus supersedes the biblical covenant established between God and the Israelites (Power 2011). Instead, critics draw from Paul's letter to the Romans to advocate for what is known as "grafting in" theology. Using a horticultural metaphor, Romans 11 suggests that through their relationship with Jesus, Gentiles might understand themselves as conjoined to Judaism, akin to the way that the shoot of one plant might be inosculated to the roots of another. The covenantal promises to the ancient Israelites are thus extrapolated to Christians, who, according to the analogy, flourish and bear fruit, even though they are not part of the root. "Grafting in" is seen as returning to the "true covenant." Thus, in the views of many Jewish Affinity Christians, this conjoining requires them to uphold certain observances of the biblical law. While mandated observances vary from group to group, most adhere to ritual observances, religious holidays and calendars, and select legal traditions.

To the outside observer, the distinctions between "replacement theology" and a "grafting in" may not appear as consequential as it does to Jewish Affinity Christians. In contrast to traditional dispensationalist thought and in line with trends found more broadly within contemporary evangelical circles, this shift allows for a new temporal map and expectation of agency. Whereas traditional dispensationalism teaches that the current era (the church age) is an afterthought and thus outside of any prophetic materials found in the Bible, "grafting in" means that the church age is part of God's initial plan and thus subject to prophetic forecasts. Human beings are thus emboldened to directly impact the world and take measures that might help usher in the last days (Webster 2013;

cf. Bialecki 2017; Frykholm 2004; Harding 2000). Participation in the covenant thus becomes a means of actively entering into a biblical promise marked by prophetic expectations and a novel conception of "Jewish" temporality.

While they follow a secular calendar in their daily lives, Jewish Affinity Christians also take note of the Jewish calendar marking the New Year and important fast dates. For example, the church hosts a yearly Passover Sedar, eagerly anticipated by many within the congregation and friends from nearby churches who joined the services for this special occasion. In 2018, Mallet made a special trip to the church for the second Friday of Passover. In the lead-up to the service, the church's email exchange saw a flurry of correspondence related to the planning and coordinating of the Seder meal. Particularly noteworthy was an email sent from Cindi, a congregation member with visual impairment. In her email, she wrote to inquire about local options for purchasing Matzah bread for the Feast of Unleavened Bread. She explained that she and her service dog Turbo had tried both Walmart and Kroger without luck. Another congregation member replied helpfully, noting that they too had tried to find Matzah locally, but that is difficult to do so at this time of year. They suggested ordering the bread on Amazon and, recognizing Cindi's low visibility, suggested that someone from the church might help her with the order.

Cindi and her service dog Turbo are new additions to the congregation at Shield of Faith, although Cindi has participated in Jewish Affinity Christianity for several years. Her inquiry about the availability of Matzah at the local Walmart is revealing about some of the key traits of Jewish Affinity Christianity found specifically at Shield of Faith. Whereas Jewish Affinity Christians in the northeast, California, or larger urban centers might have access to and knowledge about Jewish practices (perhaps even having attended Passover Seders at the homes of Jewish friends and colleagues), the congregants at Shield of Faith have next to no direct experience or knowledge of Jewish practices and traditions. Despite Cindi's assumption, it is unlikely that local grocery store chains will stock items specifically for Passover. Hence the congregation's excitement at Mallet's Passover visit and Cindi's desire to replicate elements of the meal at home. In this context, the relationship between their rabbinical leader, Larry Mallet, and Shield of Faith becomes hyper-localized. Mallet's visit enables the congregation to enter into Jewish space and time in a way that they cannot do without his presence and instructions.

Mallet's claim to Jewish kinship blurs what are already unclear boundaries similar to those found in other varieties of Messianic Judaism. Mallet was raised in a secular home. His birth mother was a Jewish and his birth father was a Catholic. Because they were not married, they abandoned him at the hospital when he was born and he was adopted by non-believers who also happened to be a Jewish mother and a Catholic father. Despite growing up in a nonreligious household, Mallet married an evangelical Christian woman and had a miraculous conversion in his bathtub, wherein God revealed to him that he was to take up the mantel of Jewish-Christianity as a Messianic rabbi. Mallet is not affiliated with any major American Messianic organizations, but he self-identifies as a Messianic rabbi. Much of the conversations around Mallet on Messianic online forums are negative. They contend that his claims to Jewish identity and rabbinical training are fraudulent and that his charismatic ministry has little to do with religion but rather is a thinly veiled snake oil venture or Ponzi scheme. For example, to indicate support for Covenant Ministries, adherents can purchase their very own *tallit*, specially blessed holy anointing oil, or Dead Sea supplements designed to prepare one for spiritual warfare.

Unlike other Messianic traditions in which Gentiles, or non-Jews, more readily take on Jewish identity, Mallet does not entertain the possibility that the Christians to whom he speaks might somehow understand themselves as Jewish. Theologically, they might encounter Judaism through belief in Jesus and through "grafting in" to Jewish temporality and biblical promises. Mallet's interpretation of the "grafting in" theology focuses on opportunities for Gentile Christians to receive the covenantal promise by being in relationship with Jewish believers in Jesus as intermediaries. As such, Mallet positions himself as the mediator through which evangelicals can temporarily embody Judaism. By financially supporting Mallet's ministries, evangelicals demonstrate to God their support of Israel and Jews and thus write themselves into God's plan and promise.

In what appears to be a unique convergence, Mallet's "grafting in" theology not only is inclusive of Jews but also incorporates Native Americans. Mallet teaches that Jews, Gentiles, and First Nations peoples are part of a binding process that he calls the "triple-bound cord." According to this perspective, American Christians are interlopers in not only the Jewish covenant but also Native American land. In order to overcome their interloper status, Mallet teaches that Christians must attend to those to whom the land and the promise were initially given: Native Americans and Jews. Mallet teaches that the Blackfoot are descendants of the lost tribes of Israel and, according to Mallet, both Native Americans and Jews share Phoenician DNA. As a Messianic rabbi who also claims to be an honorary chief of the Blackfoot Nation, Mallet stands as the fulfillment of each of these identities. He offers himself as a vessel of mediation through which evangelical Christians might surpass their status as interlopers. Within this schema,

Mallet constructs a new ethnic, religious, and national kinship system. Mallet's theological system creates a conflict for Gentile evangelicals who have no claim to this triple-bound trajectory. As a solution, Mallet offers himself as the bridge that mediates the very distance that he has constructed. The triple-bound cord serves as an imagined point of origin, which generates a hybrid ethno-religious kinship structure which, for his Gentile Christian followers, is spurned on through their distance from both Jewish and Native American identities.

Congregational Differences and the Distribution of Gifts

The forms of mediation offered by Mallet are primarily financial. Although they claim not to be a Prosperity Gospel movement—but rather situate themselves as a prophetic tradition that draws explicitly from the Hebrew Bible—one cannot overlook the similarities. The discursive content of Mallet's preaching and the promotional materials associated with Covenant Ministries is strikingly similar to the Prosperity Gospel.[3] For example, in 2016 (which in the Jewish calendar was 5776), Mallet claimed it was the year of Jubilee Abundance: when every dollar one donated to God via Mallet's ministries would see a 100-fold return in the near future. Of particular interest is the notable economic disparity between the congregants at Shield of Faith, which is located in a rural and economically disadvantaged part of Middle Tennessee, and those who attend services at Covenant Ministries, which draws its congregants from either a nearby wealthy, retirement locale or further afield from followers who travel from across the United States to attend Jewish holiday services. During my observations at the three days of Passover services at Covenant Ministries, I noted that on three separate occasions, those in attendance wrote large checks to Mallet's ministry in anticipation of an even larger, 100-fold yield.

In contrast, Shield of Faith is a non-denominational, charismatic, predominantly white evangelical church that meets in a large shed-like building in the countryside. The church was founded by Pastor Ronnie in the mid-2000s when he, a Baptist pastor, received the gift of the spirit and began to speak in tongues. As a result of his new charismatic experience, Ronnie left the Baptist Church to establish Shield of Faith. The congregation met initially in a local school and began construction of their current building about six years later, at which point the second pastor, Pastor Jim, joined the leadership team. My first visit to Shield of Faith corresponded with Mallet's second visit to the congregation. During this initial service, Mallet apostolically activated Shield of Faith to be part of his ministry network and sealed them under his holy tallit as a sign of a new covenant relationship. In order to solidify this relationship, Mallet anointed the men with holy oil and prayed over them in both tongues and Hebrew. It is important to note that apart from Mallet, the members of Shield of Faith have next to no access to Judaism. Most of them have never met someone who is Jewish and any working knowledge that they have about Judaism comes from either the Bible or their political support for the State of Israel. Likewise, their knowledge of Native American cultures and traditions is limited. Although many members of the congregation adopt the pervasive trope of claiming non-specified Indigenous ancestry through both genealogical and historical imaginaries (Deloria 1998; Green 1988; Lovett 1998; Springwood 2004). Indeed, Mallet and members of the congregation see the fact that the church is located adjacent to the Trail of Tears as spiritually significant.

The relationship between Shield of Faith and Covenant Ministries is both religious and economical.

Mallet teaches that if the members of the congregation desire to receive financial or physical blessings from God, they must invest a significant portion of their income in God and God's spokesperson, Mallet. In addition to tithing 10 percent of the church's income to Covenant Ministries, the church is also expected to give 2 percent of its income to Mallet himself (he calls this 2 percent tithe a *terumah*, the Hebrew term for an offering traditionally reserved for the priest). According to Mallet, this faith offering is intended as a sign to God that the congregants expect a blessing from God in return for this special offering. Along with the 10 percent tithe and the 2 percent *terumah*, Mallet also collects special divinely sanctioned offerings whenever he visits the congregation.

On one visit to the church, Mallet explained that God was instigating a special 100-fold blessing in which any money donated to Covenant Ministries would return to the giver 100 times over. The small congregation of approximately 200 people donated more than $25,000 over the course of 2 services. On the following Sunday, when it was announced to the congregation how much money had been raised in support of Covenant Ministries, Pastor Ronnie framed these donations as participation in Judaism and as an altruistic act of Christian surrender.

"We grew up the time of the American Dream," Ronnie explained. "Buy a house, get a good job. But Jesus is looking for people to abandon everything to him." He clarified that times were getting harder and that the failure of the American Dream to be realized is the result of a larger turn on the part of the nation away from God, from Christian values, and from support for Israel. Ronnie was particularly pleased with the presence of seven Jews in the congregation during Mallet's visit (Mallet, his wife, his daughter, his son-in-law, and three other members of Mallet's congregation). Ronnie reported that one member of Shield of Faith, who did not have any money on him during the service, had donated a dollar bill during the time of the special offering because that was all he had in his pocket. As he was leaving the church, another congregation member presented him with 100 dollars (proof that the 100-fold blessing was working, albeit in a minor form).

While the congregants themselves seemed undeterred by this large sum of money garnered on Mallet's behalf, one might be confused by the enormity of that sum from a group of individuals with little excess income to spare. It is striking that the congregation saw the 100 dollars as proof that the 100-fold blessing had occurred without contrasting it with the larger sum procured by Mallet. The discrepancies between these one-time financial dividends have parallels in the linguistic practices of Pastor Ronnie (who comes across as a genuine and simple Southern man and illustrates his sermons with references to his love of gravy, breakfast at Hardee's, and his distaste for driving on the interstate) and those of Mallet (who in dress and mannerism appears almost "nouveau riche," and whose stories are of jet-setting to Israel, meetings with Netanyahu, and the need to raise hundreds of thousands of dollars to expand his church's sanctuary and add a parking lot). These practices pertain to the performance of a particular class or economic status. Illustrative of these differences are the ways that both men interact with technology. Ronnie is hesitant and usually asks someone else to turn on the microphone for him, whereas Mallet picks up the mic with confidence and speaks directly to the sound technicians, asking, "Is this thing hot?"

Exotic Capital, Elsewhere, and Misplaced Taboo

As many of Mallet's critics do, one might easily pause at this juncture and evoke claims made about the Prosperity Gospel as a form of deception or a religiously infused pyramid scheme (see Coleman 2011). However, such conclusions fail to account for the full picture. In the context of Middle Tennessee, Prosperity Churches are ubiquitous. A question emerges: Why does this particular version that links Judaism, Christianity, and Indigenous identities gain traction within this community? The new religio-ethic territories uncovered by Mallet and the congregants at Shield of Faith emerge in the context of a multi-layered ethnic and religious landscape of the American South. Amid its historical complexities, the South, as historian James Cobb argues, is simultaneously internally and externally othered. Its diversity often goes unrecognized. Instead, the South represents a byproduct of cultural nostalgia and political and economic nativism formed in contrast to a presumed neutral North (Cobb 2005).

The Southern imaginary constitutes "a place of multiplicities" manifest through competing epistemologies and intersectionalities of race, gender, class, sexuality, and, of course, religion (Eaves 2017: 82; cf. Elisha 2011: 67). However, when it comes to religious identities, these intersectionalities exist with presumed strict divisions along the lines of race and ethnicity that mirror the imagined regional distinctions between South and North. In the aftermath of ongoing institutional and social segregation, the landscape is experienced according to the intersectional identities of its interpreters, who hold an overt awareness of other racialized claims to the religious terrain without any direct familiarity with the other forms. In many parts of the American South, Martin Luther King, Jr.'s infamous observation that Sunday morning is the most segregated hour of the week continues to hold in the divisions between Black and white churches (Abrams 2014; Emerson and Smith 2001; Shelton and Emerson 2012). More recently, as discussed later in this chapter, demographic shifts in the region have resulted in an influx of African, Middle Eastern, Latin American immigrants who also lay claim to Southern religious and ethnic imaginaries.

From the perspective of white evangelicals such as the members of Shield of Faith, there is an awareness of other Souths designated through ethnic and religious categories, such as the Indigenous South, the Black South, the immigrant South. They all exist as an "*else*where" South with the emphasis on "else" as distinguishing difference over and against a localized "where." Parallel to the way that the South is contrasted to the North, so too is the broadly conceptualized white evangelical South of Shield of Faith's congregants contrasted to the elsewhere South. While they might be unfamiliar in terms of a comprehension of their religious or cultural practices and beliefs, they are nonetheless accessible by virtue of their geographic proximity. Herein lies the first clue to the appeal of the triple-bound cord in the context of Shield of Faith: having lived in proximity to several real and imagined but safely siloed elsewheres, the possibility of the other has always lurked on the horizon.

This notion of a proximate but little understood other offers some explanation of the willingness of the congregants at Shield of Faith to incorporate alternative ethno-religious identities. It is, however, noteworthy that they have appropriated the identities of groups with which they lack any cultural familiarity and geographical proximity. This turn to absent groups generates what Craig Martin identifies as "exotic capital," a form of social capital that draws its authority from distance rather than proximity. Derived from difference and a misplaced nostalgia, exotic capital gains authority precisely because it is "*not* mastered by the user" (Martin 2014: 111). In other words, the appropriation of an ethnic or religious identity that is unknown and otherwise inaccessible helps generate a numinous modality.

Limited to the few times a year that Mallet visits the congregation, there exists an extraordinary quality surrounding Shield of Faith's participation in his genre of Judaism. The opportunity to physically interact with Jewish artifacts and individuals (in the form of Mallet and his family) provides access to an otherwise inaccessible proto-Christian other. In this schema, Judaism can be read as the point of origins of "authentic" Christianity. Likewise, the church's physical proximity to the Trail of Tears and its role as caretakers of Indigenous land further localizes the otherwise evident absence of Native Americans. At work is the essentializing trope of "playing Indian," which Indigenous scholar Rayna Green argues is the foundation of the American mythos: "In playing Indian, certainly Anglo-American players are connecting to the America that existed before European invasion" (Green 1988: 48). In Green's assessment, the pervasive power of this trope lies in the absence of Indigenous peoples. In their place, non-indigenous Americans place themselves to "reconstruct the Indian presence in an acceptable version" (48).

This physical interaction opens up what Lauren Berlant identifies as the "secret epitaph of intimacy." That is, "an aspiration for a narrative about something shared, a story about both oneself and others that will turn out in a particular way" (Berlant 1998: 281; see also Furey 2012: 22). The imagined "Jewish-self" and "Indigenous self" relate to religious and national origins and thus serve as cultural and implicitly temporal signifiers of authenticity. The triple-bound cord allows the congregants at Shield of Faith to transplant their origins into a proto-Christian and proto-American location. Intimacy with an imagined Jewish self enables evangelicals to place themselves in temporal and geographic proximity to Jesus and the early church while maintaining their reality outside the biblical narrative. Likewise, they can return to an imagined and purified national identity that departs from contemporary America, which they perceive as politically and socially immoral. At work is a form of nostalgia that reflects the forms of apostolic and nationalist nostalgia that anthropologist Omri Elisha identifies as operative in evangelical attempts to delineate themselves as distinct from liberal secular society (Elisha 2011: 171). Figuratively, they free themselves from the corrupting impact of secular America and heretical varieties of Christianity.

The collapsing of religious, ethnic, socioeconomic, and national identities evokes a larger question concerning how religious kinship is imagined. As Elisha notes, evangelicals situate their Christian identity in relation to "global and cosmic planes" (Elisha 2011: 63). Communion with the divine is reflected in their participation in fictive kinship networks that exist as part of an "imagined global ecumene" (Elisha 2011: 20; cf. Coleman 2000). While we often presume that for Christians, intimacy with God is the standard model of Christian relationality, with Jewish Affinity Christianity, we see a new, expansive structure revealed through interactions with material objects, which both disrupt "official" Christian hierarchies as well as scholarly assumptions about Christian boundary production.

The appeal of the proto-other generated through exotic capital, misplaced nostalgia, and conceptual *else*wheres at Shield of Faith can be further highlighted when we consider which identities are spirituality appropriated and which are not. Regarding their geographical and temporal location, Judaism and Native American identities are at the forefront of desirable, though mostly inaccessible, identities. Other ethnic and religious identities lurk on the margins and make themselves available for inclusion in the already proliferated hybrids endorsed by Mallet. It is possible to further understand the work of proximity and distance by turning our attention to those groups that *are* accessible but are deemed problematic. With this in mind, I offer a strange pairing of accessible others for consideration: Muslims and angels.

Middle Tennessee is one of the nation's largest resettlement areas for refugees—and has been for a significant period of time. A sizable Laotian population resettled in the region in the 1970s and 1980s. Currently, Nashville has the largest Kurdish population in North America. The small rural area in which Shield of Faith is located is home to a significant Somali population moved to the area by the US State Department's Office of Refugee Resettlement in the mid- to late 2000s. The American government selected this region for resettlement because of its low cost of living, temperate climate, and the availability of unskilled labor in factories, manufacturing, and distribution centers. Those familiar with the cultural landscape of rural Tennessee will recall the overarching xenophobia toward Muslims post-September 11, 2001. Conceptualized nationally in debates around President Obama's religious affiliation, it found local expression in the famous Murfreesboro Mosque Incident in 2010 and, more recently, in a series of White Lives Matter rallies held in 2017.

It is not difficult to identify the social impetus of these outward displays of xenophobia. It can be located historically and rooted in a larger nostalgia for the American South and the reconceptualization of race as a means of articulating regionalism. More pertinent to the context of this chapter, such xenophobia might be seen as the consequences of the perceived economic stresses that an influx of new laborers had on the types of employment many within this region relied upon (including the majority of congregants at Shield of Faith) and the further effects of the housing collapse spurred by the 2008 financial crisis. The Muslim other from the perspective of Shield of Faith is therefore conceptualized as a simultaneous religious, ethnic, and economic exotic other.

One of my first substantial encounters with Pastor Ronnie occurred while he was still trying to comprehend my presence at Shield of Faith. Long after the morning service had ended, we stood in the church's parking lot. He told me about the history of the congregation and his own experience in the community, first as a pastor at a local Baptist Church and then after he "got the spirit," as the founding pastor of Shield of Faith. In the context of discussing the region's demographic shifts, Ronnie told me a story about an incident that had occurred several months earlier.

It was a Friday at mid-day and Ronnie had just arrived at the church from a pastoral visit at a congregant's home. The church's secretary was off work that day and as he was unlocking the church, a man walked up behind him. Ronnie had intended only briefly to head into his office to complete some paperwork, so he turned to the man and told him that the church was closed. The man responded that he just wanted to pray. Ronnie apologized and said that no one was available to pray with him. At this point, Ronnie sized up this man and concluded that he was Muslim.[4] Ronnie's suspicions were confirmed for him when the man replied that he did not need anyone to pray with him but sought advice about which direction was east.

As Ronnie recounted the story to me, he related that he was bewildered by the man's request, but he nevertheless pointed him in the right direction and went into the church building to conduct his business. As Ronnie sat down at his desk, he realized that he had not seen the man pull up in a vehicle. Shield of Faith is located along an old country road outside of town and is not the sort of place one would just happen to be strolling by. Though only a few minutes had passed, Ronnie went out the door and found the man had disappeared. Several fears filled his mind: Was this an instance of a potential terrorist scrutinizing the church for a possible future attack? Had the man somehow brought a curse onto the church by worshiping a false god? Or, even more worrisome, Ronnie wondered, was the man actually a demon? In response, he hastily prayed over the space to cast out any lingering evil spirits.

I offer this story not to belittle Ronnie's account of a possible demon in his midst, but because I think it points to a larger conception of the function of religious kinship structures in the context of Shield of Faith. Comparable to the way that he does not fully understand Judaism, Ronnie's cultural literacy of Islam is also lacking. Rather than the misplaced nostalgia that Martin notes in his discussion of exotic capital, we see the evocation of a misplaced taboo. The step from Muslim to a demon is swift; it takes an unknown, yet geographically proximate, human other and places it into a category of a familiar, albeit dangerous, spiritual other. While conceptually distant, in the world of non-denominational charismatic Christianity, demons are highly accessible and spiritually proximate. Once again, we see a collapse of kinship structures rearranged in a localized, trans-religious manner.

The proximity of spiritual beings is noteworthy at Shield of Faith. God is immanent in the Holy Spirit, who regularly possesses, heals, and offers guidance (Luhrmann 2012). Access to Jesus is not limited to the biblical narrative but takes its primary form in a relationship with him and through his blessings, which are devised to be economical, spiritual, and practical (Elisha 2008). Furthermore, God is immanent in the activities of angels. At Shield of Faith, there is always the possibility that angels will appear and make themselves known to the members of the congregation. For example, on his third visit to the church, as a rush of cold air moved its way through the room, Mallet remarked that anyone who was experiencing a chilling sensation was interacting physically with an angel and should pay attention to the angel's directives concerning the tithe offering. In this context, angels materialize with a purpose and have the power to act in the human world and to alter the trajectory of individuals' spiritual (or financial) lives.

The most notable instance of angelic intervention for Shield of Faith is the occurrence of Ronnie and Jim's first meeting with Larry Mallet at a mega-church conference in Chattanooga. According to Mallet, because the rabbi is such a strong supporter of Israel, he requires extensive security detail when he speaks publicly. His guards are tasked with stopping anyone from approaching the rabbi without permission. On this occasion, Ronnie and Jim walked past his security details seeking a private consultation. Seeing them approach, Mallet said to them, "how did you get past my security team?" The two men shrugged, stating that they had just walked up without being stopped. Mallet concluded that they must have been made temporarily invisible by angels so that they could gain access to the rabbi. This miraculous occurrence became the justification for Shield of Faith's apostolic relationship with Larry Mallet.

Re-inhabiting Deterritorialized Spaces

This chapter has charted the composition of a novel religio-ethnic identity and sought to explain its specific trajectory among congregants at Shield of Faith. By way of a conclusion, however, I turn to the means through which the complexities of the triple-bound cord work to reify a white Southern place-based identity. Although the ontology generated by the triple-bound cord dominates many of the theological and outward concerns of Shield of Faith, in the absence of Jewish holidays and ritual celebrations and between Mallet's visits, the church returns to a religio-ethnic form of "ordinary time." The triple-bound cord ultimately buttresses the cultural values and identity devices associated with the congregation's regional location in the rural South.[5] This conception emerges most prominently in the context of in-group hierarchies related to gender and age, performed in both official and non-official forums.

The traditional and conservative gender ideologies of the southern United States are reflected in sharp divisions during church activities. Weekly Bible studies and church potlucks are segregated on the axis of gender. While the men's Bible study does not present itself as hierarchically superior, it is led by the pastors and church elders. Following the monthly potlucks, the cleaning and washing dishes is tasked to married women only. The basis of this division traces back to the Southern value of proper family structures and is unsurprising given the congregation's location. Its distinctiveness, however, became apparent during one of Mallet's early visits to the church. On this occasion, Mallet called the mothers and young women of marital age to the center of the room. Mallet instructed them to join hands and then called upon the male church elders to come forward and form a semi-circle around the women for prayer. As he spoke, Mallet evoked the idea that the congregation should understand themselves as a spiritual family and remain dedicated to said family's prosperity and safety. Praying over the men, he explained that they were warriors of the faith, tasked with overseeing and protecting the congregation. On the other hand, the women were tasked with birthing the congregations' heart and guarding its well-being. As the service continued, Mallet called upon the church's youth pastor to receive a blessing related to his ministry. Upon learning that the young man in his early twenties was single, Mallet commented on the importance of finding a wife. The youth pastor sheepishly agreed, much to the delight of the congregants who reinforced Mallet's observations with friendly laughter and approving nods.

A reversal, however, emerged when the focus of Mallet's message shifted to sexual relations. During a reflection on the importance of marriage between men and women, Mallet diverged from Southern norms by directly discussing sexual intercourse. While he shares the congregation's conservative Christian sentiments regarding the necessity of heterosexual marriage as a social institution, Mallet speaks openly about the importance of sex for pleasure between spouses. He teaches that women should be responsible for their husband's sexual care and churches should encourage open discussions about sex as a marital duty. In these commitments, Mallet departs from the overriding consensus at Shield of Faith that promotes sexual modesty as an indicator of God's blessing and focuses on marriage and child-rearing as the path to a full life.

In contrast to Mallet's open discussion of the benefits of sexual activity in marriage, Pastor Ronnie on one occasion disrupted his sermon to lambaste the lyrics to a contemporary Christian praise song that he saw as overly sexualized. He angrily described the song as incestual, stating that it made it seem like Jesus would greet believers in heaven with "a sloppy wet kiss." Commenting on the absurdity of this image, Pastor Ronnie retorted: "Jesus loves you, but you have to respect him like your father. And you don't kiss your father!" Incidents such as this reaffirm the community's conservative sexual categories and the assumption that young people should respect their elders. On other occasions, Ronnie railed against other trappings of youth culture such as social media, an over-reliance on technology, laziness, and resistance to hard work. The presumed celebration of vanity and youth that marks popular culture contrasts the Protestant work ethic. Ronnie regularly praises an older man in the congregation who refuses to retire at the age of seventy-six, pledging to work on his farm until his death.

In the late spring of 2015, Shield of Faith began to incorporate a new prayer into its services just prior to the taking up of the offering. This prayer, known as the "Tither's Blessing," was amended from a version of the prayer found on The Church of His Presence Website, located in Southern Alabama.[6] The brief prayer comprises three paragraphs and is bookended with Philosemitic language and ideas. It begins by explicitly stating the church's support for Israel and desire for peace in Jerusalem. Without directly referencing the chapter and verse, it quotes from Psalm 122, "Pray for the peace of Jerusalem: they shall prosper that love thee." In the second paragraph, it turns to the financial needs of the congregation, evoking a prophetic tone in which the prayer's reciter does not ask, but rather "speaks into existence" desirable outcomes:

I call forth jobs for the unemployed, meaningful jobs with good pay and benefits. I call forth raises and bonuses to those that need them and for you to have favor with your employers. I speak you will find money unexpectedly and unexpected checks come in the mail right out of nowhere as a gift from heaven just for you. (Kilpatrick 2015)

Following these worldly or everyday requisitions, the prayer then turns seamlessly to supernatural topics and beings. Angels are invited to minister to the congregation and the church itself is declared a "modern-day Goshen." In Genesis, Goshen is the land initially given to Joseph and his family by the Pharaoh and from which, according to the text, the Israelites later departed during the exodus. The prayer concludes with a blessing in the name of "Yeshua Hameshiach" and notes the biblical year (in 2015, 5775), which at Shield of Faith is a "year of double grace."

While the prayer promotes a broad Prosperity Gospel theology, Shield of Faith has constructed a localized interpretation. The practical nature of the prayer is highlighted in requests for "meaningful jobs with good pay and benefits." It is no surprise that rural Tennessee residents are concerned with securing a job with benefits since few employers in the area offer positions with full benefits. The fuller version of Kilpatrick's prayer also includes concerns that would speak to individuals with more job security. For example, it includes prayers on behalf of employers and entrepreneurs, and requests for employment at locations where the adherent will "fit in and have a bright future." Similarly, Mallet's congregants have never wasted their prayers asking for middle-of-the-road benefits from employers or raises to their hourly wages.

In contrast, at Shield of Faith, the anticipation that unexpected checks will serve as a solution to financial and psychological hardships is muted by the miraculous appearance of angels. Since, as previously mentioned, angels do show up at services on occasion, this portion of the prayer has already been fulfilled. The angels reify the spiritual capital of the church over and against any actual financial or economic impact of the prayer's request. While angels might be frequent visitors, they are difficult to tie down and even more difficult to count. Like unexpected checks, one can hope for their arrival and possibly evoke them through acts of devotion, prayer, and worship, but, given their nature as spiritual beings, they escape enumeration. As such, they cannot be counted in the same way that Pastor Ronnie counts the number of Jews present in the congregation or the triumph of the 100-fold blessing (cf. Engelke 2010). The angel's presence enables Shield of Faith to lay claim to its own spiritual capital in lieu of an exotic or financial one and, as such, write themselves into the receiving end of prosperity. The angels work to position the members of Shield of Faith into a larger "global ecumene" of proliferating religious identities and the providential nature of prosperity. I do not want to go so far as to say that angels represent an ethnic kinship structure akin to Jewish, Gentile, and Native American ones, or a merger of several, but, in the context of Shield of Faith, we may identify them as occupying a proximate *else*where.

Mallet's incorporation of the triple-bound cord moves outside of traditional categories of kinship, ethnicity, and religion toward a novel Jewish imaginary. While certainly Christians often imagine themselves as tied directly, or indirectly, to biblical communities and characters—both within the Hebrew Bible and the New Testament—evangelical interest in, and affinity with, Judaism as an identity that they might themselves take on vis-à-vis a rabbinical model, because it is somehow reflective of the religion of Jesus, is particularly fascinating. In the case of Mallet, the evangelical desire to return to the religion of Jesus conflates with particular constructions of contemporary and rabbinical Judaism in order to generate a hybrid affinity Judaism. In many ways, this hybrid then responds to Christian expectations of promise that conflates the intimacy imagined between Christians and God to a new expectation of intimacy between Christians and their construction of a Jewish other whose identity they then subsume: evangelical interpretations of Jewish scriptures are replete with the assumption that God has made certain promises to Israel that are then transposed to Christians through Jesus. Judaism then becomes a space where evangelicals can act out new expectations about God's immanence in the world, including economic ones. In this sense, Mallet embodies the hybrid and offers himself and his particular ways of being rabbinical and wealthy as the necessary displaced mediation through which the incorporation of multiple ethnicities and religions occurs. These processes are made possible through a continual renegotiation of proximity and distance to many hybrid modalities. Mallet's option, however, is not the only possibility, as hinted by his inclusion of a secondary Indigenous other at Covenant Ministries and the empirical experience of limited financial prosperity at Shield of Faith. Of course, there is the option for further confluence of Jewish, Gentile, Native American, Muslim, insider, outsider, wealthy, poor, Southern, Northern, angelic, demonic, and perhaps other identities. When the evangelicals at Shield of Faith wrap themselves in the *tallit* or blow the *shofar* during their services, they are not simply "playing Jewish," rather, they are forging new Christian spatial and temporal modalities.

Part Three

Transformations

8

Landscape as Expressive Resource in Materializing the Bible

James S. Bielo

"For fifty years, travelers along Route 8 and Interstate 84 in Waterbury [Connecticut] have found an unexpected landmark rising from the well-worn and rocky heights of Pine Hill. To the uninitiated, the gigantic illuminated cross remains a curiosity, as much a question mark as a crucifix."[1] So writes a contributor to a popular Connecticut travel magazine in 2008. The cross in question draws eyes (and perhaps cars) to Holy Land USA: a defunct Christian attraction hoping to be born again (see Figure 8.1).

Holy Land USA dates to 1955 when a local Catholic lawyer, John Greco, was inspired to create the biblically themed shrine. Using a mélange of discarded materials, concrete, religious statues, lumber, tin, plastic, and other items, Greco led the construction of Bethlehem and Jerusalem in miniature: 200 buildings spread throughout 17 acres, focusing on the New Testament accounts of Jesus but arranged in no particular narrative sequence. At its peak popularity in the 1960s and 1970s, the attraction drew roughly 40,000 visitors annually. With Greco's death in 1984, the park was willed to a local Catholic convent. Despite the sister's devotional labor, Holy Land USA entered a decades-long period of disrepair. Crumbling and corroding structures were a constant problem, while theft, vandalism, arson, and even murder onsite were occasional. The attraction's future shifted in 2013, when the city mayor and a local business owner purchased the land from the convent with a singular ambition: return the park to its former popularity.[2]

Their first order of business in 2014 was to restore and illuminate again the hilltop cross. Waterbury's rolling topography is pivotal in the park's lost and hoped for glory. The cross sits atop Pine Hill, a 450-foot rise: not the highest elevation in the city but the highest in the downtown vicinity.

Figure 8.1 Hilltop cross at Holy Land USA (Waterbury, CT). Photograph by Dave Williams.

Standing atop Pine Hill today, your panoramic view is unobstructed and includes diverging rivers, crisscrossing freeways, residential neighborhoods, church steeples, treetop hills in the distance, and the characteristic Rust Belt imprint of a de-industrialized economy.

It is difficult to imagine Greco and his fellows not seeking to capitalize on the hill's visibility from all angles in the city. Intended or not, Holy Land USA's illuminated cross resonates with biblical and nationalist tropes of a "city on a hill," a destination where something greater than happiness awaits: salvation. The unavoidable visibility of the cross also marks it as an act of public religion. Perhaps as a reclamation, in response to narratives of embattled faith, and perhaps as a proclamation of a pious nation, Holy Land USA resonates ideologically and politically. In this simple but powerful way, Holy Land USA mobilizes its local landscape as an expressive resource on behalf of its evangelical and devotional work.

In this chapter, I hone in on a particular affordance found in landscapes everywhere: their capacity to serve as expressive resources and, through their materiality, to shape the contours of cultural expression. I bring this insight to attractions that "materialize the Bible," a place-making phenomenon in which Christian individuals and communities transform the written words of scripture into experiential, choreographed environments. Holy Land USA was not the first place of its kind; it joined a long history of re-creating biblical narratives in physical form. At its core, materializing the Bible is about fostering an affective intimacy with scripture for creators, caretakers, and visitors. This intimacy is anchored by the imperative that scripture is not merely to be engaged hermeneutically but should be felt and internalized so that the membrane between scripture and self is permeable. Our organizing question is this: How do materializing the Bible attractions mobilize landscapes to bolster this affective imperative?

Landscape as Expressive Resource

Landscapes are "an intertwining of the flesh of the body and the flesh of the world" (Tilley and Cameron-Daum 2017: 6). The history of humanity can be told as a history of land use, alteration, dwelling, and imagining lifeworlds via land. As setting, media, and agentive interlocutor, anthropologists have recognized landscape as a nature-culture hybrid that is central to human evolution and experience. Our varied interactions with landscapes are a fundamental ingredient for cultural difference and contestation.

Scholarship in the anthropology of landscape works from the premise that "landscape" is always more than the physical setting for human action and a determinant of local meaning. Rather, landscape is "a cultural process" (5) because its meaning, use, and material form can morph over time in relation to practices of human settlement and imagination. This chapter works within this tradition, as I focus on the interaction between religious ambitions, the materiality of landscape, and its expressive affordances. Landscapes are mobilized as a resource, but not an inert resource, never a blank canvas through which any meaning is possible or likely. Landscapes are mobilized to tell the stories people want to tell, but their physicality lends them to certain stories over others.

As a cultural process, the distinctiveness of landscapes as places emerges in the relationship between physical form and the meaningful forms of dwelling people engage. "What could be truer of placed experience," Feld and Basso ask, "secure or fragile, pleasurable or repugnant, comforting or unsettling— than the taken-for-granted quality of intense particularity" (1996: 11)? This sense of particularity was integral for Basso's analysis of Western Apache landscapes (1996). Basso's primary fieldwork took place throughout the Fort Apache reservation in eastern Arizona. A mountainous region dense with pine forests, this terrain mixes desert dryness and heat with rushing streams, juniper cottonwood trees, and tall prairie grass. For readers who are familiar with Basso's evocative writings, we know that the Western Apache landscape is ultimately more than the sum of these topographical, climatic, and botanical elements. The Western Apache saturate physical land forms with memories of the ancestors, stories told and re-told when wisdom is needed, a living tradition that binds the present to the past and orients exemplary lives.

The empirical focus of this chapter—attractions that materialize the Bible—occupy a different position than the Western Apache. They are not working with an autochthonous claim to place. They arrived in modern time. Their arrivals were documented and, more to the point, plotted. Their creators selected the land forms they inhabit. Features of topography, climate, flora, and the built environment act as not only brute spatial facts but also figure in the strategic calculus of "why here." The central problem we are examining in this chapter is how this interaction unfolds, how the expressive resource of landscape is mobilized to enhance acts of Christian place-making.

Materializing the Bible

Throughout the world, more than 450 extant attractions materialize the Bible; that is, transform the written words of scripture into experiential, choreographed environments. Attractions are found in more than 40 nations and are produced by a wide range of Protestant, Catholic, and ecumenical individuals and communities. They appear in diverse forms, self-identifying as "theme parks," "museums," "gardens," "grottos," "replicas," "models," and more. Some concentrate on select biblical stories (e.g., Noah's ark, Moses' tabernacle, Solomon's temple, the life of Jesus), while many are a jumble, mixing multiple scriptural references to create a biblically saturated landscape.

Attractions that materialize the Bible variously combine elements of devotion, pedagogy, entertainment, and evangelism. Irrespective of their emphasis or self-identification, they make a promise to visitors. They promise that the power and meaning of sacred texts will be revealed or rediscovered. Visitors are invited to "experience," "engage," "interact with," "see," and "step into" the Bible. Through this physical encounter, attractions seek to persuade visitors to develop an affective intimacy with scripture.

The invocation of "affect" is pivotal. As a conceptual apparatus, affect is valuable because it draws our attention to the entanglements that develop among structural forces, sociality, ideology, materiality, and subjectivity (Supp-

Montgomerie 2015). Places that materialize the Bible join a rich and varied tradition that recognizes "the Bible" as a cultural category that is not reducible to a printed text to be read, interpreted, memorized, and discursively circulated (Beal 2012). "The Bible" appears historically through a wide range of experiential registers: from stained glass and other artistic media to film, video games, and toy objects. We have the story of Noah's ark in Genesis 6–9, and we have (among many others) Edward Hicks' widely reprinted 1846 painting, the 1928 romantic melodrama film *Noah's Ark*, the 1991 *Bible Adventures* game for Nintendo, craft and mass-produced wooden playsets designed throughout the nineteenth and twentieth centuries, and in 2016 a young earth creationist "theme park" centered on a "life-sized" replica of Noah's ark (Bielo 2018).

These transmedial performances certainly have multiple functions—religious pedagogy, devotion, fun, evangelism—but their capacity to be efficacious in any function is grounded by an affective relation. Knowledge that religious actors develop about scripture is anchored by the development of intense bonds with scripture (e.g., love). While these affective bonds can certainly support an authoritative view of scripture, they also engage religious actors in an ongoing authorizing process in which the aura of scripture is internalized. The ambition is to experience scripture from as many angles as possible, in as many sensory configurations as possible, because just as "the Bible" is inexhaustible for readers it is also experientially inexhaustible.

Attractions like museums, gardens, and theme parks testify to the power of affect. The arrangement of material and sensory experiences in choreographed space registers effects on and through the bodies of visitors. This echoes historian Vanessa Agnew's depiction of re-enactment as a form of "affective history," in which the past is imagined through the "physical and psychological experience" of individuals (2007: 301). This mode of performing history aspires to provoke the body, for the body to respond in ways that may or may not have the consent of language or cognition. For example, Agnew (2014) describes the sensorial ambition of "gooseflesh," which affective history seeks to achieve as an involuntary aesthetic evaluation. Contrary to the fact that bodies are enculturated to respond to particular stimuli in particular ways, gooseflesh promises the consumer of affective history that they are experiencing something timeless and unmediated.

Attractions work toward this affective intimacy through multiple means. It is pursued through artwork, architectural design, the materiality of building items, onsite signage, sensorial effects, visitors' guides, and other elements of experiential choreography. As created places, they must be created somewhere particular. They are built out of and into local landscapes. How, then, are local landscapes mobilized as expressive resources in the affective work of materializing the Bible?

The earliest examples of this phenomenon originated as surrogate sites for Holy Land pilgrimage. For example, consider the Sacred Mount of Varallo in Italy's far northwestern corner. The attraction was started in the 1490s by a Franciscan monk who, inspired by his stay in Jerusalem in the 1470s, wished to re-create some of the holy city and its biblical past for those who could not (or would not) make the long and difficult trip east. Built on a hilltop above the town, the finished attraction features more than forty chapels, connected by walking paths, each filled with elaborate murals and life-sized clay figures re-creating scenes from the life of Jesus.

In his analysis of the attraction, David Leatherbarrow (1987) argues that Varallo's location is integral to its design and efficacy. Built at a time when pilgrimage to the Holy Land was becoming increasingly difficult yet pilgrimage as a form of popular piety was becoming increasingly popular, the town's off-the-beaten-path location satisfied pilgrim desires for experiencing a journey, separation from the everyday, and entering into the liminality of pilgrimage. The mountain setting resonated in two further ways: with the rich scriptural tradition of mountaintop experiences (think: Moses on Mt. Sinai, Jesus tempted in the wilderness), and with the fulfilling rituality of ascending slopes to reach a pinnacle experience. "Up steep slopes and across the terraces," Leatherbarrow writes, "the pilgrim was directed through dense woods, openings in tree screens and architecturally built-up areas. . . . The rule of uniqueness of place is beautifully celebrated at Varallo" (114). The site capitalizes on tree lines and topographic changes to heighten the immersive experience, keeping visitors on the intended route while obscuring subsequent chapels on the ritual path. Early site designs reveal that this spatial choreography was purposeful: "it is clear that the route up the hillside was designed very carefully to structure the sequence of spaces that would aid the memory of the pilgrim" (115).

The Sacred Mount of Varallo initiated a long history of re-creating scriptural narratives and geographies in order to provide surrogate experiences of "the Holy Land." Each replication has reckoned with how its local landscape might figure in its immersive efforts. What can be accentuated? What must be obscured?

For example, at Palestine Park in western New York state land was transformed in multiple ways. Built in 1873 by Methodist leaders in the American Sunday School movement, its primary functions were to be a pedagogical aid for teaching scripture and an attractive destination for devotional leisure. Originally

170-feet in length, though extended to 400 after several years, the park is a scale topographic model of Bible lands with cities and bodies of water marked. Not only was earth moved and shaped to resemble "biblical Palestine," it was positioned so that Chautauqua Lake served as the Mediterranean Sea. Classes were typically brought to the model by boat and visitors were encouraged to imagine themselves as Holy Land pilgrims, stepping off at the port of Jaffa. The park was "an immediate success," teachers and visitors alike attended lectures dressed in Middle Eastern garb, adding elements of theatrical role-playing to the virtual reality fostered by the materialized replica (Davis 1996: 89). As Burke Long observed, "Realism was the driving aim, fantasy the enabling impulse" (2003: 30).

Nazareth Village in Nazareth, Israel highlights a markedly different affordance of engaging the local landscape in order to re-create the biblical past. Opened in 2000, this "living history" biblical museum re-creates domestic and pastoral scenes from first-century Galilee. Marketed primarily for evangelical Protestants on Holy Land tours, Nazareth Village aims to conjure what the everyday world of Jesus of Nazareth would have looked, felt, sounded, and tasted like (Ron and Feldman 2009). The attraction is located within the urban boundaries of contemporary Nazareth, just west of the Old City. On the one hand, the surrounding landscape poses an immersive challenge: evoking a rural past when an urban present is audibly and visually immediate. To counter this, natural landscape features are mobilized in the spatial choreography: namely, botanicals such as olive trees, wildflowers, and almond trees offer visitors sensorial access to the biblical past in the form of cultivated nature.

While some attractions focus on the sites, geography, or lifeworld of the Christian Holy Land, others focus on single biblical scenes, stories, or events. A prominent example is the Holy House of Loreto. According to Catholic tradition, the Basilica della Santa Case in Loreto, Italy, contains the original house from Nazareth where Mary and Joseph raised Jesus. To avoid destruction, angels transported the house from Judea to Loreto. The earliest known example is a 1631 replica in Prague, but perhaps the best-known example is found near England's eastern coast in a village named Walsingham.

As tradition has it, it was here in the eleventh century when a local noblewoman, Richeldis, was visited by the Virgin Mary and instructed to build a replica of the Holy House. The popular pilgrimage shrine was destroyed during Henry VIII's sixteenth-century anti-Catholic purge, and it lied dormant until the late nineteenth century. Between 1896 and 1934 Walsingham birthed two shrine complexes, one Anglican and the other Catholic, each making claims of an authentic link with the Marian miracle, including two different replicas of the original Holy House replica. While some contestation persists, the site attracts Anglican, Catholic, and heritage tourists who seem to happily experience the place in a mixed company (Coleman 2004).

In Simon Coleman's analysis of Walsingham, landscape is a crucial factor in the attraction's emergence and ecumenical appeal. Because rurality is a potent symbol of English national identity, "the landscape surrounding the village is often seen by visitors and pious residents as adding to the medieval feel, providing a generalized sense of a rural and bucolic England, untouched by the modern age" (60). Coleman reports the experience of a group of pilgrims who, despite their own expectations, were profoundly affected by a theatrical re-enactment of the Stations of the Cross onsite. They described the difficulty they anticipated of imagining "hot, dusty Palestine" amid the snowy chill and "slushy, cold" of Walsingham in winter. Despite this material disconnect, they were emotionally stirred when a member of the crowd—a mimetic Simon of Cyrene—used their coat to comfort the wet, shivering Jesus. "What [the actors] actually did," the woman explains, "was cleverly use the conditions we were actually in—the cold, the damp, and snow—to make the points, to incorporate them into the devotions" (63-4). Here, the rural English landscape functions as both "an unchanging symbol of continuity" and "the launching point for liturgical and interpretative creativity" (65).

At Walsingham, the potency of landscape's expressive potential relies on multiple symbolic and iconic associations. Yet another mobilization focuses on the physicality of landscape items. Attractions around the world use local things—wood, sand, stones, and soil—as architectural material, layering theological significance into the physical properties of these items.

Consider, for example, the Grotto of the Redemption: a Roman Catholic shrine in north-central Iowa.[3] The Grotto emerged from the good part of a life's work by Paul M. Dobberstein, a German-born priest who immigrated to the United States in 1892 at age twenty and was called to lead a rural Iowa parish in 1897. As the story goes, Dobberstein fell ill and promised Mother Mary that he would build a shrine in her honor if she delivered him back into good health. After gathering construction materials for years, he began work on the Grotto in 1912. The project consumed "the waking hours of his earthly existence," up through his death in 1954.

The Grotto is comprised of cement, Italian marble, and thousands of "precious and semi-precious stones"; jade, sapphire, and at least forty other kinds collected by Dobberstein and donated to the project from around the world. Nine core scenes materialize "the story of the Redemption. . . . Man lost the friendship of God and regained it through the Incarnation, Passion, Death and Resurrection of Jesus." It begins with the Garden of Eden then moves to the Stable of Bethlehem, Home of Nazareth, the Trinity, the 10 Commandments, Garden of Gethsemane, 14 Stations of the Cross, burial of Jesus, and finally the Resurrection.

Unlike many Catholic shrine sites, the Grotto boasts no miraculous heritage. "There have never been miraculous apparitions of any kind connected to the Grotto. No claim for cures or miracles have been made." It is, rather, a testament to the devotional labor of Dobberstein; material witness to what is borne of dedicated faith and dedicated work. Like so many attractions, the Grotto's stated ambition is to make the stories of scripture newly real, to collapse the distance of space-time between a scriptural then and there to a present here and now. "To bring people of today, who live centuries removed from those blessed [biblical] days into closer touch with the things of God, is the aim and effort of the builder of the Grotto of the Redemption."

In its self-presentation, the Grotto maintains a self-conscious sense that its method and media is perfectly suited to human faculties. "It is the aim of the Grotto to present, in palpable form, this reunion of Man and God, the reconciliation between fallen human nature and offended divine Justice; because truth reaches the mind most easily by way of the senses." The Grotto promises to mainline truth through its physical qualities: a somatically rich environment where visitors can walk, touch, and be immersed. This promise is extended by the builder's reflections on the affordances of construction materials. The following was first observed as a guidebook epigraph, a recontextualized quote from Dobberstein on why "precious stones" were his media of choice:

> Spoken words are ephemeral: written words remain, but their durability depends upon the material upon which they are written: but if carved into bronze or sculpted into stone they are well nigh imperishable. This *imperishableness* is the outstanding feature of the Grotto. Thus the story of the *redemption* will continue to tell its edifying story long after the builder has laid down his trowel, and will be a silent sermon expressing in permanently enduring precious stones, the fundamental truths of Christianity. (*emphasis in original*)

Dobberstein begins critically, drawing legitimacy away from oral discourse, the media associated most directly with sermonizing. He sizes up written discourse more favorably, but not without immediate pause. Facts of materiality separate the perishable from the imperishable. Facts of time separate the wheat from the chaff. Imperishability is prized for its durability into the unforeseen future, its capacity to withstand the pelting storm of time in ways more fragile media cannot, human, human-made, and natural alike.

If imperishability organizes the Grotto of Redemption, impermanence organizes the Biblical Sand Sculptures of Ocean City, Maryland.[4] Since 1974, born-again evangelist Randy Hofman has used the oceanfront setting of local beaches to craft scenes and stories from Christian scripture. His subjects range across favorites of the evangelical imagination: Daniel in the lion's den, David and Goliath, Noah's ark, Jesus' baptism, the Last Supper, and Jesus' crucifixion, ascension, and the Second Coming.

Born in 1951 into a Catholic household, Randy entered art school in New York City in the late 1960s with hopes of doing visual communication work in advertising. This ambition faded as he explored the industry; he describes a moral repulsion to a "skanky" business. In the early 1970s he became a born-again evangelical, prompted by reading Hal Lindsey's best-selling book *The Late Great Planet Earth*. When he first arrived in Ocean City he apprenticed with another evangelical sand sculptor and divided his time between oil paintings of local nature scenes, sand sculpting with his mentor, and chalk drawings of biblical scenes on city sidewalks. His oil painting continued, exhibiting in his studio near the beach, but he abandoned the chalk drawings because this seemed less "indigenous" than working with sand. For Hofman, one attraction of sand as a media to work with was its attachment to place, an indexical marker of belonging and local experience.

Randy works throughout the summer tourist season, and his sculptures are viewed by as many as 10,000 visitors every day for 2 months. Each sculpture requires roughly fourteen hours of construction, from digging out the sand to completing the artwork to finishing it with a mixture of water and Elmer's glue. The latter was a particularly important innovation, one he learned on a visit to California to work with sand sculptors there. By spraying the sculptures with this mixture, their lifespan is extended from a single day to at least one week and as long as a month. Still, even the occasional month-long display is defined by temporariness and tenuousness, as the interventions of weather and passersby could destroy the creation at any time.

When I asked Randy why sand is his chosen media, he reflected on two motivating interests. First, he noted the widespread popularity and affectively charged nature of "playing in the sand," an activity many in the United States associate with play, childhood, and summer vacations. By capitalizing on the powerful familiarity of sand, he likened his work to Jesus' use of agricultural imagery in parables, "he knew just what would resonate [with his audience]."

Second, Randy observed a "delicious little spiritual parallel" between a sand sculpture and our mortal lives on earth. Both, he said, were defined by their ephemerality, "here today and gone tomorrow," as the proverbial saying goes.

Hofman's biblical sand sculptures are a fascinating mix of devotional labor, attachment to place, and the temporality of materiality. Perhaps in spite of, perhaps because of, the hours he invests in a single sculpture, it is the quality of temporariness that defines his material theology. Each sculpture's short-lived tenure on the beach is inextricable from sand's physical affordances, which Hofman treats as an iconic sign for human earthly existence. We disappear as quickly and as easily as the sculptures.

* * *

As a global phenomenon, materializing the Bible fascinates because it presents cases of religious tourism that jumble familiar categories: popular and official religion, sacred and secular, devotion and pedagogy, entertainment and evangelism, play and piety, faith and fun. Be it the mountainside of Varallo or the countryside of Walsingham, landscape plays an integral role in the location and efficacy of attractions. The reason exceeds mere scene-setting; it is landscape's capacity as an expressive resource that brings it to the fore of analytical attention. Dynamically engaged with the particular ambitions of particular attractions, landscape bolsters the promise of building an affective intimacy with scripture via the media of material replication. To observe this interaction between landscape and attraction in closer detail, we move to an ethnographic account of a site in northern Kentucky.

Garden of Hope

Covington is a small city, just across the Ohio River from Cincinnati. On its southwestern edge—tucked away on the backside of a working-class residential neighborhood, at the end of a No Outlet road, set atop a steep rise that affords a gorgeously unobstructed view of the Cincinnati skyline, is a place called the Garden of Hope.

The Garden opened to the public on Palm Sunday in 1958, consummating the nearly twenty-year vision of a Southern Baptist minister, Reverend Morris Coers. After three pastorates in Indiana, Illinois, and Michigan, and two terms in the Indiana state legislature, Coers accepted the senior pastor position at a Baptist Church in Covington in 1945. Well known at the time as a local radio minister, Coers' ambition exceeded pulpits, politics, and mass media preaching. He had been inspired—akin to Varallo's Franciscan monk nearly 500 years earlier—by a pilgrimage to Jerusalem in 1938. In particular, he was inspired to create a place at home that would be a beacon for all who would never make a Holy Land trip themselves. Coers says it this way in a 1956 interview with the *Cincinnati Times-Star*: "we expect to attract thousands of tourists from all parts of the world—persons who will never have the privilege of walking in the Holy Land." After years of fundraising, he purchased the 2.5-acre hilltop plot in 1956 and commenced construction immediately.

Today's Garden of Hope is a jumble of elements, inspired by scripture, the Holy Land, and elsewhere. For Coers, the centerpiece was always a 1:1 scale replica of Jerusalem's Garden Tomb (see Figure 8.2).

As a biblical site, the Garden Tomb is controversial. Many Protestants claim that the tomb, located outside Jerusalem's Old City walls, is where Jesus was buried and resurrected. However, this claim is rejected by mainstream biblical archeology and dismissed by the majority of the world's Christians who claim that the Church of the Holy Sepulchre inside the Old City houses both Golgotha and the burial-resurrection site. The Garden Tomb emerged as a Protestant alternative in the nineteenth century. The site was first identified in 1867, fully excavated in 1883, and purchased in 1894 by a British Anglican ministry

Figure 8.2 Garden Tomb replica at the Garden of Hope in Covington, Kentucky. Photograph by the author.

founded with the express purpose of preserving the tomb (Kark and Frantzman 2010). Garden Tomb supporters will sometimes recognize the site's contested history; for example, the Garden Tomb Association guide book does when it admits "whether this particular tomb be the real Holy Sepulchre is a matter of conjecture" (1960 [1944]: 17). But, the site has proven to be more satisfying among Protestant pilgrim-tourists who favor the open-air feel over the Old City Church, which is busily adorned with Catholic and Eastern Orthodox ritual elements and actions (Bowman 1991).

As a thoroughly Protestant site, Kentucky's Garden of Hope erases any sense of disputed legitimacy. In Coers' newspaper interviews at the time of the opening, the written text of onsite signage and visitor pamphlets, or in tour guide performances, the Church of the Holy Sepulchre is never mentioned and archeological arguments against the Garden Tomb's veracity are elided. The Garden of Hope's appeal to authenticity happens instead through the immersive experience of leaving Kentucky for Jerusalem.

Coers' primary claim to creating an "exact" replication of the Garden Tomb was his relationship with the Tomb's warden. From 1953 until his untimely death in 1967, Solomon Mattar helped care for and guided pilgrim-tourists at the Tomb. As Coers' noted in a 1956 interview with the *Cincinnati Enquirer*, "I have been collaborating long distance with the warden of the garden in Jerusalem. He arranged for an architect to draw exact plans of the tomb of Christ. I have arranged to have these plans followed in the minutest detail." To accompany this architectural precision, Coers flew in numerous botanical species indigenous to Jerusalem. Just as Nazareth Village hopes to mobilize the sight, feel, and aroma of biblical flora, Coers planted "cedars of Lebanon," juniper, and various flowers to help transport visitors via the natural world of scripture.

Today, only a few of these varietals remain and the botanical immersion is lost from Coers' original vision. However, Palestinian floras were not the only materials Coers brought back from his travels. Scattered throughout the Garden are four stones, still sitting just where Coers placed them. Two reside near a small collection of picnic tables, the first area visitors encounter, housed in decorative wrought-iron cages. Signage explains the first stone as "from Good Samaritan Inn, over 2,000 years old from Jerusalem" and the second as "from Jordan River where Jesus was baptized over 2,000 years ago." The third stone is positioned differently, embedded into a floor. It is located inside the Garden's chapel, a replica of a sixteenth-century Spanish mission church. Along with worship services, the chapel was primarily intended for weddings, a practice that Coers initiated in 1958 and that continues today. During the ceremony, couples stand atop a pink stone, which signage explains "is from the Horns of Hatton where Jesus delivered the Sermon on the Mount." Just past the chapel, at the end of a small downhill walking path, is the final stone, also resting in an ornate iron cage: "from Solomon's Temple, 500-pound block from Wailing Wall."

Reverend Morris Coers realized his twenty-year vision, but he enjoyed it for only two years. He died in his sleep in late February 1960. With his passing, the Garden fell into a lengthy cycle of selling, buying, disrepair, repair, and further disrepair, through both natural processes and human vandalism. The site was purchased again in 1993, and following a major restoration effort was re-opened to the public in 1998. The primary tour guide today, a seventy-year-old Covington native named Steve, has "shown it to over eight thousand people" since he began guiding in 2003.[5] As of summer 2016, the site entered a new, and newly popular, phase of its life. The opening of Ark Encounter, a creationist theme park 40 miles south of Covington, has sparked the organization of bus tours to the area. For example, the company Ohio Travel Treasures arranges for groups to take a gospel music-centered Ohio River cruise, and visit the Ark, the Creation Museum (another creationist ministry open since 2007, located 20 miles due west of Covington), the Cathedral Basilica of the Assumption (a replica of Paris' Notre Dame Cathedral) in downtown Covington, and the Garden of Hope.

During the nearly two-year construction period, Cincinnati newspapers published seven stories about Coers and his devotional labor. Each story celebrates the location's visual experience of looking out over the cityscape. For example, paraphrasing Coers, the Garden's chapel is "so designed that visitors entering to pray and attend religious services may view the panorama of two cities, separated by the beautiful Ohio river." In a 1957 interview with the *Cincinnati Post*, Coers reflects on the link between the landscape view and the attraction's affective ambitions: "Surely this reminder of the past, with our industrial valley, our rivers, Carew Tower and Mt. Adams in the background, will appeal to those seeking closer contact with Christianity. In fact, peoples of all faiths should find inspiration here."

For Coers, the landscape affordance was not strictly visual. In the same 1957 interview he proudly declares: "I truly believe it will be an inspiration to all who come here. In fact I have called the point where the chapel is to be built Inspiration Point. From there you can see 18 churches in the valley of the Ohio and Licking Rivers—at Angelus time, the sound of the bells is thrilling." Given this prized aural experience, one wonders if Coers' untimely death owed in part to the I-75/71 highway construction that began soon after the Garden opened.

While the cityscape still dominates the visual field facing north, looking west now means looking down on six lanes of zooming traffic. Today, the soundscape at the Garden is saturated by the constant rush of automobiles, washing out anything else from below—including distant church bells chiming. Perhaps the new Interstate's sounds, an aural obstruction to Coers' devotional ideal, tolled a death knell of disappointment.

Despite the aural disruption, visitors still appreciate the Garden's devotional appeal and the celebrated cityscape view. When tour bus groups unload they invariably move, with magnetic predictability, to the main overlook. At times, this proves frustrating for the primary guide Steve, who prefers to gather groups in front of the welcome sign and explain the attraction's first few features (e.g., the Jordan River stone) before inviting them to disperse for picture-taking (see Figure 8.3).

The cityscape view has always been a central experience of the attraction, but guiding performances seem to transform it into something more than merely scenic beauty. One hint of this surfaced when talking with Steve about the guiding decisions of Jim, a guide who began assisting when the tour groups became difficult for Steve to handle alone. When they guide together, they alternate among the Garden's four main areas, with Jim handling the introduction. Jim's strategy is to begin with the city's founding and the Ohio River's role in western

Figure 8.3 Welcome sign, with city skyline in backdrop. Photograph by the author.

settlement, moving through time until he reaches Coers in the 1950s. For Steve, this is a mistake. Without being overly disparaging of his partner, he stated firmly, "People don't wanna hear about Lewis and Clark, they care about this place." Steve wanted the guiding focus to remain fixed on Coers' devotional labor and the attraction's extant features, such as the Holy Land stones and a gift to the Garden that sits on the overlook.

The Garden received some regular visitors in its early years, including a married couple from Michigan who traveled to Cincinnati for business trips. While her husband was in the city working, Katharine Smarr's preferred place to visit was not the downtown area or museums, but the Garden. After her death, Mr. Smarr commissioned a memorial statue, "Christ's Sermon on the Mount," to be built in Rome, Italy, and then sent to be installed at the Garden of Hope (see Figure 8.4).

The statue is elevated off the ground and faces the overlook and cityscape view. When I first encountered the statue I wondered if guides or visitors were drawn to a biblical parallel: just as the historic Jesus looked over Jerusalem, this sculpted Jesus looks out over Cincinnati. When Steve lent me the tour guide script—a twelve-page document, author unknown and likely written after the 1998 re-opening—this suspicion was confirmed. The script directs guides to relate the statue to scripture: "When you look at the eyes of the statue and see where rain and

Figure 8.4 Sermon on the Mount Statue at the Garden of Hope. Photograph by the author.

Figure 8.5 Jesus weeping at the Garden of Hope. Photograph by Rory Johnson.

weather have discolored it, the eyes seem to have been weeping. We are reminded that the Bible tells us that Jesus wept over the city of Jerusalem" (see Figure 8.5).

The practice of transforming this Kentucky hill traces to its founding. For the Palm Sunday 1958 opening, one of Coers' congregants, Alice Kennelly Roberts, wrote a commemorating hymn, "Garden of Hope," that was sung during the worship service. Its opening lines anticipate the biblical parallel that the Sermon on the Mount statue would later elaborate:

A Garden of Hope on a hillside/
A Chapel of Dreams on high/
Inspiring men's thoughts to reach upward and pointing their hearts to the sky/
Where One who knew hills of Judea awaits with compassion and love...

The second verse continues the parallel, inviting visitors into the typological poem:

A place where the lonely find solace above and apart from the crowd/
For Jesus found peace in a garden when death marked the path that He trod.[6]

The Garden of Hope presents a useful case study in the broader analysis of how biblically themed attractions mobilize landscape as an expressive resource. A particular insight from the Garden centers on this sacralizing transformation of the cityscape view. Scenic beauty is certainly not antagonistic to the Garden's devotional ideal, but perhaps it overlaps too much as a standard of secular tourism. From the commemorating hymn to Steve's preferred guiding practices, the visual aesthetics are transformed from simply "a magnificent view" to an emplaced experience with biblical resonance.

Conclusion

This chapter has explored the capacity of local landscape to be mobilized as an expressive resource in the context of religious tourism. The analysis proceeds from an organizing premise in the anthropology of landscape, which understands landscape as a cultural process rather than a static setting. The material facts, uses, and symbolic imaginings of landscapes change with time, social engagement, and strategic performance. In the context of attractions that materialize the Bible, landscapes exist as potent expressive resources, bolstering the work of building an affective intimacy with scripture.

Across the examples presented here, we see a range of landscape affordances. Physical features, such as Varallo's mountainous slopes and tree lines, help choreograph ritual action and experience. The physical properties of local materiality can also be celebrated and invested with theological significance, as with the case of biblical sand sculptures. Forms of cultivated nature, such as Holy Land botanicals at Nazareth Village and the early Garden of Hope, can foster the immersive experience of shifting frames from the present to the biblical past. Landscapes are marshaled to claim the particularity of place, as with Walsingham's appeal to English rurality so that a diverse group of visitors are equally satisfied. And, attractions can seek to transform how visitors interact with the landscape, as with the Garden of Hope's cityscape view, altered from something scenic but common into something biblical.

To close, I want to highlight a dynamic that has been implicit throughout this analysis. As the opening case of Waterbury's Holy Land USA illustrated, place-making is always also place-claiming. These religious attractions do not only mobilize landscapes, they integrate into them, join them, become part of them, and, ultimately, help define them. Devotional or pedagogical, entertaining or evangelistic, they can always be read as territorial acts of power. They do not only create biblical environments in order to attract religious tourists, they seek to create biblically saturated landscapes, where all who travel might encounter a redeemed place.

This facet of the attractions calls to mind their quality as part of public life. Their public-ness is not confined to a legal register, but rather, as Sally Promey (2001) has discussed, a sensory register. They matter as public displays of religion insofar as they are part of a shared visual experience; they are accessible to all who encounter them and are able to see. As such, they contribute to the range of identities and ideologies that constitute our public experience of place. While the presence of attractions is obviously interpreted differently, they are part of shared experience nonetheless, part of what define the landscapes we call home.

9

When Mountains Move

Athonite Processions, Sacred Performance, and Overlapping Topographies

Veronica della Dora

Christianity dwells on the tension between the macro-scale of global redemption and the micro-scale of the sites in which biblical events took place. Alongside these sites, a number of non-biblical places have long constellated the sacred geographies of various Christian denominations. Holy mountains were the most characteristic topographic features of Byzantine spiritual culture. Scattered across the empire, from Asia Minor to the Balkans, they came into being between the fifth and the eleventh centuries and operated as centers of spiritual resource and pilgrimage. Initially, they were attributed an aura of holiness thanks to the presence of charismatic holy men who had been attracted by their isolation and wilderness, and later thanks to the establishment of organized monastic communities (Talbot 2001; Greenfield 2000).

Mount Athos, a 50-kilometer north Aegean peninsula topped by an imposing granite cone rising from the sea for over 2,000 meters, was the first Byzantine holy mountain to be established in the Balkans. It was also the most isolated and hardest to reach of all. Described as "the Holy Mountain" par excellence since the mid-tenth century, Athos is the only surviving example of Byzantine holy mountain to have experienced uninterrupted occupation to our days and to have survived Crusaders, Slavs, and Ottomans practically untouched. Today, with its twenty Byzantine monasteries and a population of nearly 2,000 monks, it is the largest monastic community and one of the most important holy sites in the Orthodox world.

Athos' survival has been ascribed to its seclusion and to its ability to control external forces (Speake 2002). Today, the flow of male visitors remains strictly regulated, whereas access has been interdicted to women for over a thousand years on the grounds of the *avaton*, the ancient right of an Orthodox monastery (either male or female) to shut its doors to the opposite sex—in this case, the entire peninsula is regarded as one single "large monastery" bounded by the sea for most of its perimeter. Yet, as with other holy mountains and famous Christian holy sites, Athos has always transcended its physical boundaries— whether through flows of prayers, objects, or people (della Dora 2011a; Talbot 1996). This chapter considers one such flow. It focuses on *litaneies*, or open-air processions, performed by the monks of Mount Athos during major liturgical feasts within and outside of the peninsula.

While pilgrimage as a spatial phenomenon has long captured the interest of anthropologists (Badone and Roseman 2004; Morinis 1992; Eade and Sallnow 1991; Turner and Turner 1978), cultural geographers (Maddrell et al. 2014; Scriven 2014), tourist studies scholars (Andriotis 2009; Cohen 1992), and scholars of religion (Gothoni 2013), religious processions have received far less attention. And yet, this practice has historically played, and continues to play, an important role in the way in which Christians of different denominations, and Orthodox Christians in particular, experience and imagine the land, and are in turn "shaped" by it. With pilgrimage, religious processions share a liminal status. They are temporary phenomena. They are transitory sites of convergence of people, sacred objects, and prayers; of embodied performances, images, smells, and sounds; and of visibilities and invisibilities. Processions and pilgrimage also share a symbiotic relationship with the land. While they are fluid assemblages that are always in the making, processions rely on fixed landmarks and pre-established routes. As with pilgrimage, they produce an experience of space that is intimately grounded in local topographies. As with pilgrimage, they are articulated through a slow, horizontal movement through places that challenges the tropes and rhythms of modernity and can have a transformative power on their participants (Coleman and Eade 2004; Frey 1998).

As it often happens on Mount Athos, a procession can be part of a pilgrimage. However, the two phenomena are by no means the same. While pilgrimage can be an individual practice undertaken at any moment in time, religious processions are usually carefully choreographed collective performances repeated on specific days in the liturgical calendar. They are complex mobile assemblages interacting with and transforming local topographies on a cyclical basis; or rather, they are extraordinary assemblages that are periodically articulated and sustained within ordinary landscapes. More significantly, while pilgrimage is usually defined by a centripetal movement toward a place, usually a holy shrine (Bajc, Coleman, and Eade 2007), processions, and Orthodox *litaneies* in particular, rearticulate the sacred space of the shrine *outside* of its walls by way of liturgical performance. Not only do they move people, holy relics, charismatic icons, and other objects around, but they do also move *places* around—and they have the power to transform places. What happens though when the place is not a manmade holy shrine, but a holy mountain? Can mountains move? Can Mount Athos move?

In order to address these questions, it is important to grasp the cultural specificity of Orthodox *litaneies*. The first section of the chapter thus sets up the context by exploring the origins, meaning, and historical significance of Byzantine religious processions, and their ability to transform the landscape. Drawing on *typika* (monastic rules) and monks' accounts,[1] the second section focuses on liturgical processions on Mount Athos and their deep intertwinement with the complex topographies of Holy Mountain and its monasteries; in other words, it shows different ways in which the sacred space of the monastery's church is rearticulated and extended beyond its walls through local processions. The third section expands the focus beyond the precinct of the peninsula and discusses *litaneies* as part of a series of practices through which the Holy Mountain has historically transcended, and continues to transcend, its geographical boundaries. The final section of the chapter turns to a contemporary procession to the Athonite monastery of Docheiariou's female dependency in the Lagkada region (northern Greece). Ethnographic observations are used to illustrate how the Holy Mountain is "transposed" outside of its physical boundaries by way of spatial archetypes that are inscribed in the landscape through liturgical performance both physically and imaginatively.

Litaneies: Liturgical Performance and Topography

As they left the village, shoes were heard on the cobbled streets, thousands of them. Then the narrow path that led to the fields began and they would not fit but in a single line, one after the other. The procession stretched like an endless black snake clotting its coils among the trees. They reached Omalas, which is the only flat area in the uphill olive grove. There the head of the procession stopped and the snake began to curl, clasping its blackness, until the end of the tail stopped wrapping up. . . . Everyone fell on their knees, crossed themselves, looked at God in the blue eyes of the sky. Men, women, children, they all forcefully cried "Ameen!" May the dry ravines hum and their voice reach the feet of the Lord. (Myribēlēs 1995[1949]: 402; my translation)

According to John Baldovin, liturgical practice is "not simply and immediately God-given, revelation itself, but rather part of the human grace-prompted response to revelation" (1987: 253). In other words, worship is always embedded in a specific cultural context. Subject to the contingencies of history and geography, this context, argues Baldovin, is "as important as text for the history of worship" (1987: 35). This claim holds especially true in the case of Orthodox *litaneies*. While the English word "procession" comes from the Latin verb "*procedere*," or "to move forward," therefore stressing the experience of moving through space, the Greek word "*litaneia*" embeds a different meaning. It comes from the verb "*lissomai*," "to supplicate." Rather than physical movement, the Greek word thus stresses the emotional intensity of a petition. It evokes an intimate spiritual act externalized through repeated, insistent prayer, and perhaps even tears. The word also points to the origins of the practice. One of the most ancient and characteristic forms of worship in the Orthodox Church, *litaneies* were initially enacted by the Byzantines as responses to threats such as natural disasters, invasions, and heresies. In Robert Taft's words, they were "the usual response to unusual danger" (1992: 30).

While there are mentions of religious processions in the Old Testament (Ps. 118:27; Josh. 6:1-27), according to Baldovin, the origins of Byzantine *litaneies* are to be traced back to ancient Greek festivals, whereas the first evidence of Christian stational liturgy comes from Jerusalem at the end of the fourth century. Stational liturgy was a mobile form of Christian worship enacted sequentially in multiple urban shrines on different days of the week and of the liturgical calendar. The choice of the shrine depended on the feast or commemoration being celebrated on that specific day. This form of worship was therefore intimately connected with the urban topography, to the point that the whole city was transformed into a single sacred place and its walls ended up including "not just a geographical area, but also an idea" (Baldovin 1987: 266). It was by way of stational liturgy, Baldovin argues, that Jerusalem and then Rome and Constantinople became "the" loci of the Church.

Bridging different shrines, processions formed the bulk of stational liturgy, especially in Constantinople, the first city to be consciously planned as a Christian imperial capital (Walker White 2015). While in Jerusalem and Rome religious processions were usually reenactments of key events in sacred history (e.g., Palm Sunday, or Good Friday), Constantinopolitan *litaneies* served different purposes. Early liturgical processions (fourth to fifth centuries) were connected with the translation of martyrs' relics. Enacted by both Arians and Nicaeans, these processions had a powerful symbolic and propagandistic function: they showed which ecclesiastical party "controlled" the streets of the city. In other words, they displayed the power of the established Church in the midst of ecclesiastical strife, while at the same time transfiguring the urban topography and sometimes extending it to the surrounding waters (Taft 1992: 31–2; Mayer 1998). Saint John Chrysostom, for example, famously describes a nocturnal torchlight procession led by his own party, which stretched along the coast making it "a river of fire" and turning the sea into "a church."[2]

Featuring crosses, miraculous icons, relics, and other sacred objects, Byzantine *litaneies* were also enacted as petitions against enemy sieges and other threats, such as pestilences, droughts, and other natural disasters. Over time, they became manifestations of imperial power and expressions of thanksgiving (Berger 2001). For example, the Virgin's robe preserved in the shrine of Blachernae acted as the palladium of the city when processed around its walls during the Siege of the Avars in 626. Processions commemorating this and other similar events (e.g., the Russian Siege of 860) continued to be enacted throughout the Middle Ages. By the tenth century, the *Typikon of the Great Church*, a book containing liturgical directions for each feast and fast of the year, mentioned no less than seventeen processions dealing with specific historical events other than translations of relics or church dedications. Nine memorialized earthquakes, five enemy sieges, and three the hail of cinders from the eruption of the Vesuvius of 469, the Great Fire of 461, and the foundation of Constantinople on May 11, 330 (Baldovin 1987: 197).

Whether connected to civil or natural calamities, *litaneies* were therefore deeply woven into the history of the city and its identity. Even before that, however, they were also materially woven into its fabric. Lewis Mumford's evocative words effectively capture the dynamic, if not transient, interplay between the processing crowd winding about the streets and the built environment:

> Here is no static architecture. The masses suddenly expand and vanish, as one approaches them or draws away; a dozen paces may alter the relation of the foreground and background, or the lower and upper range of the line of vision.
> (cited in Baldovin 1987: 256)

Over the centuries, *litaneies* physically transformed Constantinople: key shrines were connected through major street axes, whereas dedicated public infrastructure, such as galleries and arches, added to the solemn theatricality of the events. At the same time, the cyclical enactment of these events turned the city, including what were perceived to be secular everyday spaces, into sacred space. For example, during the Tuesday ritual, the icon of the Mother of God Hodēgētria (which was believed to have been painted by Saint Luke the Evangelist) was carried around a market square, where she performed a regular miracle, so that that "most profane" place was transformed into "the most sacred" (Lidov 2006: 351). Indeed, according to Alexei Lidov, "the iconic space" that was established at the Hodegon square extended over a much larger territory: "through the procession, the miraculous power emanating from the Hodegetria icon of the Mother of God spread through the entire city, making it an enormous icon in space and bringing to the fore its status as earthly embodiment of the Heavenly Jerusalem" (Lidov 2006: 355). In this way, argues Lidov, a mystical link was established between geographically distant areas: the Holy Land, where the icon came from, and Constantinople, or "the New Jerusalem."[3]

While *litaneies* originated and blossomed in urban environments, they were by no means restricted to cities. Two non-urban outdoor processions are mentioned, for example, by the Byzantine monk, itinerant preacher and holy man Nikon Metanoeite (930–98). Both took place in the village of Amykleion in the southern Peloponnese: the first was enacted by the villagers to thank God for freeing them from a devastating plague, whereas the second was initiated by the saint on the following day to cast the foundations of a new church (Thomas et al. 2000: 251–2). While no detailed description is provided, these rural processions would have lacked the pomp and sophisticated choreography of their urban counterparts, and yet they would have preserved, and perhaps even amplified, their "petitioning" and thanksgiving qualities. Modern examples of rural *litaneies* punctuate Greek literature and folk culture (Chatzēphōtēs 2002). For example, in a famous novel set in Lesvos shortly after the Great Fire of Smyrna in 1922, Stratēs Myribēlēs provides an evocative description of a supplicatory procession of islanders passing through the yellow dust of sun-burned fields and olive trees to "pray God, who hang the land upon the water, to send the spirits of the rain upon their trees" (1995[1949]: 179).

Liturgical processions are also mentioned in medieval monastic *typika* (or "rules of observance"). Their patterns and outreach varied greatly according to the nature of the confraternity and its location. For example, the *typikon* of Empress Irene Doukaina Komnēnē for the convent of the Mother of God Kecharitomenē (1110-16), which strictly banned men other than eunuchs and designated priests from its precinct, maintains that processions "should not last long" and should take place within its walls. The nuns were thus instructed to conduct their *litaneies* between the church, the oratory and the common dormitory, while the convent itself, the *typikon* states, should remain "unobserved from all sides" (Thomas et al. 2000: 703-4). At the other end of the spectrum is the eighth-century *typikon* for Stoudios, the most famous monastery of Constantinople, which was also responsible for the revival of late antique coenobitic monasticism (Thomas et al. 2000: 84-7). The *typikon* provides instructions for a *litaneia* taking place on Bright Monday (the Monday after Easter). The procession, we are told, should depart from the church of the Forerunner, circle the vineyard close to the monastery, move down to the sea, then to the church of the all-Holy Mother of God, and finally head back to the Forerunner. Vested in priestly garments and carrying crosses and icons, the monks would recite an *ektenēs* at each of these stations and proclaim "Christ is Risen" "in a loud voice" (Thomas et al. 2000: 101).

Litaneies and Athonite Topographies

Litaneies have inscribed the landscape of Mount Athos at least since the foundation of its first coenobitic monastery, the Great Lavra by Saint Athanasios (Mamalakēs 1971). Liturgical processions on the peninsula are first mentioned in Lavra's *typikon*, which was originally compiled by the saint in 963 (though probably edited around 1020) and was based on the Stoudite model. The *typikon* describes a procession taking place on Holy Saturday:

> At the completion of the fourth hour, the wood is struck and we are led into the church. Taking up the litany, we go off to Saint Nicholas, if the weather is clear, and to the Forerunner. There we turn around and begin vespers, without reciting the Psalter. Then we enter for the complete liturgy. (Thomas et al. 2000: 227)

As with its Stoudite counterpart, the liturgical procession described here is signposted by manmade landmarks, in this case the chapels of Saint Nicholas and of the Forerunner. The weather is also taken into consideration. The Lavra can be imagined as a small city with its own shrines, or rather, as a small microcosm embedded and integrated within the larger microcosm of Mount Athos and within a wider sacred network stretching as far as to Constantinople (and the Stoudios monastery).

Today, *litaneies* continue to be enacted on the peninsula on major liturgical feasts and, occasionally, as special petitions, for example, for the relief from a prolonged drought, or from sudden threats, such as fires. Festive processions take place on three main distinct occasions: on Bright Monday and Tuesday (tou Diakainēsimou); on the Sunday of Orthodoxy (the first Sunday of Great Lent);

and finally, on the feasts of the patron saint to whom a monastery is dedicated, or of a miraculous icon preserved in the monastery. Each of these feasts imprints the *litaneia* with a distinctive character, which is in turn reflected on the topography of the monasteries and their surroundings.

During the Bright Week processions, for example, icons and relics are taken around the monastic complex and matching hymns are chanted at different stations, which are usually marked by chapels (as in the *typikon* of Saint Athanasios) and other more or less prominent landmarks and topographic features. On the way, the monastery's gardens, vineyards, and animals are blessed with holy water and through the recital of special prayers at pre-established stations, where different members of the brotherhood (both living and dead) are also commemorated. While the general form of these litanies is more or less the same, their routes, meticulously scripted in the *typikon* of each foundation, vary from monastery to monastery. These variations generally reflect the topographic peculiarities of the monastery. For example, at Simonopetra, a "fortress" hanging from a cliff 330 meters over the sea, the monks process down the road to a high point where there is a kind of small platform, on which an *hagiasmos* service (blessing of the water) is held, whereas at Docheiariou, which is located down on the shore, the *hagiasmos* is performed on the dock of the monastery.

The other two kinds of *litaneies* usually involve shorter processions, which are generally confined to the courtyard. As in the rest of Greece, during the Sunday of Orthodoxy, icons are taken out of the *katholikon* (the monastery's main church) and walked around it in commemoration of the defeat of iconoclasm in 843, whereas on the monastery's main feast holy relics are taken to the *phiale* (well), where an *hagiasmos* service takes place and faithful venerate the relics and the cross used to bless the water. On that occasion, the monks of Docheiariou also perform a small procession to the monastery's cellar, which culminates with the blessing of the wheat, oil, and wine (a tradition imported by their abbot from the monastery of Saint John the Theologian on the island of Patmos, where he was tonsured). On these feasts, icons and relics become spiritual magnets drawing together hundreds of faithful from different parts of Greece and other Orthodox countries. Each monastery becomes a small "Constantinople" (see Figure 9.1).

As processions move upon the land, they connect and sanctify places; as with their Constantinopolitan ancestors, they produce "spatial icons" (Lidov 2006). Indeed, some of them consciously inscribe the landscape with symbolic patterns. The monks of Lavra, for example, perform four *litaneies* per year, each of them following a different cardinal direction, so that together they form a cruciform pattern—the same pattern Saint Athanasius saw inscribed on the

Figure 9.1 Procession of the miraculous icon of the Mother of God Quick to Hear around the *katholikon* of Docheiariou monastery, Mount Athos. Photograph by Elder Apollò of Docheiariou.

Mountain when he first arrived.[4] During each procession, the sign of the cross is repeated by the priest's blessing hand, as it moves from North to South, from East to West, and from West to East. The micro-scales of the human body and of Athos are thus made symbolically converge with the macro-scale of the cosmos.

Athonite processions are intimately woven into the topography of the peninsula, as well as into its multiple temporalities. This intersection is especially palpable in *litaneies* commemorating local miracles, such as the landing of the icon of the Mother of God "Portaitissa" on the shore of Ivēron during iconoclasm, and its retrieval by monk Gabriel (a canonized saint of the Orthodox Church) (Savvas Philotheitēs 1936: 27). The event occurred on Bright Tuesday and is commemorated annually on that day. On Saturday of the Holy Week, prior to divine Liturgy, the icon is transferred from its chapel to the *katholikon*, where it remains until the second Monday after Easter. On Bright Tuesday morning, the Resurrection Canon and odes to the icon are chanted during the matins service, after which the icon is processed to the cemetery, the vineyards, and to the chapels outside of the walls of the monastery. The icon is then taken to a chapel on the seashore where the divine Liturgy is completed. After that, it is carried to the spot where it was placed for the first time by monk Gabriel. Through the procession, the miraculous journey of the icon is thus reactivated. Time is mapped on space. Or rather, space becomes an elaborate palimpsest in which different temporal dimensions overlap and interpenetrate: the historical past in which the miracle took place; the present time of the procession; and the eternal time of the divine Liturgy.

Athonite *litaneies* are also closely interconnected with the cyclical time of the year. In particular, Bright Week processions are connected with the Lord's Resurrection, as well as with the arrival of the spring and the "awakening of the landscape"—and therefore with the agricultural cycle on which Athos depends. Out of the peninsula, Bright Week *litaneies* are usually meant "to bless not just villages and their houses, but also fields and crops, as far as the community's eye can reach" (Chatzēphōtēs 2002: 272). In the case of Mount Athos, the entire peninsula—which is also called by the monks "the Garden of the Virgin"—is simultaneously brought to life (Kourilēs 1953: 69). Special prayers for the prevention of the drought are read, crops and gardens are blessed, while Athos is filled with flowery scents and birds' songs. Pilgrims have long described the experience as a spiritual and emotional rebirth. For example, a Greek journalist writing in the early twentieth century defined these processions as "one of the most beautiful customs of Athonite religious life" and claimed to "have never seen a more picturesque ceremony." One could call it "the flower festival of the monks" (Athanas 1926, quoted in Chatzēphōtēs 1977: 13). Similar sentiments are echoed in a monk's account written ten years later:

> We should say that truly not only the people who take part to the *litaneia* rejoice and cherish their souls in this glorious procession of the icon of the Queen of Heaven, who with her invisible presence blesses her servants, but the entire creation rejoices and chants hymns of thanksgiving. . . . The flowers emanate their sweet scents. . . . With their varied colours, the hazel trees and the groves elevate hymns to the Virgin's infinite charismas. From the branches of the trees, the nightingales take part in our joy with their songs, . . . while the angels fly around in invisible flights and merrily chant: "Hail, Full of Grace, the Lord is with you," and through you with us. (Savvas Philotheitēs 1936: 13)

Here the *litaneia* seems to transfigure the landscape. The cycle of the liturgical year is aligned with the cycle of life, as visible and invisible worlds come together in a joyful hymn of cosmic praise.

Situated somewhere between contingency and eternity, between place and space, *litaneies* are by definition liminal phenomena. Spring, itself a transitional season, reflects and reinforces their transitory and transformative character (Varvounis 2014). Likewise, their routes, whether following a coastal path, encircling the perimeter of the *katholikon*, or marking the boundaries of a monastic precinct, give geographical expression to liminality. By encircling an area—be it Imperial Constantinople during a siege, the space of a newly built church awaiting to be consecrated, or a field awaiting to be blessed—Orthodox *litaneies* sanctify it and protect it from external threats. They trace an invisible boundary between sacred and profane space (Eliade 1959), or rather, they activate sacred space through their very enactment.

The largest Athonite *litaneia* encompasses an entire village, Karyes. Located in the heart of the peninsula, Karyes is the seat of the Holy Community (Iera Koinotēta) which consists of the representatives of the twenty monasteries, having as executive committee the four-membered Holy Administration (Iera Epistasia). The representatives are lodged in cells (or small cottages) belonging to the various monasteries (Sideropoulos 2010). The church of the Prōtato, situated at the center of Karyes, hosts the miraculous Axion Estin icon of the Mother of God, which on Bright Monday is taken on procession around the village (see Figure 9.2).

The route was first established in *c.*1508 and it has been faithfully followed ever since, except for a few new stations added between the mid-nineteenth century

Figure 9.2 Procession of the miraculous icon of the Mother of God Axion Estin in Karyes, Mount Athos. Photograph by Elder Apollò of Docheiariou.

and the early twentieth century (Ioustinos Simonopetrētēs 1987: 14). The route described in the original document encompasses twelve stations, including cells belonging to the different monasteries, various crosses located along the route, and the nearby monastery of Koutloumousi. Today, the procession takes over five hours (see Figure 9.3).

The *litaneia* departs from the Prōtato. It is led by a choir of monks and by priests and deacons carrying icons, lanterns, chandeliers, and censers. At each station, Easter odes and odes to the Virgin are followed by the hymn to the saint to whom the cell (or monastery) is dedicated and by a related passage from the gospel. As they stop at the various cells, monks and pilgrims are offered cheese, wine, and eggs by the local Fathers. The *litaneia* therefore becomes a site of hospitality, as well as a multi-sensorial experience in which all the five senses are involved. It gives full expression to the sensual richness of the Greek Orthodox tradition. Orthodoxy does not make a dualistic division between the spiritual and the material worlds, but rather the latter is understood and experienced as a vessel and a precondition for making the former manifest (Ware 1963). The Greek landscape, and the landscape of Mount Athos in particular, is itself

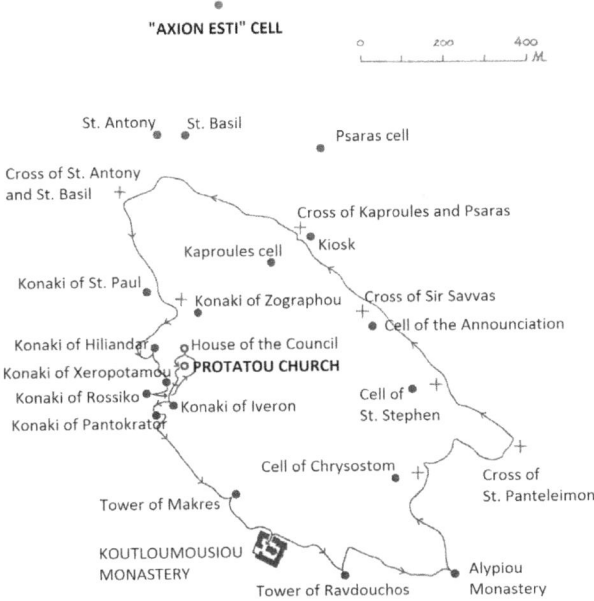

Figure 9.3 Route of the procession of the icon of the Mother of God Axion Estin around the village of Karyes, Mount Athos (source: the author after Hieromonk Ioustinos Simonopetrētēs).

a tangible manifestation of the holy, dotted as it is with churches, monasteries, chapels, and roadside shrines (Dubisch 1995: 61). Each of these shrines belongs to a topography connected to the cycle of the liturgical year, which, in this case, is activated during the procession.

Along the way, special prayers are also recited: a prayer for the prevention of life-threatening diseases is read at the cell of Saint Panteleimon (a famous healing saint), one for the drought at the cell of the Annunciation, and finally one for the protection against the threats of thunder and lightning near the cross of Zōgraphou (Kourilēs 1953: 69–71). The procession of the icon is essentially regarded by the monks as an act of love: "it takes place to sanctify our homes, to bless our crops, to cast away every noxious insect from our gardens and vineyards and trees. And finally to clean the air from unhealthy exhalations, and make it tempered for the health of our bodies" (Ioustinos Simonopetritēs 1987: 13). In this sense, the *litaneia* of the Axion Estin makes no exception: all the Athonite monasteries consider *litaneies* essential for their prosperity and for the good production of their gardens and vineyards, and when this was not done in the past, local stories report, they were often struck by natural disasters (Ioustinos Simonopetritēs 1987: 15–16). What makes this *litaneia* stand apart from other Bright Week processions, however, is its pan-Athonite quality: as it moves around the village and the representatives' cells, the procession weaves an invisible thread through the various monasteries; it brings them together in a symbolic circle, or rather, in a warm embrace.

Taking the Holy Mountain Outside of the Holy Mountain

The *litaneies* of the Axion Estin and those of the individual monasteries are represented on a number of post-Byzantine topographic engravings. A general view of Mount Athos and its monasteries produced by monk Dionysios of Karyes in 1889, for example, features the church of the Prōtato during the procession of the miraculous icon guarded by a local *chōrofylax* and presided by a bishop. Earlier engravings of the individual monasteries likewise feature often elaborately executed thanksgiving processions in which the monks exit the main gate and walk their icons around the monastic precinct. Their circular (or semi-circular) movement reinforces the insular self-enclosure of the monastic space. For example, on an eighteenth-century engraving of Vatopaidi, the procession of black-robed monks forms a sort of "outer wall" encircling half of the monastery. The abbot and the deacons can be seen at the head of the procession, followed by the priests carrying a holy icon under a lavish baldachin, followed by the rest of the confraternity (Deluga and Zych 2002: 128–9).

Likewise, on an engraving of Docheiariou printed in Venice in 1819, the procession stretches from the gate of the monastery along the shore and half the way up its northern walls, forming a sort of "sacred barrier" against external threats, including pirate vessels and frightening sea monsters (see Figure 9.4).

On the engraving, one can discern most of the stations of the Bright Monday *litaneia* mentioned in the original 1815 manuscript *typikon* (Docheiariou cod. 356): the gate of the monastery (where the first ode of the Resurrection Canon is chanted), the garden and chapel of the Transfiguration (where the current gardeners are commemorated and the *kontakion* of the Transfiguration is chanted), the watermill, the chapel of the Mother of God, the dock, the graveyard (where the reposing fathers are commemorated), the chapel of Saints Onoufrios and Peter (where the founders of the chapel are commemorated), and the *katholikon* (where the procession ends).

Portraying processions on the threshold between the sacred space of the monastic precinct and the outside world, in their own way, these engravings stress their liminal quality, as well as their centrality in the liturgical life and identity

Figure 9.4 Engraving of Docheiariou monastery, Mount Athos. Venice, 1819. Photograph from author's private collection.

of each monastic community. As "sacred maps" and visual representations, they offer snapshots of a practice that has remained largely unchanged through the centuries. They also speak of perceptions of place articulated through the repetition of pre-existing spatial archetypes and iconographies. For example, topographic views of the entire peninsula were built on the model of similar engravings of Sinai produced for the monastery of Saint Catherine as early as in the seventeenth century (see Figure 9.5).

On both the Athonite and Sinaite representations, mountain slopes featured as "ladders" joining threatening seas (or deserts) to celestial heights populated by saintly figures. By adopting similar patterns and iconographies (including processions), Athos was thus presented as a "second Sinai," as key node within an extended network of Orthodox holy places in an Ottoman-dominated world (della Dora 2011b).

If considered as material objects rather than simple visual representations, however, these engravings also speak of the difficult circumstances under which they were produced, while at the same time offering fascinating insights into the circulation of Mount Athos outside of its physical boundaries. Often led to the edge of bankruptcy by heavy taxations imposed by the Porte, in the eighteenth

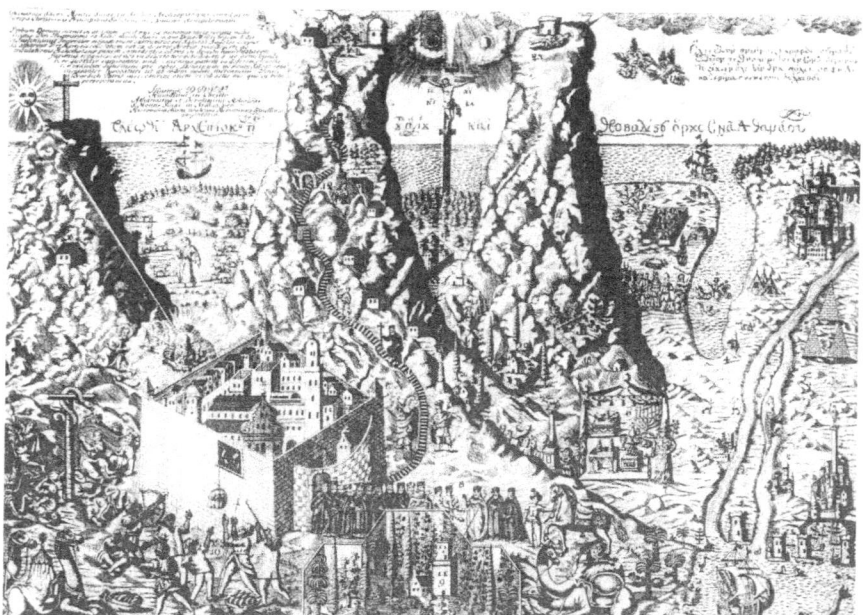

Figure 9.5 General view of Mount Sinai, by anonymous engraver. Venice, 1710. Photograph from Istituto Ellenico di Studi Bizantini e Postbizantini, Venice.

and nineteenth centuries most Athonite foundations used to send their monks on alms-begging expeditions (a practice known as *zēteia*) in the hope of raising funds and attracting pilgrims (Aggelomatē-Tsougarakē 2007). Some of these engravings, which were originally printed in the great centers of the Greek diaspora (e.g., Venice or Vienna), and later in Karyes, were used by the monks as illustrated "brochures," or "visual pedigrees" of their own foundations. The detailed plans of the monasteries framed by local saints and miracles (e.g., see Figure 9.4) enabled potential benefactors to conjure up a monastic foundation in their mind's eye and therefore increase the chances of donations (Papastratou 1990). The engravings also allowed prospective pilgrims to undertake short "visual tours," which might have eventually encouraged a visit to the peninsula. In other cases, as it is explicitly stated in the inscription of the 1819 engraving of Docheiariou, the engravings were given away to Orthodox pilgrims by the monasteries as "blessings" and mementos of their visits. Their ability to be cheaply reproduced and transported made these prints ideal media for circulation. In other words, whether acting as subtle instruments for persuasion and armchair travel, or as sacred souvenirs, topographic engravings helped the monks "take Athos outside of Athos."

It was, however, mainly thanks to the charismatic presence of the relics the monks usually carried with them on their alms-begging expeditions, and thanks to the monks themselves, that the Holy Mountain was enabled to travel outside of its boundaries and stretch as far as to Wallachia and Russia. Ranging in scope from nearby cities to remote Orthodox countries, alms-begging missions generally featured fragments of the Holy Cross and relics of saints preserved in the monasteries (Mamalakēs 1971: 518; Aggelomatē-Tsougarakē 2007). In this way, women and often distant faithful unable to travel to Athos were presented with a unique opportunity for veneration. For example, the famous eighteenth-century monk and intellectual Kaisarios Dapontes of Xēropotamou traveled with a relic of the Holy Cross for no less than eight years, in order to collect funds to restore the *katholikon* and other parts of the monastery which had been damaged by a severe fire. The journey, which took him to Constantinople, the Danubian principalities, and the islands of Chios, Samos, Psara, Evia, Skopelos, is vividly recorded in his autobiographical poem "The Garden of Graces" (1768) (see Polyvios 1992).

Sometimes, it was nearby villagers and even distant rulers that invited the Athonite monks and asked them perform *litaneies* to exorcise epidemics and natural disasters (Aggelomatēs-Tsougarakē 2007: 256). On these occasions, relics were received with great solemnity, as a nineteenth-century Protestant missionary in Constantinople skeptically describes:

> The girdle of the Virgin arrived last Friday, from Mount Athos. It was received with great pomp by the Patriarch and other dignitaries of the Greek Church, who carried it to the Church in Phanar, attended by an immense crowd of people, who formed such a procession as is rarely seen in Constantinople. The Greeks suppose that by this relic the cholera will be exorcised from the city. I wonder what the intelligent among them think of this, and still more what those in the West, who have such an admiration of the Greek Church, will say of it. (*Evangelical Christendom* 1872: 85)

In some instances, the miraculous outcome of these *litaneies* turned into a commemorative recurrence. For example, in 1768 the inhabitants of Petrokerasa in northern Greece, about 70 kilometers northwest of Mount Athos, contacted the monastery of Xēropotamou asking the monks to help their village, which had been hit by a deadly disease. "The Fathers, immediately after receiving word, and with great honours and a grand procession, brought a piece of the True Cross to the village, and upon its procession around the village, [Petrokerasa] was saved and the disease that plagued its inhabitants was eradicated" (Frangos 2005). In memory of this event, every year on Palm Sunday, the monks of Xēropotamou have since continued to take the relic to the same village to be venerated by its local inhabitants and pilgrims.

In different ways, flows of monks, engravings, and, more importantly, of relics enabled the Holy Mountain to transcend its physical boundaries, as they continue to do today in multiple ways. While strictly regulated by the Holy Community, relics and famous icons continue to be the key protagonists of both occasional and periodical processions out of the Holy Mountain and to be received with the same solemnity as in the past. Sometimes these processions have the flavor and pomp of the sensational event. For example, in 2012 the Axion Estin icon paraded in Thessaloniki with state honors in occasion of the 100th anniversary of the liberation of the city (*Iefimerida*, October 13, 2012), whereas the visit of the Girdle of the Virgin to Moscow attracted no less than 285,000 believers, after 2 million Russians had venerated it in the course of its journey to the capital (*New York Times*, November 23, 2011). Other times, relics are simply taken out of Athos on a small boat by the monks, in order to be venerated by women stationed on another boat 500 meters off the coast (Kotsi 1999). Other times, yearly processions with relics and wonderworking icons form a geographical extension of the liturgical life cycle of specific Athos' monasteries, as in the case of Xēropotamou and the village of Petrokerasa.

Ranging from a few hundred meters to thousands of kilometers, staged in urban, rural, and even marine settings, these different types of "Athonite journeys into the world" produce different engagements with the landscape of the Holy Mountain: as a distant landscape of the mind conjured up by images and descriptions (including topographic engravings); as the backdrop of a floating pilgrimage observed from the boat; and also as a presence pulsating with life, as an extraordinary reality periodically inscribed in familiar landscapes by way of Athonite processions. The last section of this chapter considers one such procession.

Sacred Performance and Overlapping Topographies

Every year, on September 7, an entire village is turned into an open-air church. On that day, the vigil of the Feast of the Nativity of the Mother of God, the miraculous icon of Our Lady the Quick to Hear (Gorgoypēkoos) is transported from the monastery of Docheiariou to Sochos, a rural village 70 kilometers northeast of Thessaloniki, in northern Greece. From there it is carried on procession to the convent of the Mother of God Theoskepastē, Docheiariou's female dependency, which is located on a hill overlooking the village. As the icon enters the village's main square, she is greeted by the sound of church bells and hymns, by small flags and pennants set up for the occasion, and by a vast crowd of faithful. Some of them have come a long way to ask for a miracle, others to thank her, others just to honor her. Adorned with fresh flowers and sheltered by a parasol, the icon is kissed, touched, and blessed with holy water (see Figure 9.6).

The square is turned into a stage for sacred and civic performance, as religious rituals alternate with speeches by Docheiariou's abbot and the town's mayor. Carried across the square over creaky loudspeakers, melodic chants and charismatic words mix with the crowd's background noise and with the wind. As the icon parades through the main street, villagers cross themselves; small icons and altars are improvised on sidewalks; incense is burned; candles lit; colored rugs unrolled on her pathway; and music played by a local brass band. Rhythmic drumrolls and the sound of trumpets mingle with random conversations; the scent of the incense blends with the fragrance of fresh basil; the black hoods of the monks with the colorful shirts of the faithful; the silky vestments of the priests with cotton summer dresses and jeans. Traffic is stopped. Time is suspended. For a day the sacred space of the church is taken outside of its walls. For a day the sacred space of the Holy Mountain of Orthodoxy is transposed outside of its boundaries (see Figure 9.7).

Unlike the Petrokerasa procession of the Holy Cross, this *litaneia* is not rooted in a century-long tradition. The convent was founded by a small group of

Figure 9.6 Reception of the miraculous icon of the Mother of God Quick to Hear outside of the church of Saint George in the village of Sochos, northern Greece. Photograph by the author.

Docheiarite Fathers in 1994 and the first procession of the Quick to Hear took place shortly thereafter. Since then, it has been enacted on an annual basis in occasion of the Feast of the Nativity of the Mother of God, to which the convent is dedicated. In spite of the convent's recent construction and its location off beaten tourist and pilgrim tracks, every year the event attracts villagers from Sochos and nearby towns, as well as hundreds of pilgrims from different parts of Greece and beyond. Most of them (both male and female) have a personal connection with Docheiariou and attend the event on a regular basis as a form of "spiritual maintenance" (Ron 2012). Indeed, many of them take the feast as an opportunity for confession and spiritual counseling with the Fathers. Others often join in either individually or on pilgrimages organized by local parishes. The *litaneia* thus becomes a mobile site of gathering, where different life narratives and geographical scales intersect, or where, as the abbot put it in a sermon, "the children of the Mother of God all come together—from the village, from Thessaloniki, from Athens, from the rest of Greece, and from abroad."

Today many Greek parishes hold a procession on their feast day (*panēgyri*). Whether taking place in urban, rural, or insular settings, these *panēgyria* are an

Figure 9.7 Procession of the miraculous icon of the Mother of God Quick to Hear moving through the village of Sochos. Photograph by the author.

important part of Orthodox spiritual culture and liturgical practice, as well as of Greek folk tradition (Chatzēphōtēs 2002; Du Boulay 2009; Dubisch 1995). However, what makes the Sochos *panēgyri* and procession stand apart is first of all its focus, that is, a miraculous icon that comes out of the Holy Mountain only on that occasion, and second, the fact that the entire feast (including procession, *hagiasmos* service, vigil, and liturgy) is celebrated by the monks of Docheiariou according to the Athonite *typikon*, that is, as it is celebrated on Mount Athos (as opposed to the abbreviated rituals of parishes, or even of non-Athonite monasteries). For women and other faithful unable to visit the Holy Mountain, the feast therefore represents a unique occasion to experience, or rather to take part in, Athonite liturgical life. While most of the services take place indoors (in the convent's *katholikon*), the *litaneia* forms one of the most poignant aspects of the feast, not least because of its insistently physical and symbolic interaction with the landscape.

As the procession leaves the village, the carpets end, the band parts; the loud instrumental music gives way to Byzantine chant. A lower mingling of human voices fills the air. As they walk, the monks and the congregation chant, mostly by heart, a long chain of hymns from the Supplicatory Canon to Our

Lady the Quick to Hear composed by Nikodēmos of Mount Athos in 1792. Each describes a miracle performed by the Quick to Hear to those coming to her in a state of compunction and repentance (Nikodēmos Agioreitēs 2001). Out of the village, the atmosphere becomes more somber. The topography changes and the embodied experience of walking changes too: it becomes more demanding. A small chapel and a sign mark the beginning of the ascent to the convent, and the boundary between the village and "the wilderness." The faithful no longer walk on the flat smooth surface of asphalted streets and paved sidewalks; they often step into the rugged terrain on the sides of the road in order to get a glimpse of the icon. Their engagement with the terrain becomes more tactile, as wild grass and thorns scratch their legs, and dust and small stones occasionally get into their shoes. As the surface of the land is inscribed by the procession, the surfaces of human bodies are also inscribed by the land. The faithful becomes a pilgrim (see Figure 9.8).

The change in the landscape evokes archetypal topographies and spiritual journeys: the ascetic's movement from the city to the wilderness, Moses' ascent of Mount Sinai (Exodus 19), Saint John's ladder (Ignatios 1998), the pilgrim's ascent to Athos' summit. The hill becomes a transitional space between the

Figure 9.8 Procession of the miraculous icon of the Mother of God Quick to Hear on the way to Docheiariou's dependency. Photograph by the author.

"world" (the village) and the spiritual space of the monastery. This tripartite scheme brings to mind the structure of the abovementioned post-Byzantine topographic engravings of Sinai and Athos, with their threatening deserts and seas at the bottom, ladder-like mountains in the middle, and celestial space at the top (see Figures 9.4 and 9.5).

The threefold scheme is deeply rooted in the Byzantine spiritual tradition. Drawing on the life of Moses and the symbolic places of the Old Testament, Saint Gregory of Nyssa (c. 335; after 394) mapped the three great stages of spiritual life on the physical landscape of Sinai; or rather, he described spiritual life itself as a journey through space. *Katharsis*, or the purification of the soul from egoistical passions, *phōtisis*, the enlightenment of the soul by the Holy Spirit, and *theosis*, or union with God, were compared respectively with the entry into a moonlit desert night, followed by a movement to a fog-covered mountain, and finally, into an impenetrable gloom (Gregory of Nyssa 1978). While surely less demanding than ascending Sinai (or Athos), the embodied experience of the ascent of the Greek hill marks an inner path of *metanoia*, of inner transformation. Indeed, in a speech preceding the *litaneia*, the abbot of Docheiariou invited the faithful gathered in the square to join in the procession and "ascend the holy mountain" (meaning here a spiritual, rather than physical ascent; an inward, rather than upward movement).

Geography, it has been observed, has a unique capacity to give expression to the deepest longings of the human soul (Sheldrake 2001; Lane 1998). In the Orthodox tradition, it holds a symbolic function. In the same way churches, chapels, and other holy landmarks in the landscape reflect and assert an intimate relationship between material and spiritual worlds, so do "archetypical" landscape features make invisible spiritual paths visible. For example, in the Supplicatory Canon to the Quick to Hear, life is repeatedly compared to a stormy sea and the Mother of God to "a tranquil port," a recurrent topos in Byzantine Patristic literature (della Dora 2016: 240–4).[5] Likewise, the symbolic shape of Sinai superimposed on the northern Greek countryside allows pilgrims to visualize and, ultimately, walk their inward pathway of *metanoia* (Figure 9.9).

At the same time, however, the procession also transposes and activates a different "earthly" topography—the topography of Mt Athos. Like on the Holy Mountain, here the procession stops at pre-established stations where the Fathers read special prayers and chant matching hymns. For example, as the procession exits the village and passes by the neighboring monastery of the Transfiguration, the monks chant the *kontakion* of the feast of the Transfiguration

Figure 9.9 Procession of the miraculous icon of the Mother of God Quick to Hear approaching Docheiariou's dependency. Photograph by the author.

(as they do during the Bright Monday procession at Docheiariou, when they stop by the same-named chapel) and commemorate the abbot of that monastery (as customary in the Axion Estin procession). Likewise, prayers related to the waters and the crops are read in proximity of a fount; prayers for the animals' health are recited as the procession passes by the stalls with the cows; and matching hymns are chanted at the chapels near the convent, as the procession nears its destination. We can thus think of the Sochos procession as an Athonite procession in miniature, or rather, as an ephemeral space in which different topographies and "spatial icons" converge and overlap—Sinai, Athos, and Docheiariou.

The slow movement of the procession produces a pre-modern experience of space. As opposed to mechanized journeys, the *litaneia* does not turn space into an abstract geometrical dimension; movement does not reduce space to mere time or distance, but rather, it transforms it into a meaningful sequence of micro-places. From scenic view, landscape is morphed into a sacred topography in the literal meaning of the word (Malpas 1999). With its slow pace, the procession seems to "subvert or transcend the rushing, mechanized world of modernity." As with pilgrimage, it emphasizes "a slowing down rather than speeding up of life"

Figure 9.10 Procession of the miraculous icon of the Mother of God Quick to Hear approaching Docheiariou's dependency at dusk. Photograph by the author.

(Coleman and Eade 2004: 11). Following the setting sun, it realigns the pilgrim with the rhythms of nature and the cosmos (see Figure 9.10).

As the procession reaches the monastery in the twilight of the dusk, it is joyfully greeted by the sound of bells and *sēmandra* (the instruments used outside the church to call monks to the services). An *hagiasmos* service takes place, followed by a long night vigil celebrated by the monks. Children move around, while a steady flow of faithful venerates the icon. Animated by chants and candle lights, the monastery shines in the quietness of the countryside like one of the many bright stars crowding the terse sky above.

*

As Gregory of Nazianzus argued in the fourth century, vivid landscape imagery helps "spell out things more clearly" (Greg. Naz. Hom. 26.10). For the Byzantines, landscape could act as a vehicle of revelation. Landscape uttered stories. Nature was a vast reservoir of familiar symbols through which the Creator revealed Himself. God had spoken to the Hebrew through "landscape utterings": "the burning bush, the rock that gushed with water, the jar of manna, the fire from God that came down from the altar" (John of Damascus 1997). He continued to speak to humans through His works, which Basil called "visible memorials of His wonders" (Basil *Hom.* 8.8). In this sense, Creation was understood as a spiritual map; a map that revealed invisibilities through its own visibilities and materialities.

Rooted in the Byzantine tradition, Orthodox processions continue to activate this spiritual map and produce a multi-sensorial and quintessentially topographic experience of space and landscape. Indeed, their slow, sequential, and repetitive movement through specific sites (or landmarks) makes *litaneies*, and Athonite *litaneies* in particular, inherently place-based phenomena. At the same time, Athonite processions are also sites of convergence of different materialities and temporalities; returning every year, as in a spiral, they are always the same and yet never the same. Athonite *litaneies* can thus be interpreted as mobile intersections between different spatial and temporal scales. In bringing the church outside of its walls, and Mount Athos outside of its perimeter, they temporarily transfigure villages into churches, hills into holy mountains, and the earth itself into a cosmic temple. In the words of Saint Nicholas Velimirovitch, *litaneies* "have the meaning of communal open-air prayers [enacted] under the light of the sun and under the dome of the universe" (*O Sōtēr* 2016).

Litaneies sit in between the ordinary and the extraordinary. While processions enacted during the consecration ceremony of an Orthodox church (or the blessing of a field, or a village) set it apart from its surroundings, paradoxically, they also link the space of the church with the outside world—or rather, they turn the outside world into a vast church (Christo 2005: 60). Likewise, not only do Athonite processions inscribe the surface of the peninsula and activate its sacred topographies, but they also rearticulate its sacred space outside of its boundaries, often in forceful, multi-sensorial, and deeply embodied fashions. As such, Athonite *litaneies* generate intense and diverse atmospheres: the solemn and the intimate, the spectacular and the homely, the strange and the familiar. They invite us to reflect on the complex relationship between multi-sensorial experience, topography, and time. More broadly, they also call for a reconceptualization of sacred space from static receptacle or abstract dimension to a fluid entity that is always in the making.

10

The Garden of Eden in an Era of Over-Tourism

(Managing) New Testament Sacred Groves in the Holy Land

Amos S. Ron

This chapter tells the story of three sacred groves in the Holy Land: the Mount of Beatitudes, the Garden of Gethsemane, and the Garden Tomb. It illustrates the ambivalent view of gardens in Christianity: on the one hand, the garden is the origin of all that is good and godly. It is an oasis at the heart of the spiritual and physical desert that surrounds us; on the other hand, unlike the wilderness, which is sparse and pure, the garden is replete with temptation. Historically, both views have left their mark on the landscapes of Christianity, but this chapter will elaborate on the first approach, by interpreting their "gardenscape." Moreover, this chapter will elaborate on these sites on two levels: the instrumental-tangible level, as pilgrimage centers in an era of over-tourism, and the symbolic-intangible level, as centers of meaning for Christian individuals and denominations.

Introduction: From the Sacred Grove to the Garden of Eden

Sacred groves have been a very common form of religious landscape, from antiquity to the present day (Baumann, Grimm, MacCulloch, Pliny, Porteous, Quantz in Dafni 2006: 11). Literally, a sacred grove is a group of trees to which sanctity is assigned: But what indeed is a sacred grove?

Dafni provides several definitions. For example, "a sacred grove is a stand of trees in a religious context" (Birge, in Dafni 2006: 1). In another definition, a sacred grove is "a patch of forest or natural vegetation protected and managed by the community considering it to be the reside place of the deities or ancestral spirits" (Pandey, Rao, in Dafni 2006: 2).[1]

According to several scholars, in antiquity the terms "Garden of Eden" and "Sacred Grove" overlapped to a certain degree. For example, according to Schachter (2013: 74), "Eden is not only a lush garden but also a sacred space, sharing characteristics with other mountain-top shrines found throughout the ancient Near East." Other studies describe the Garden of Eden as a primordial temple for humankind (Lioy 2010: 25).

The Garden in Jewish and Muslim Traditions

According to Ron (1989), ancient Judaism was ambivalent toward gardens and vegetation. During the Second Temple Period, for example, few plants were grown in Jerusalem. According to Semple, "the Israelites . . . frequented them [pleasure gardens] and thereby provoked the denunciations of the prophets" (Semple 1929: 427). According to another source, "the Temple of Jerusalem was an exception because the Jews feared that trees in the courtyard might savor of the hill-top gardens or groves of Baal-worship" (Semple 1971: 194).

In Islam, gardens in general, and sacred groves in particular, played an important role in architecture and in theology. Sacred groves are found in Iran (Ron 1993), India (Singh et al. 2017), Morocco (Deil, Culmsee, and Berriane 2005), Israel (Dafni 2002), and elsewhere, and are also perceived in the context of the veneration of sacred trees (Dafni 2006; Dafni, 2011). In his monumental work on Islamic art and spirituality, the famous Iranian scholar and philosopher Seyyed Hossein Nasr (Nasr 1987) wrote that in Islam,

> the architectural forms and the gardens have a definite traditional and symbolic character, the garden being a form of mandala which closes upon an inner centre and serves as a "reminder" and "copy" of paradise. (p. 70)

Sacred groves can appear in reality both as full size visible and visitable gardens, as well as in shapes and patterns in rugs. According to Nasr,

> Like the good Persian rug and the genuine Persian garden, the miniature serves as a reminder of a reality which transcends the mundane surroundings of human life. The space of the miniature is the space of that "imaginal world" where the forms of nature, the trees, the flowers, and the birds, as well as the events within the human soul, have their origin. (Nasr 1987: 182)

The Garden in Christian Traditions

Christian traditions have an ambiguous and ambivalent view of the garden. On the one hand, the garden is the origin of what is good and godly and represents an oasis at the heart of the spiritual and physical wilderness that surrounds us; on the other hand, the garden is full of temptations, while the desert is pure. Hence, this is where the true garden lies. Both approaches have left their mark on the landscapes of Christianity.

This chapter will elaborate on the first approach by analyzing three contemporary sacred groves in the Holy Land: the Mount of Beatitudes, the Garden of Gethsemane, and the Garden Tomb. We should note, though, that in Christianity sacred groves are just one example of a landscape centered on vegetation. Other examples include monastic gardens (Zoran 2020), Christian-oriented botanical gardens (Prest 1981; Ron 1989), biblical gardens (Bielo 2018a; Bielo 2018b; Hepper 1997; Ron 1989), biblical-themed environments (Ron and Timothy 2019), and Christian-oriented allotments and community gardens (Wilson 2007).

A Personal Introduction

In addition to my academic occupation and career, I have been working as a licensed tour guide in Israel for approximately forty years. My first visits to the Christian sacred groves in Israel took place during the tour guide course; I recall the pleasure of the shade, the beauty, and the calm, but at the same time I kept remembering, as a Jew, that our prophets did not approve of the concept of a vegetative sacred place, and that they were very critical of such sites (Hos. 4:13; Jer. 2:20).[2]

As a tour guide, I participated in hundreds of rituals performed by the groups I guided and observed many more performed by pilgrims of a variety of languages, skin colors, and dress codes. As an Israeli living in a rural community setting, I was amazed to see gardens become sacred groves; eventually, I learned to ignore the admonitions of the Old Testament verses from Jeremiah and Hosea, and these sacred groves and others (e.g., the Bahai gardens in Haifa) served, to a certain extent, as a home away from home. Undoubtedly, visiting these sacred groves repeatedly as a guide and participant observer was one of the reasons that led me to write an MA thesis on gardens in cultures (Ron 1989).

Theorizing Christian Sacred Groves

If we were to compare the academic research world to an enormous forest, there is considerable tree volume on the subjects of theorizing the *sacred* (e.g., Beckford and Walliss 2017) and on theorizing *groves* (e.g., Hunt 2000; Ikutegbe 2016). When we turn to the subject of *theorizing sacred groves*, the forest becomes far less dense. The few who wrote about it include (in alphabetical order): Thomas Barrie (2010; 2012), Michal Bitton (2012; 2016), Michel Conan (1999; 2007), John Dixon Hunt (2000; 2004), Malte Koeditz (2011), Lindsay Jones (2000), Belden Lane (2001), and Lily Zeng (2018). The contribution of these sources to theorizing Christian sacred groves can be divided into three perspectives: *social, temporal, and spatial.*

The social perspective is represented here by the works of Michel Conan, John Dixon Hunt, and Thomas Barrie. Conan, a garden theorist with a background in sociology and anthropology, emphasizes the following, and in several studies how rituals which involve spiritual and religious experiences often take place in gardens:

> The gardens provided a number of symbolic features that supported the enactment of the rituals, but primarily they enabled their visitors to engage in performances that carried them away to a supernatural world by promoting them to unusual types of actions. (Conan 2007: 9, in Bitton 2016: 202)

Hunt, an Englishman by origin, was a professor of history and theory of landscape at the University of Pennsylvania. Although several of his books are relevant to the theme, I chose to elaborate on his 2004 book titled *The Afterlife of Gardens*. The book introduces the reader to *reception theory*, as developed by Stuart Hall (Hall 1973). Although he does not mention the term, Hunt is also a devout follower of the landscape interpretation concept (see Chapter 1, Duncan and Duncan 2010; Ron 1989), which suggests a very clear distinction between "writing" the landscape and "reading" the landscape. According to Verdi, in her review of the book,

> The extraordinary journey on which Hunt takes the reader is filled with surprises and begins with landscape architecture. Gardens like Versailles, Villa d'Este, Stowe and Central Park do survive because of their original design, but also and especially, Hunt says, because of their reception. In a word, *its meaning is in its use*. That is, the new research questions no longer linger on the design meaning from the designer's point of view, and instead inspect the interaction between the garden and his consumers and explore the consumer's experiences, reactions, and practices inside the garden. (Verdi 2005: 375; my emphasis)

This approach was further developed by other garden scholars (Bitton 2012; 2016), anthropologists (Conan 1999; 2007), and geographers (Cosgrove 1984;

Ron 1989), who suggested a new research horizon to explore the ways in which human practices in gardens contribute to the creation of their cultural, social, and political environment. In Hunt's words,

> This book is about how gardens can be experienced, not about how they have been designed. . . . Yet it must be acknowledged that how gardens are visited, how they are used (and perhaps abused), and how they are absorbed into the experiences of generations of people who explore them after their creation constitute a very different and just as fascinating a story. . . . That, then, is the subject of this collection of essays—to study how gardens may be experienced and to explore the *longue durée* of reception rather than the often more brief moment of design or inception. (Hunt 2004: 11)

In his book entitled *The Sacred In-Between: The Mediating Roles of Architecture*, Thomas Barrie, an American professor of architecture, elaborates on the in-betweenness of sacred architecture. According to him,

> It is in the "in-between" of the complex forms, media, agendas, and ritual uses that constitute sacred architecture that new understandings, from a contemporary perspective, might be gained. (Barrie 2010: 8)

Like Conan, he elaborates on rituals performed on sacred ground in general and in sacred groves in particular. His book is on sacred architecture, sacred groves being but one example. His examples are taken from a medieval church in Saint Foy in Conques, France; Carl Jung's house in Bollingen, Switzerland; Tongdosa, a Korean Zen Buddhist monastery; the modernist Saint Benedict's Abbey at Vaals, Holland; the Pantheon in Rome; and the Hagia Sophia in Istanbul, and some Ottoman Era mosques (Barrie 2010:12). These examples reflect the connections established between the cultural intentions, symbolic agendas, and ritual requirements, and the architectural means utilized to achieve them.

The temporal perspective is represented here by the works of Lindsay Jones (2000), Malte Koeditz (2011), and Lily Zeng (2018). Lindsay Jones is a comparative religion scholar and an archeologist. According to Michal Bitton, Jones suggested that the creation of a new sanctuary, including sacred groves, involves three essential phases:

> The first is selecting or discovering the place of hierophany, usually by adopting or confiscating a natural piece of land. The second is setting the place apart, providing it as a marked-off space. The third phase is sanctifying the place,

mostly by purifying and cleansing it to the extent that it will ensure the appeal, integrity, and efficacy of the subsequent rites and ceremonies. (Jones 2000: 264-7, 272-4; in Bitton 2016: 72)

Malte Koeditz, a design architect, wrote his dissertation on timeless architecture. It is noteworthy that when Edward Relph wrote on "placelessness" in urban design, the word bore a negative connotation (Relph 1976), whereas "timelessness" usually has a positive connotation. According to Koeditz (2011),

> Timeless architecture is often considered to be something which has been designed in such an intentionally reduced manner to endure time. . . . Architecture deals as much with the future as with the past, and is therefore expected to achieve a relative permanence.

Elaborating on this term, Koeditz relies on classic examples from architecture. Vitruvius (first century BCE), for example, had a clear idea of what constitutes lasting, or timeless, architecture: *firmitas* (strength), *utilitas* (utility), and *venustas* (beauty). This is one of his best-known principles and is a good summary of his theory, but timelessness in architecture is not something which can be designed based on rules—it is a mindset.

Although Koeditz's dissertation does not deal directly with sacred groves, the idea of timelessness is highly relevant for our discussion. Thus, when a group of pilgrims enters the Garden of Gethsemane, the ancient olive trees and other elements such as stone walls and traditional terraces evoke timelessness.

Lily Zeng is a social scientist at Yale's School of Forestry and Environmental Studies. Her research combines cultural anthropology and ecology and examines the dynamic relationship between indigenous communities and their sacred forests. Her work also emphasizes timelessness. She observes four narratives of nature and culture based on ideas of timelessness: (1) sacred groves are remnants of pristine forests; (2) nature is made sacred through the absence of human activity; (3) sacred groves are a-historical; and (4) sacred groves are removed from modernity (Zeng 2018).

The spatial perspective is represented here by the works of Belden Lane. Lane is an American professor Emeritus of theological studies. In the context of sacred groves, he is best known for his writing on the four axioms for the study of sacred places. Possibly influenced by Pearce Lewis' *Axioms for Reading the Landscape* (Lewis 1979), Lane's second axiom asserts that "sacred place is ordinary place, ritually made extraordinary" (2001:19). In other words, sacred groves do not necessarily look more divine.

Histories in a Nutshell

At this stage it is worthwhile to elaborate somewhat on the structure of this chapter. The first two sections ("Introduction: From the Sacred Grove to the Garden of Eden" and "Theorizing Christian Sacred Groves") are relatively abstract. The next four sections are more concrete and tangible and elaborate on three case studies. This section is historical, and it aims to unfold three Christian sacred groves in the Holy Land—"the Mount of Beatitudes by the Sea of Galilee," "the Garden of Gethsemane," and "the Garden Tomb"—the latter two in East Jerusalem.

The Mount of Beatitudes

The Mount of Beatitudes, located near the northwestern shores of the Sea of Galilee, is the traditional site of Jesus' delivery of the Sermon on the Mount to the multitudes (Matthew 5). The site has a relatively small church, surrounded by very large gardens. The contemporary church was built over archeological remains of an earlier Byzantine church, and was designed and built by Antonio Barluzzi, a famous Italian church architect, between the years 1937 and 1938 (Halevi 2009: 58). The owners of the site were, and still are, an organization called ANSMI (Associazione nazionale per socorrere i missionari cattolici iItaliani) (Halevi 2012: 77). According to Halevi, the plan for vegetation around the church emphasized the harmonic integration between Italian and local flora (Halevi 2009: 166; Halevi 2012: 100).

The vast amount of land around the church was designated to be part of an Italian colony (Halevi 2009: 166), which never materialized. The availability of this land enabled the subsequent construction of beautiful gardens that function nowadays as a sacred grove.

Garden of Gethsemane

The name, meaning "olive press" in Aramaic, refers to the olive-oil industry located on the slopes of the Mount of Olives. Here, at the edge of the Kidron Valley, Jesus meditated and prayed with his disciples the night before his arrest (Mt. 26:36-46; Mk 14:32-42). This is where he was betrayed by Judas, and then taken captive (Mt. 26:47-56; Mk 14:43-52). Adjoining the garden's remaining eight ancient olive trees are three churches: the Church of the Agony, the Church of Mary Magdalene, and the Grotto of Gethsemane. Our discussion here is limited to the Church of the Agony (also known as the Church of All Nations), designed and built by Barluzzi (Davidson and Gitlitz 2002), and completed in 1924.

The Garden Tomb

The Garden Tomb is an alternative to the Church of the Holy Sepulchre, marking the actual site of Jesus' burial. Located near the Old City of Jerusalem, it serves the non-Catholic and non-Orthodox denominations (i.e., Protestant, Anglican, and Latter-day Saint [LDS][3]) as a sacred grove without a church. The place was discovered in 1867 and is operated by the London-based Garden Tomb Association.

A brief comparison between the three sacred groves brings to light the following points:

- Two of the sites (Mount of Beatitudes and Gethsemane) have important churches that were designed by Antonio Barrluzzi, the famous Franciscan church architect.
- The third site (the Garden Tomb) emphasizes its "churchlessness."
- All three sites have significant archeological remains.
- When times are "normal," that is, prior to the Corona pandemic, all are heavily challenged by over-tourism.
- Although less relevant for this volume, the historical information concerning the three sites is impressive, and includes a master's thesis on the Garden of Gethsemane (Bitton 2012), a PhD dissertation on the Barluzzi-designed churches in the Holy Land (Halevi 2009), which include very detailed chapters on the Mount of Beatitudes and on the Garden of Gethsemane, and a PhD dissertation on the Garden Tomb (Bitton 2016).

Authenticity

We are shifting now from history to the present day. In cultural geography this shift can be regarded as a distinction between writing the landscape (or producing it) and reading the landscape (performing it). The next three sections will elaborate on issues of authenticity and pilgrimage.

"Authenticity" is a very important and widely used term when it comes to the context of sacred space and pilgrimage studies. In my book (with Dallen

Timothy) on contemporary Christian travel (Ron and Timothy 2019) the words "authenticity" and "authentic" appear eighty-one times, as part of terms such as "environmental authenticity," "spiritual authenticity," "cultural authenticity," "religious authenticity," and more. Lior Chen's work is another indication of the importance of this subject. According to him,

> In general, there are three approaches to the study of the "authenticity of a place." The first two, the "objective" and "constructed" approaches, focus on an object, whereas the third, the "existential" approach, focuses on the subject.... This threefold typology illustrates the lack of standardization in the use of the term "authentic." (Chen 2019:25)

This section will discuss the relevance and importance of two additional types of authenticities: "locational authenticity" and "visual authenticity"—both (to the best of my knowledge) not mentioned before in the context of tourism and pilgrimage.

"Locational authenticity" refers to the question of whether the event that the site commemorates actually took place at the said location. For example, the New Testament locates Jesus' birth in Bethlehem, and this is the basis for popular belief throughout the world. However, most biblical scholars place it in Nazareth. The site of the Tomb of the Virgin Mary is even a better example. Some identify her burial site at Gethsemane, while others identify her tomb in Ephesus, Turkey (Davidson and Gitlitz 2002: 170). Recent papal visits to Turkey and to the Holy Land confirm the status of Ephesus as the correct location (Davidson and Gitlitz 2002: 170), but much of the scholarship suggests that Gethsemane is more likely to be the authentic location (e.g., Rubin 2009: 56).

The term "visual authenticity" refers to the question of how the place looks like nowadays in comparison to how the place looked like then. In most cases, Protestants will prefer visual authenticity, whereas Orthodox and Catholics appreciate locational authenticity.

Trying to fit the three sacred groves discussed into this terminology suggests that the Church of the Beatitudes has a strong locational authenticity based on the biblical description[4] and the Byzantine archeological remains under the church; the surrounding gardens do not look like the natural mountain side at the time, but since the whole area is rural and agricultural, it feels authentic to visitors. Consequently, Stephanie Stidham Rogers perceives them as "real" (see Figure 10.1):

> In the same way, Protestants gather on the grassy banks of the Mount of Beatitudes. Most often they do not go inside the shrine—but rather are content to sit on the

Figure 10.1 A group of American pilgrims at the Mount of Beatitudes. This group I guided preferred to gather outside the sacred grove, as per Stidham Rogers quoted earlier. The Church of the Beatitudes is in the background among the trees. Photograph by the author, March 2012.

grassy slope under the sky and read from the New Testament. Seeing too much of the contemporary religious scene in Palestine is an obstacle to getting back to the "real" Holy Land of the Bible that they seek. (Stidham Rogers 2011: 26)

The Garden Tomb has very strong visual authenticity. The ancient tomb with the rolling stone and other archeological elements contribute greatly to the biblical appearance; however, the common archeological view is that the site of the Church of the Holy Sepulchre is at the correct location (Barkay 1986). This led Rev. Bill White, the secretary of the Garden Tomb Association in the 1980s, to claim that "it may not be the correct location, but it's a marvelous visual aid" (several personal communications during the 1980s). This view is somewhat simplified: If the Garden Tomb has only visual authenticity, why not go to Orlando to the Holy Land Experience? (See Figure 10.2.)

Analyzing the sacred grove at Gethsemane from the perspective of authenticity is important. According to Halevi (2012), the contemporary garden and church were designed by an Italian team, including Barluzzi himself. At roughly the same time, the British took over Palestine from the Ottoman Turks (1917?). The Catholic

The Garden of Eden in an Era of Over-Tourism 211

Figure 10.2 The tomb of Jesus at the Garden Tomb. Photograph by the author, March 2012.

approach to the holy sites was not well considered by the new regime, including the first governor of Jerusalem, Sir Roland Storrs. Storrs' view of authenticity was typical of the Church of England and praised the natural look (see Figure 10.3):

> Of all the places hallowed by the Passion of Christ none is more beautiful, few so authentic, as the Garden of Gethsemane. Times unnumbered have I wandered there, . . . in the ancient olive grove under the moon and stars. The upper part of that Garden belongs to the Russian Orthodox Church, . . . the lower half is the property of the Franciscans. They discovered in an evil hour traces of the foundations of a Basilica, said to date from Justinian. The Custos, while disposed to agree in private conversation . . . that Terra Santa was over-doctored, over priested (especially by other denominations) and over-policed, somehow could not perceive that it was also somewhat heavily over-churched. His ambition and his application was to complete (in other words to build anew) the Basilica of Justinian, . . . over this last, still far the wrong side of the Turkish lines, I felt but a limited competence. The thrice holy site of Gethsemane I longed to save, so temporized and discouraged. . . . My prayer that it should be allowed to remain as it was in the time of Christ was a final proof of the narrowness of my outlook. Military Commands are not resigned in war-time, and even if they were, I had no particular reason to suppose that my successor would prove more zealous for Jerusalem or less amenable than myself. (Storrs 1937:315–16)

Figure 10.3 The Garden of Gethsemane. In the background we see some of the ancient olive trees, surrounded by pilgrims, during the picking season. In the foreground we can see a much younger tree, planted by Pope Paul VI, on January 4, 1964. Photograph by the author, October 2012.

To conclude, we can say that the three sacred groves discussed here are authentic in more than one way. The Mount of Beatitudes has strong locational authenticity and some visual authenticity. The Garden Tomb has very strong visual authenticity despite the possibly wrong location—its proximity to the Old City and to the Church of the Holy Sepulchre compensates for the inaccuracy, and therefore Orlando is not really an option. The Garden of Gethsemane has an exceptional degree of authenticity, since both the locational and visual authenticities are very much present.

Pilgrims and Pilgrimages to the Sacred Groves

My last visit to the sacred groves was in October 2019, while guiding an American pilgrimage group. The tourist season then was at its best (i.e., the most crowded), and no one suspected the upcoming Coronavirus pandemic. These days, the sacred groves are relatively empty, which also indicates that most visitors are incoming tourists rather than locals.

In the following section, I will elaborate on aspects of the management of the sites, and describe what goes on in the minds and hearts of some of the pilgrims visiting these sacred groves.

Crowd Management and Spirituality

When tourism is at its height, the sacred groves, like other sacred sites in the Holy Land, get very crowded, to the extent that they easily meet the criteria of over-tourism, which is defined by Fontanari and Berger-Risthaus, as "the phenomenon of a popular destination or sight becoming overrun with tourists in an unsustainable way" (2020: 44). Some people find the idea of being at a sacred site with great multitudes stimulating (e.g., Malcolm X. in Mecca in 1964: Malcolm 2001: 213); for many, however, over-tourism poses a great threat to the spiritual atmosphere that they seek. Yet, the groves must be managed one way or another in order to provide the conditions for spirituality.

At the Garden of Gethsemane, the site is divided into two parts. The southern part—the main part—includes the Barluzzi church and a garden with the ancient olive trees. The pedestrian pathway in the garden is arranged as a one-way path to ensure a constant flow. The northern part of the garden is enclosed, has basic seating arrangements, and groups can reserve (for a fee) a time slot for prayers, taking communion, and so on. The proximity to the main road is a constant source of noise, which adds to the tension between earthly and heavenly Jerusalem.

At the Garden Tomb the spatial arrangement is interesting: apart from the vegetation, there are important archeological remains, including the sepulchre and a huge water cistern, as well as fourteen different "classrooms" (see Figure 10.4), which vary in size and protection from the weather. Clearly, the Garden Tomb caters very well to the organized mass tourist (Cohen 1972), or even more to the organized mass Christian pilgrim. Their way of coping with over-tourism is to expand their capacity by increasing the available time slots, having longer days, and accepting visitors seven days a week. Moreover, the visit must be booked in advance, and time allocations are regulated by guiding by the site's own guides, who are often volunteers (Ron and Timothy 2019, chapter 5).

The Audible and the Visible

"And seeing the multitudes, he went up into a mountain: and when he was set, his disciples came unto him" (Mt. 5:1) (see Figure 10.5).

	THE GARDEN TOMB	
Date: Time:		Number of People
Communion requirements		
Location	Centre Platform	
	A	
	B	
	C	
	D	
	E	
	Cistern	
	Dell	
	Pines	
	Nook	
	Deck	
	Chapelside	
	Small Chapel	
	Large Chapel	
Guide: Tour Company:		

Figure 10.4 Communion request form, indicating fourteen individual spots for the use of groups, at the Garden Tomb. Photograph by the author, December 2011.

Figure 10.5 The bus parking lot at the Mount of Beatitudes. Photograph by the author, October 15, 2012.

The multitudes Matthew referred to, who came to hear Jesus two millennia ago, were most likely Galilean Jews; the multitudes that come nowadays to hear the Sermon on the Mount are, for the most part, Christians from other countries and nations. One would expect the site to be very crowded when there are so many busloads with visitors, but the following photograph, taken a few

Figure 10.6 The Mount of Beatitudes. The pilgrims are in the garden, but barely visible. Photograph by the author, October 15, 2012.

minutes earlier, gives the false impression that the garden is empty. The garden is very large and located on the slopes of a mountainous area overlooking the Sea of Galilee. The entire area is rural, agricultural, and very peaceful. The garden has several "outdoor classrooms" for reading scriptures, praying, and so on. Some are small, others are large, and reservations are essential (see Figure 10.6).

Apparently, all three sacred groves use the same method—the outdoor classroom; the Mount of Beatitudes, however, differs for at least three reasons: size, acoustic qualities, and textual uniformity.

(a) *Size*: The size of the site is approximately 8 acres,[5] which makes it much larger than Gethsemane and the Garden Tomb.
(b) *Acoustic qualities*: Numerous biblical students and scholars have noticed that the acoustics around the Mount of Beatitudes are very good—one can literally hear almost everything that is said. Here is an example of such a description, provided by Swisher:

> The hillside is situated in an agricultural valley which overlooks the Sea of Galilee, and it serves as a natural amphitheater with incredible acoustics. (Swisher 2017: 127–8)

(c) *Textual uniformity*: Despite the lack of research in this field, my own forty years' experience suggests that most organized groups read the Sermon on the Mount, and few read anything else during the visit. The result is a high textual uniformity, although the readings take place in several languages. The high textual uniformity, together with high linguistics diversity, makes this site particularly spiritually powerful.

Inside Their Hearts: Collecting Data in and on the Sacred Groves

Most pilgrims do not come for the purpose of visiting the three sacred groves; they come to the Holy Land. A typical ten-day Holy Land itinerary includes fifty to seventy sites, most of which are considered meaningful, spiritual, and sacred. Consequently, there is a need for visitors to relate to and process their experiences. The following list shows the two ways and procedures that have developed over the years:

- Writing a personal diary, or journal.
- Attending praise meetings in the hotel, after dinner.

These praise meetings (also known as evening meetings) are very important to the participants. In general, in group pilgrimages the sightseeing part takes place from breakfast till dinner. This is the main time frame, in which the travel itinerary is followed carefully. In addition, there are also the "in-between times," which are described by Jackie Feldman as

> in lunch cafeterias or in tourist shops—when the guide's choices are open to disagreement and even dispute. Times during which he or she is silent—like at prayer services. And, of course, evening meetings, back-of-the-bus conversations, and group reunions. (Feldman 2016: 61)

Despite their importance, the evening meetings are seldom mentioned in travel itineraries. For the purposes of writing this chapter I scanned through fifty itineraries of groups and unsurprisingly, only two itineraries mentioned "a lecture in the evening" (Ron 2007) or "This evening, we will have a lecture on the Savior in this area [The Sea of Galilee]" (Ron 2001).

Although the evening meetings are not mentioned in writing, they are frequently talked about among participants—the meetings often start on the intellectual side, but then rather quickly drift into something very emotional, tearful, and spiritually moving. Such occurrences are very common, yet almost totally unresearched in academia.

So, how does one learn about what is in their hearts? The path is not clear, but I can suggest three possible ways:

Yael Guter's Ranking of Significance

For her PhD dissertation, Guter circulated 134 questionnaires to pilgrims of various denominational backgrounds, concerning the subjective significance of the various sites visited, and the sacred groves were ranked very high. More specifically, for the Catholics, the order of significance was Gethsemane first, followed by the Mount of Beatitudes;[6] for the Protestants, Gethsemane first, the Garden Tomb second, and the Mount of Beatitudes third; for the evangelicals, the Garden Tomb first, Gethsemane second, and the Mount of Beatitudes third; for the Latter-day Saint, the Garden Tomb first, Gethsemane second, and the Mount of Beatitudes third; and for Christian Zionists, the Mount of Beatitudes first, Gethsemane second, followed by the Garden Tomb (Guter 2004: 92–6).

Informal Attendance of Guides

The tour guides are not expected to attend these meetings because they fall in their free time, but when they do—they might observe these emotional moments, but unless they need these occurrences for an academic degree there is no reason for collecting this data.

Reading about the Sacred Groves in Travel Literature, Travel Accounts of Religious Leaders, and so on

To illustrate the potential of this method, I chose two such sources: a well-known Franciscan guidebook written by Eugene Hoade, an Irish priest who served as the Custodian of Gethsemane Basilica, and the writings of Harold B. Lee, the eleventh president of the Mormon Church.

Father Hoade describes the significance of the Mount of Beatitudes as follows:

> So, while our boat glides by swiftly and gently on the shining waves, before our eyes develop, as if on a magic film, the different places on the western shore rendered forever renowned by the Gospel story. Here are the ruins of Magdala; the smiling plain of Genezareth; Bethsaida, birth place of three of the Apostles;

higher up the Mount of Beatitudes; there on the shore he sat in a boat and told them the parable of the sower of the cockle, of the growing seed, of the mustard seed, of the leaven: "I will open my mouth in parables. I will utter things hidden from the foundation of the world." (Hoade 1962: 722)

He is deeply involved with Gethsemane, probably since he served as the Custodian of Gethsemane Basilica. Here are his words:

> The Garden of Gethsemane. We enter with deep respect the enclosure of the Garden of Gethsemane, where Jesus, on that last night, spent perhaps the most sorrowful hour of all his sorrowful passion, the hour in which as a man he chose to suffer the awful pangs of human nature which trembles before martyrdom and is affrighted at the sight of death; the hour in which he chose to struggle, to conquer and to teach his disciples the art of Christian struggle and the divine secret of Victory. "Father, not my will but thy will be done." (Hoade 1962: 261)

Here are some of President Lee's impressions, after his visit to the Garden Tomb:

> My wife and I were in the Holy Land. We have spent some glorious days visiting those places. . . . But a strange thing happened after we had gone to the garden tomb, and there we felt it was definitely the place. It was in the hill, it was a garden, and here was a tomb. . . . But the strange thing was that when we moved it seemed as though we had seen all this before. We had seen it before somewhere. (Galbraith et al. 1996: 506)

In other words, we scholars still need to find ways to their hearts. In my opinion a promising path for a future project would be to recruit students in tour guide courses who will most certainly have the professional motivation to participate.

Concluding Thoughts

This research can be regarded as an introduction to the topic of sacred groves in general, and biblical sacred groves in particular. More specifically, it is a case study highlighting three sites in Israel/Palestine: the Mount of Beatitudes by the Sea of Galilee, and Gethsemane and the Garden Tomb—both in East Jerusalem.

The uniqueness of this research lies in its in-betweenness, or multi-disciplinarity. This research aims to bridge between several academic fields and disciplines: anthropology of religion, cultural geography, comparative religion, landscape architecture, and tourism studies.

Due to its multi-disciplinary nature, it might seem incomplete, and readers might wish that certain aspects could and should have been expanded upon—more ethnography, more about the universal significance of these groves, about special visitors such as the last four popes, other religious leaders, and so on. So, certainly, there is a need to elaborate and expand.

As an end note, I would like to illuminate on the theoretical terminology that was introduced earlier in this chapter. From Conan (1999; 2007) and Hunt (2000; 2004), we learned about the importance of rituals; Barrie (2010; 2012) and Zeng (2018) elaborated on timelessness in sacred architecture, and Lane introduced his second axiom asserting that *sacred place is ordinary place, ritually made extraordinary* (2001: 19). In other words, sacred groves do not look more divine. For example, a sacred olive grove, such as Gethsemane, can look just like the adjacent olive groves that are on the Mount of Olives, or almost anywhere in the Mediterranean. The sacred groves are what they are because they have been sanctified by people. The botanical contribution of these groves can be interesting and significant, but undoubtedly the cultural and spiritual contributions are the pivot of their existence for so many believers. The power of traditions, the understandings of nature, and the prayers and rites performed on the sites is what make them what they are.

Afterword

The Work That Landscape Does
On Placing and Displacing in Christianity
Simon Coleman

In reflecting on the rich contributions that this volume makes to the study of Christian landscape, I want to begin with a little-known image, produced by a largely forgotten artist. Thomas Seddon (1821–56) was born in London, the son of a cabinet-maker, and became a friend of the celebrated Pre-Raphaelite artist William Holman Hunt (1827–1919). The two men were devout, if unconventional, Christians, and in 1854 they set off to produce paintings of the Holy Land. Hunt was rather dismissive of his companion's talents, referring to him as "an amateur friend of our circle" (Hunt 1905: 362; see also Coleman 2002). Nonetheless, the trip did produce at least one notable work by Seddon, his *Jerusalem and the Valley of Jehoshaphat from the Hill of Evil Counsel*, which was first exhibited in London in 1855.

Seddon's portrayal of biblical landscape was the result of painstaking and pious labor. He had ventured out of the holy city, leaving Hunt behind and pitching his tent at a vantage point from which he could gain an uninterrupted view of sites associated with the Garden of Gethsemane and the Mount of Olives. Yet, at first glance, the scene he created seems rather somnolent, even static. Very little is happening. We look down into the valley, with the distant walls of Jerusalem occupying the top left of the picture, glowing red in the blazing sun. In the foreground, a shepherd slumbers under the shade of a tree while sheep and goats graze on a nearby slope.

Why should we give this peaceful prospect a second glance? It is worth noting that no less a figure than John Ruskin reputedly called Seddon's views of Egypt and Palestine "the first landscapes uniting perfect artistical skill with topographical accuracy . . . giving to persons who cannot travel trustworthy knowledge of the scenes which ought to be most interesting to them."[1] As

Ruskin appreciated, the aim was to depict a landscape without ambiguity or distortion, to create an image that was literally and metaphorically *faithful*. To be sure, no dramatic event was taking place in the scene, but for the biblically informed viewer the work was replete with narrative nonetheless, pointing to both scriptural past and prophetic future: not only a reminder of Jesus' anguish in the Garden before the events of the Crucifixion but also an anticipation of the end of the world, given the association of the Valley of Jehoshaphat with the Last Judgment. The very "emptiness" of the landscape provided by Seddon thus served two key purposes: it removed unnecessary distractions from the Protestant imagination (Hummel and Hummel 1995) and it invited the believing viewer imaginatively to step into the frame, to gain more intimate access to the Holy Land known previously only through scripture and sermon. Indeed, Seddon believed that he was treading "the same soil which our Lord trod," while assuming that his duty was to convey to others a direct experience of such soil without "misrepresentation" (1854: 85).

In suggesting how we might gaze at Seddon's landscape through his own Orientalist, Victorian, Christian, Pre-Raphaelite lenses, I also wish to argue that his work alerts us to many of the broader themes that we encounter in this volume: landscape as simultaneously encountered and represented; the many and complex linkages between land and narrative; the intertwining of temporal with spatial dimensions in human experiences of place; and—above all—landscape as neither inert nor merely given, but always an ongoing result of, and catalyst for, human action. James Bielo tells us in his contribution that landscape is no blank canvas: rather, it is a material resource that directs our attentions in dynamic ways, mobilizing "to tell the stories people want to tell." In these terms, Seddon's painting purported to give viewers an accurate and uninterrupted vision of the Holy Land and the Bible, yet mediated such vision in multiple ways. The specific affordances of paint, wood, and canvas permitted him to frame and focus attention on a landscape that he could transport from the Holy Land to London; and the careful detail, the topographical accuracy, served to remind viewers of the urgent truth of the text underlying his vision. I am also reminded here of Eric Hirsch's (1995: 1) observation that landscape entails establishing chronic relationships between the foreground and background of social and cultural life, with the former emphasizing the realities of the present and the latter often pointing to more distant, aspirational, even ultimate, goals. The power of Seddon's landscape is that it has the capacity to keep these perspectives in permanent dialog. He shows us the shepherd and the sheep in the front of his canvas, but behind—on the hill above and the valley below—we are invited to contemplate the storied landscape of the living Bible, rendered as tangibly as any Protestant sensibility might permit.

Much of the early development of the so-called anthropology of Christianity was founded on a new appreciation of Christianity—especially in its Pentecostal and charismatic guises—as an inherently globalizing form, capable of adopting cartographic perspectives and traversing territories with seeming ease (Dempster, Klaus, and Petersen 1999; Coleman 2010). A focus on landscape forces us to keep our eyes not only on the bird's eye view but also on the social, spiritual, and material grounding of religious life; to appreciate multi-scalar interactions between human and divine agency, immanence and transcendence. What this volume's numerous depictions of Christianity share with such characterizations of Pentecostalism is a sense of the Christian capacity to transform and translate place. Christianized landscapes often embody dwelling and stability and yet awareness of the likelihood of spiritually motivated change—or the possibility of looking toward divine "elsewheres" (compare King, this volume)—is usually also present. Such landscapes easily become restless, and are inherently liable to be *dis*placed—to be developed, domesticated, diffused, and so on—as background challenges foreground, and as spiritual aspiration entangles with fallen reality. Yet, if Christianity works on and through landscapes, so landscapes work on and through Christians, helping to form and reform religious subjects—such as Seddon himself, practicing an austere piety through laboring to paint a harsh landscape within which he also immersed himself. In the space that I have, I shall explore this theme of placing and displacing in Christianity through four modes that I see operating in this volume (of course there are more): mediation, domestication, appropriation, and temporalization.

Mediation

Christianity mediates between realms—between the immanent and the imminent, the everyday and the transcendent, whether or not the specific practices enabling such mediation are valued or acknowledged. Seddon, after all, claimed that his artfully and painstakingly produced work could somehow provide undistorted access to biblical settings and truths: a form of mediation through its denial. Ultimately, his aim was to propel us toward the Lord and not only the Land, and the specific dimension of mediation I want to emphasize initially involves the interactions and tensions that we see occurring between "person" and "place" in the establishment of Christian experience and authority (see also Eade and Sallnow 1991). My point is exemplified by Michael Giovine's chapter, which provides a wide-ranging analysis of the Catholic landscape gathered around and diffusing from the figure of Padre Pio, as centripetal and centrifugal tendencies become mutually entangled around a man becoming an icon. Pio is "of" Pietrelcina and much of his holy presence derives from his rootedness in his place of birth. Indeed, Di Giovine suggests that Pio is made for and by the people, so that his saintly reputation emerges from the "ground up." Nonetheless, Pio's influence also diffuses beyond any single place, not only because of his miraculous powers of bilocation but also—more prosaically—because of the ways in which a "Pio-centic hagiography" is transported by his followers across the globe, ultimately helping to form a system of what Di Giovine (following Tambiah 1977) calls "galactic shrines." Pio's translated presence in relic, narrative, and image both invokes and transcends his territorial origins as his saintly career takes off, establishing him as a considerable force within a worldwide, contemporary Catholic landscape of devotion and liturgical labor.

The spiritual terrain created by, through, and around Pio might seem utterly remote in ideological and geographical terms from the evangelical landscapes described by Rebekka King, though many of the believers she describes are as cut off from wider forms of cultural and social capital as are inhabitants of remote Italian villages. King's interlocutors are situated in the American South but are attempting to negotiate their relationships with various forms of "elsewhere," ranging from Jewish Covenantal theology and Native American land rights to the recent influxes of Muslim immigrants. In this context, the extraordinary figure who resonates with the congregants of Shield of Faith is not an ascetic monk but a mobile hybrid. As a prosperous Messianic rabbi who claims to have been made an honorary chief of the Blackfoot Nation, Larry Mallet offers access to otherwise inaccessible identities and prerogatives. He articulates and negotiates a very different regime of distance and proximity to that provided by Pio. Yet, in both cases spiritual capital not only emerges out of offering that which is exotic to and transcends everyday existence but also works through the complex medium of landscape, where regional belonging and biblical legitimation become reconciled. Both Pio and Mallett represent forms of spiritual entrepreneurship, expressed through Catholic and evangelical idioms respectively. Both have come to embody certain principles of mobility. However, neither has been able to operate in a spatial vacuum. Charismatic person is never fully separated from place.

The theme of mediation is extended by James Bielo's discussion of *trans-mediation*, where the reconstruction of biblical landscape not only provides the latter with three-dimensional qualities that may promote powerful religious experience but also relocates it in strategic spots within American space and public culture. Thus the Garden of Hope just outside Cincinnati is a translation of scriptural space into contemporary form, and like Seddon its makers claim authenticity through enacting particular, marked forms of exactitude: the centerpiece of the site is a 1:1 scale replica of Jerusalem's Garden Tomb, for instance. Bielo's case studies point to the further ways in which Israel/Palestine is multiply instanciated in this volume, as it acts not only or even primarily as stable point of orientation but also as catalyst for numerous reframings and remodelings of place.

Domestication

Pio—like many powerful spiritual figures—has become a significant yet ambiguous presence within the global Catholic Church. His mediation of miraculous saintly powers presents a potential challenge to the still more extensive galactic landscape centered around Rome. Thus it seems to me that in 2018, when Pope Francis visited sites associated with Pio's life, he was not only marking out significant shrines through what Di Giovine calls "a precision-oriented visit" but also working to incorporate and domesticate the saint's charisma within his own. Francis confirmed the continued salience of Pio's spiritual traces by traveling through a carefully constructed landscape of commemoration; but as the potency of the saint was being indexed and acknowledged, it was also being partially encompassed by the chief representative of centralized Catholic authority.

A useful comparison can be made here with another pilgrimage tradition that is discussed in this volume. John Eade's chapter ingeniously follows the numerous manifestations of water in the emergence and development of Lourdes. He draws our attention not only to unruly mountain streams but also to a river that becomes increasingly confined and redirected, tensions between secular spa and sacred source, ambiguities of ordinary and healing water, hidden pipes and a visible spring, even the potential for climate change to permit wild water to take a destructive revenge on the site. Eade is keen to emphasize the sensual materialities of pilgrimage experience, and water seems to seep through every paragraph of his paper, confirming its existence as a risky but powerful substance, not unlike the spiritual seductions of a Padre Pio or a Larry Mallett. As we have long known, sustainable religious institutions often depend on negotiating a balance between charismatic and institutionalized forms of authority, and it seems that Lourdes—well established but always vulnerable to the vagaries of religious trends—works hard to maintain "the shape of water" (with apologies to Guillermo del Toro[2]), to keep its charisma on tap through elaborate physical infrastructures that not only permit but also regulate the intimate, embodied encounters between bathers and *brancardiers*.[3]

Also striking about contemporary Lourdes, however, is its attitude toward the original mediating human figure who was crucial to the foundation of the site. Bernadette Soubirous—the young woman who had the original Marian vision—was eventually moved from the town after staying eight years in a local hospice, thus effectively being shunted into the ecclesiastical and topographical background. In her case, rather more than that of Pio, carefully orchestrated place came to predominate over idiosyncratic person. I therefore find it usefully provocative to juxtapose her fate—and the silencing of her voice—with the two female figures described by Sara Patterson in her discussion of Mormon captivity narratives. Bernadette was also confined and redefined by authoritative male figures, but in the case of Ann Eliza Young and Elizabeth Smart the female captives proved much less amenable to being domesticated and moved into a silent background.

If comparing Pio with Mallett allows us to juxtapose "old" Europe with the New World, so we can perform the same move in placing Lourdes alongside Utah. The church that Bernadette helped revive perceived itself to be in trouble, challenged by French secularism and European urbanism, and thus attempted to draw on the spiritual energies provided by a young, largely mute girl situated in a rural landscape. Mormonism, by contrast, was an upstart and controversial religion on the rise in the untamed American West of the nineteenth century, with its transgressive polygamous practices expressive of unregulated practices that were still possible to conduct in the territory of Utah. An important trajectory in Patterson's analysis is the transition of Mormonism over the past century or so from scary Other to accepted, if still minority, faith. It is in the context of this institutional transformation that we should acknowledge the disturbing (on many levels) accounts of the perhaps appropriately named Young and Smart, as they insist on rearticulating their own experiences and identity in the face of not only the sexual violence of individual men but also the structural violence involved in institutionalized attempts to redirect or mute their voices. As Patterson points out, Elizabeth Smart's position is especially interesting in this regard, as she attempts to tell her story while remaining within the confines of Mormon morality and narrative. She must allow herself to be partially domesticated even as she searches for a means of expression. It turns out that an effective way for her to do so is to speak through the medium of landscape, as she contrasts comforting and orienting images of home with the impropriety of both unfettered sexuality and dangerous, disorderly nature.

Appropriation

The Mormonism that Patterson describes plays out over a century when the American West is rendered relatively civilized if still occasionally dangerous, and as the frontier of European settlers pushes against the remnants of Native American ways of life. In this sense Mormonism both resists and contributes to a mainstream Christianizing of the continent—and one that, in Rebekka King's account, hosts new and threatening non-Christian religionists in the present day. The familiar colonial trope of the twin appropriation by Christianity of local landscape and local faith is given productive twists by Jonathan Miles-Watson's and Sitna Quiroz's juxtaposition of West African Pentecostals with the communities that inhabit Christchurch Cathedral in the Indian Himalayas. Both case studies involve the Christian animation of postcolonial landscapes through movement, though the trajectories of such movement seem rather different: while the pastors drive from their homes in southeastern Benin to a large Pentecostal campus situated to the side of an expressway in southwestern Nigeria, the majority of those who enter Christchurch Cathedral engage with a self-consciously historic space that attests to the virtues of dwelling over the long term. Although I have not yet been to Christchurch, I can attest from personal experience to the power of Canaanland, and its formation of an exurban oasis outside the more chaotic streets of Lagos. In fact, it is one of a number of such camps built outside the city, many of them broadly Pentecostal but some Muslim, which claim to exemplify the positive characteristics of an alliance between religion and modernity in the reconstruction of both urban space and individual lives. In the language I have been using in this chapter, we might therefore see many of such spaces as placing theological aspiration in the foreground, with prosperity theology suggesting the possibility of linking secular and sacred worlds in ways that do not require the sacrifice of one to benefit the other.

The initial point I want to make about appropriation applies to both Christchurch and Canaanland. One looks hyper-traditional and the other hyper-modern, yet both gain power from their spectacular contrast with the surrounding terrain. The Cathedral extends vertically in a style familiar to

European landscapes of faith, while the camp expands horizontally across a considerable tract of land. In practice, both represent ambiguous and materially mediated forms of reconciliation with colonial heritage. Christianity, the religion brought from Europe, is not rejected but reappropriated through the adoption of two rather differently "awesome" architectures of privilege and prestige: the long-established cultural capital of the Cathedral and the prosperous camp that is a place not only of prayer but also of determined study and strategic commerce.

Some of the spiritual camps situated around Lagos are said to have been built on "pagan" land, so that the modernism of the architecture also signifies the partial eradication of the dangerous spiritual powers of the bush, even though camp-dwellers and -visitors must always remain on guard against the infiltration of evil forces. While these modernist Christian spaces therefore gain some of their power from maintaining the constant possibility of the resurfacing of non-Christian features of the landscape, they do not approach the subtleties of appropriation that we see in Brett Hendrickson's analysis of the Santuario de Chimayó in New Mexico. The dynamism of the latter site emerges through the continuous interplay between indigenous origins and Christian superimposition. The palimpsest-like quality of pilgrimage sites is well known (e.g., Smith 1987; Lousteau and DeConinck 2019), but here I emphasize the way it reinforces my earlier point about the particular affordance of landscape as a religious medium: its ability to retain and even display multiple orientations at once—not only the foreground and the background but also the power of the present to strategically disinter and reveal the powers of the past. It seems telling that at the center of the sanctuary at Chimayó there lies a hole full of soil—an invitation to delve into what lies below the surface to unearth and appropriate connections with worlds whose contemporary salience is not denied, but reframed. The differences from the West African or Indian examples of both moving on from and reinvoking elements of the colonial past may not after all be so great.

For my final example of appropriation I want to highlight a further variation on the theme of mobility and appropriation. Veronica della Dora's discussion of the Byzantine Holy Mountain at Athos depicts a landscape that is both remote and restricted, with women banned from entry. Such interdictions make the occasional horizontal flows from the sacred landscape all the more significant, as a "mountain" periodically exceeds its normal boundaries. The latter entails a form of controlled appropriation of landscape through liturgically charged movement—much more disciplined in its choreography than the formation of shrines to Pio that diffuse out in all directions into global Catholic space. One way of interpreting Athos' processional culture is to say that it reminds us not only of the power of the sacred to permeate wider worlds, especially in Orthodox contexts, but also of the ways in which the mountain is itself recharged with spiritual power through such mobility and such veneration—much as Pope Francis is reenergized by tracing (over) the footsteps of Pio. As we have seen already, Christian space tends to be restless, and to shift between placement and displacement. The moving of the mountain becomes in this sense a means of retaining spiritual relevance by publicly demonstrating its power to "transfigure villages into churches, hills into holy mountains, and the earth itself into a cosmic temple" (quoting della Dora). By periodically "turning the outside world into a vast church" such processions not only invert but also reanimate the normally restricted landscape of the holy mountain.

Temporalization

Considerations of time have been present in every case I have discussed so far, most notably through the numerous ways in which the Christian landscapes encountered have balanced the past, present, and future in ways that have generally kept them in dynamic dialog. Joseph Webster's piece allows fresh qualities of time to come even more spectacularly to the foreground of our ethnographic and analytical attention, as he considers the operation of "eschatological agency" within a Scottish geography that is itself expressive of rather unrelenting apocalyptic urgency. Unlike the Athos model of periodic forays into a landscape in order to resacralize it, the Christian fisherfolk whom he studies in Gamrie are constantly surrounded by urgent and demanding signs of the (last) times, discerned even in the swirl of the wind or the surge of the sea. In this sense, landscape offers no resting point, no firm and static ground through which to fix identity, as ceaseless spiritual aspiration is permanently placed to the fore—a dimension of engagement with landscape that we also saw, in a different register, among West African Pentecostalist pastors. As Webster points out, inhabiting the Gamrie landscape means not only always being on the lookout for spiritual as well as meteorological storms but also constantly posing awkward questions about one's agency in relation to the world's slide toward the end times. Believers learn to "read" the landscape, and there is always the assumption that behind the surface there lies a deeper significance.

Webster's informants may be located in the north of Scotland but they retain acute awareness of events occurring in political and religious landscapes located far from their own—the chaos of Brexit, the seemingly overweening powers of the European Union, the fate of Israel, and so on. He also hints at the potential significance of another temporality that may increasingly be coming to the fore, in line with a different but perhaps still more threatening temporal development. It seems that elderly Christian informants are becoming cognizant of how for younger villagers Sabbatarianism is a largely dead tradition, incompatible with modern forms of trawling. Avoidance of work on the traditional day of rest is no longer always perceived as a possibility. So further questions may be posed: Does this shifting relation to the seascape and the Sabbath itself point to a wider transformation in religious and working lives? Can the Sabbath be pushed to the background without wider consequences—not only economic and cultural but also spiritual?

It may be fitting that I conclude my reflections on this volume with questions rather than statements, for these echo my central theme: the ways in which Christian landscape so often contains within itself the tensions and the energies required for its own, chronic, replacement and displacement.

Notes

Introduction

1 This volume is a compilation of chapters by thirteen scholars who were raised (academically speaking) by three main academic disciplines: anthropology (Bielo, Coleman, Di Giovine, Eade, Knibbe, Miles-Watson, Quiroz, and Webster), religious studies (Hendrickson, King, and Patterson), and cultural geography (Della Dora and Ron).

Chapter 2

1 Bernadette initially referred to the apparition in local dialect as "Aquero," the Thing, but later told the priest about the self-identification. Carroll interprets the change as providing evidence that the apparition was prompted by an unconscious desire to gratify a parental figure (Carroll 1985: 56).
2 The pioneer filmmakers, the Lumière brothers, significantly chose Lourdes in 1897 as one of their first sites to film. Significantly, they concentrated on the square which had been constructed for the new public rituals such as the afternoon Blessing of the Sick procession, https://www.wdl.org/en/item/356/ (accessed August 5, 2018).
3 For a discussion of the issues raised by American scholars concerning the abuse crisis see, for example, Ronan (2008), Petro (2015), and Orsi (2017).

Chapter 3

1 The terminology of ethnic signification is complicated in New Mexico. Generally, the terms "Hispano" and "Nuevomexicano" are used for people in the state who trace their ancestry to Spanish colonists. The majority of Native Americans in the northern Río Grande valley in the vicinity of Chimayó belong to a variety of Pueblo tribes.
2 For an analysis of the Santuario's art, see Gavin, Mauldin, and Lucero (1990) and Boyd (1974: 69–76).
3 The information is gleaned from the author's fieldwork in 2014 and 2015.

4 This account of the origin of the Santuario is not so much a composite as an overlapping display of almost identical accounts that are likely drawn from the same oral traditions. See especially Borhegyi and Boyd (1982: 32) and González (2013: 11).
5 The following sections on Pueblo and Catholic origins for the holy dirt draw from research I completed for *The Healing Power of the Santuario de Chimayó: America's Miraculous Church* (Hendrickson 2017: 41–55).
6 Quoted in Harrington (1916: 342).
7 See Bunting (1976: 54).
8 See Martin (2001), especially chapter 1.
9 The town in Guatemala is spelled "Esquipulas," without an accent and with stress on the penultimate syllable. The anthropologist Stephan de Borhegyi introduced a misspelling of the word as "Esquípulas," a mistake that has been reproduced many times throughout the scholarly literature. I have elected to correct the error here.
10 Other sources suggest that "Esquipulas" is a Hispanicization of a Maya name, perhaps "Eskip'urha." See, for instance, Sinclair, John. "The Earth—The Faith—The Blessing," pg. 7. John Sinclair Papers, box 10, folder 3, Center for Southwest Research, University of New Mexico, Albuquerque, New Mexico. One author creatively but probably mistakenly posits that "Esquipulas," given the healing related to his cult, is a corruption of "Aesculapius," a Roman god of healing (Carrillo 1999: 54).
11 Borhegyi (1954: 391–5). Borhegyi's conclusions are confirmed in Kay (1987: 30–2).
12 For example, see Howarth and Lamadrid (1999: 19).
13 Wall placards, El Rincón de Don Bernardo Abetya Welcome Center, Chimayó, NM, viewed June 29, 2014. The quoted material on the placard has no attribution.
14 The Catholic Church's analysis, rather surprisingly, echoes that of the historian of religions Mircea Eliade, who endeavored to find shared religious meanings behind the ritual facades appreciated by actual religious practitioners. For a discussion of the axis mundi and this universalizing project, see Eliade (1957: 32–42).
15 This datum appears in microfilmed records of Spanish colonial documents housed at the Archive of the Archdiocese of Santa Fe. Further cataloging details were not available at the time of research.
16 Bernardo Abeyta's letter to Fray Sebastián Álvarez, November 15, 1813. Document 1, Churches in New Mexico Collection, folder 17, New Mexico State Archives, Santa Fe, New Mexico. My translation.
17 Fray Sebastián Álvarez's letter to the Lord Provisor and Capitular Vicar of the Diocese of Durango, November 19, 1813. Document 2, Churches in New Mexico Collection, folder 17, New Mexico State Archives, Santa Fe, New Mexico. My translation.
18 Howarth and Lamadrid (1999: 18) and Kay (1987: 35).
19 Borhegyi (1954: 395) and Gutiérrez (1995: 73–4).

20 "Popular Legends Surround Building of Santuario," (April 1984). A copy of this periodical can be found in the Chimayó Vertical File, Center for Southwest Research, University of New Mexico, Albuquerque, New Mexico. *People of God* is the official newspaper of the Archdiocese of Santa Fe. The article is unsigned but claims to be based on a 1982 brochure published by the Sons of the Holy Family, the order that has administered the Santuario since the 1950s. I have not been able to locate a copy of this brochure.

Chapter 4

1 Mitchell taught that there were eight key texts, which he called the "Seven Diamonds Plus One." Those books included the Bible, the Book of Mormon, the Doctrine and Covenants (all three are LDS scriptures), as well as *The Book of Isaiah* by Avraham Gileadi, *The Final Quest* by Rick Joyner, *Embraced by the Light* by Brett J. Eadie, and *The Golden Seven Plus One* by C. Samuel West. The "Plus One" was a book of Mitchell's own revelations titled "Book of Immanuel David Isaiah." Smart 3; 16; 120.

Chapter 5

1 Most of the rainforests in this area have gradually disappeared due to the introduction of cash crops since the nineteenth century and urbanization.
2 Palm oil became the main cash crop that the French established in this area after the abolition of the slave trade.
3 These military checkpoints are meant to control the illegal traffic of gasoline; however, it is known that they usually profit from bribes.
4 Illegal trade between borders is a phenomenon that dates from the colonial period (see Asiwaju 1976:186). Personal connections between people on both sides of the border, the landscape and weak surveillance of borders present the ideal conditions for illegal trade.
5 In the "word of faith" movement, monetary offerings operate as "spiritual transactions" to incite divine intervention. This form of giving is accompanied by the claiming of things such as health, wealth, or success, through positive affirmations that affect the "spiritual realm" before they can manifest themselves in the material world. During Shiloh, after each service or prayer session, people were encouraged to place their monetary offerings, called "seed offerings" inside paper envelopes provided for this purpose.

6 When he speaks of knowledge, it mainly refers to religious knowledge and the principles of prosperity that he preaches.
7 These two categories are not intended to close the possibility of other, further, systems of Christian sacred space.

Chapter 7

1 Mallet employs the term "First Nations" when discussing Native Americans (a term which has little resonance among conservative Christians in Tennessee but lays claim to a political identity by which Indigenous persons in North America underscore their rights to sovereignty and the land).
2 When discussing Jewish Affinity Christianity, it should be distinguished from both Jews for Jesus and Messianic Judaism. Jews for Jesus is a Christian proselytizing organization that seeks to convert Jews to Christianity without retaining Jewish identity or practices post-conversion. Messianic Judaism is a distinct movement with its own history, practices, and institutional structures. It focuses less on the conversion of Jews to Christianity but rather on the construction of what they called "believing synagogues," which seek to integrate Jewish practices and traditions with a belief in Jesus (whom they refer to as Yeshua) under the assumption that the majority of their congregants have some claim, or perceived claim, to Jewish ancestry. Services at Messianic synagogues combine non-denominational evangelical services with Jewish rituals and traditions. At a typical service, one may witness prayers in Hebrew, Jewish *siddurim* (prayer books), blowing of the *shofar* (ram's horn trumpet), and wearing of *tallitot* (prayer shawls) and *kippot* (skull caps), sometimes alongside spontaneous, charismatic, or spirit-filled tongues, eschatological expectations, and upbeat Christian worship songs. That being said, despite their claims to a genealogical link, most research suggests that these connections to Judaism are not as solidified as the movement's rhetoric suggests (Dulin 2013, 2015; Kaell 2015; Kollontai 2004; Wasserman 2000).
3 I do not intend to indicate that I think that the Prosperity Gospel is a monolithic entity, rather it is a loosely related theological movement or hermeneutical practice that takes many forms (see, for example, Bowler 2013; Cahn 2011; Coleman 2011; Frederick 2013; Haynes 2012). In fact, I should note that both Mallet and Pastor Ronnie are adamant, theirs is not Prosperity Gospel, or, as Ronnie terms it, "the health, wealth, prosperity message."
4 Unfortunately, I did not ask for clarification but my assumption is that Ronnie came to this conclusion based on the man's attire and physical appearance.

5   For this section of the chapter I am indebted to my former research assistants, Stephen Tyler Haggard and Ethan McHugh, who along with conducting ethnographic and media research related to this project served as key informants concerning rural Southern cultural norms and values.

6   The full text of the "Tither's Blessing" prayer is widely available online. It can be found on the downloads page the Church of His Presence's website (https://churchofhispresence.org/downloads). The church's pastor, John Kilpatrick, is a prominent figure in the Prosperity Gospel movement. Kilpatrick became a public figure as the head pastor of the famous Brownstone Revival and outpouring of the Holy Spirit that occurred at the Brownsville Assembly of God in Pensacola, Florida, during the mid-1990s (Poloma 1998).

Chapter 8

1   Source: ctexplored.org/a-pilgrimage-to-waterbury-where-a-lighted-cross-stood-sentinel-over-a-miniature-holy-land/ (accessed January 19, 2018).

2   See: holylandwaterbury.com/ (accessed January 19, 2018).

3   The following is based on a c.1975 guidebook for The Grotto of the Redemption and a 1946 radio interview with P. M. Dobberstein (source: http://www.westbendgrotto.com/history/; accessed February 18, 2019).

4   The following is based on the following data sources: author interview with Randy Hofman (November 7, 2017); a ninety-seven-minute DVD, *Biblical Sand Sculptures*; and three periodical profiles sent to the author by the artist (*Clubhouse* by Focus on the Family, July 2004; *Shore Living Magazine*, December 2006; *Charisma*, December 2008).

5   With the Garden's increased popularity since summer 2016, Steve has recruited several part-time guides to help lead the bus tours. As part of my participant observation work with the attraction, I accepted a request from Steve to serve as a volunteer guide on several occasions. Over the course of three months, I observed nine bus groups that included the Garden in their regional circuit of religious tourism. Groups ranged in size from twenty-five to fifty, and hailed from Protestant churches as distant as Wisconsin, Pennsylvania, Virginia, and Tennessee. With one exception (a youth group from a private Christian school near Milwaukee), the busses were primarily filled with retirees.

6   I am grateful to the Garden of Hope tour guide, Steve, who provided access to the attraction's records, which include a copy of the original sheet music and lyrics.

Chapter 9

1. The accounts include interviews with the Fathers of Docheiariou, as well as written accounts by other monks dating from the early to the late twentieth century. I am deeply indebted to Father Amphilochios, Father Apolló, and Father Theoktistos of Docheiariou for all their assistance and for granting me access to many of the primary sources used in the chapter, including the original manuscript of the *typikon* of Docheiariou (cod. 356) and the *typikon* of the *litaneia* of the Axion Estin icon of the Mother of God. I am likewise thankful to Father Maximos Constas of Simonopetra, Georgios Sideropoulos, and Christos Kakalis for their precious bibliographical suggestions and insights into liturgical processions in other Athonite monasteries, as well as to Maria Alexandrou and Nicoletta Isar for the stimulating conversations on processions which inspired some of the ideas presented in this chapter.

2. "Yesterday our city was aglow, radiant and famous, not because it had colonnades, but because a martyr arrived in procession from Pontus. . . . Did you see the procession in the Forum? . . . Let no one stay away from this holy assembly; let no virgin stay shut up in her house, no woman keep her own home. Let us empty the city and go to the grave of the martyr, for even the emperor and his wife go with us. . . . Let us make of the sea a church once again, going forth with lamps" (cited in Baldovin 1987: 183).

3. Not least, Constantinopolitan stational services and *litaneies* left an indelible stamp on the divine Liturgy and other rites of the Orthodox Church, as well on the church buildings themselves. Entrances, processions, and accessions, Taft observes, all came to characterize Byzantine liturgy. The church thus became both the culminating point of the large outdoor urban processions, as well as a site for the enactment of "miniature" indoor ones. Indeed, processional activity was directly responsible for the characteristic shape of early Constantinopolitan churches, with their multiple entrances on all four sides and an atrium enclosed by a portico, where the procession would pause. "Inside the church, the longitudinal axis between entrance and apse was emphasized, and the processions were guided to the sanctuary by floor markings and the walled pathway of the *solea*" (Taft 1992: 33). The church building thus took processions "outside in." With the construction of Haghia Sophia, the image of the church as a cosmos in miniature, reaching from God's heavenly throne to the lower realm of humans, was given material shape in the most literal sense. "The awesome splendors of its vastness and the sparkling brilliance of its light," Taft comments, "led observers to exclaim with remarkable consistency that here, indeed, was heaven on earth" (Taft 1992: 36).

4. "The seashore along the mountain was precipitous and without any harbors on both sides, to the north, that is, and to the south, for more than eighty miles. The mountain resembles a peninsula which extends toward the sea in the shape of a cross" (Thomas et al. 2000: 253).

5. "From sea storm and swelling waves of certain death / hast thou saved them that invoked thy divine name: / preserve us also from outward destruction / and from the

shipreck of soul in eternal deeps, / and bring us to the tranquil port/ of salvation, O Mother of God Most High."

"Most grieviously tossed/ upon the stormy sea of life, / and all-overwhelmed / with swelling waves of sufferings, / we take flight, O Virgin, to thy blest Icon as to a tranquil port: / wherefore, stretch forth thy hand to us, / and save us from tempests as thy Son saved Peter" (Nikodēmos Agioreitēs 2001: 19).

Chapter 10

1. For a comprehensive list of definitions of sacred grove, holy tree, and so on, see Dafni (2006: 1–3) and Singh et al. (2017: 1).
2. For example, Hos. 4:13: "They sacrifice upon the tops of the mountains, and burn incense upon the hills, under oaks and poplars and elms, because the shadow thereof is good: therefore your daughters shall commit whoredom, and your spouses shall commit adultery"; Jer. 2:20: "For of old time I have broken thy yoke, and burst thy bands; and thou sadist, I will not transgress; when upon every hill and under every green tree thou wanderest, playing the harlot."
3. Short for the Church of Jesus Christ of Latter-day Saints, also known as the Mormon Church.
4. "And seeing the multitudes, He went up on a mountain, and when He was seated His disciples came to Him. Then He opened His mouth and taught them" (Mt. 5:1-2).
5. Measured by Adam Ron, using arial photographs.
6. As expected, the Garden Tomb was not on their list, as they believe that the Church of the Holy Sepulchre is the correct place.

Afterword

1. This quotation appears in the 1911 *Encyclopaedia Britannica* entry on Seddon.
2. The Oscar-winning film *The Shape of Water*, directed by Guillermo de Toro and released in 2017, depicts water as both prison and medium for escape.
3. *Brancardiers* are volunteer assistants who work at Lourdes, including the key task of enabling and regulating the flow of bathers through the shrine.

References

Introduction

Badone, Ellen. 2007. "Echoes from Kerizinen: Pilgrimage, Narrative, and the Construction of Sacred History at a Marian Shrine in Northwestern France," *Journal of the Royal Anthropological Institute*, 13: 453–70.

Ballesta, Jordi. 2016. "John Brinckerhoff Jackson, within Ordinary Landscapes: Field Research and Amateur Photographic Practices," *L'Espace Géographique*, 45 (3): 211–24.

Bowman, Glenn. 1991. "Christian Ideology and the Image of a Holy Land: The Place of Jerusalem Pilgrimage in the Various Christianities," in John Eade and Michael Sallnow (eds.), *Contesting the Sacred: The Anthropology of Christian Pilgrimage*, 98–121. London: Routledge.

Carter, Thomas. 2015. *Building Zion: The Material World of Mormon Settlement*. Minneapolis: University of Minnesota Press.

Chidester, David and Edward T. Linenthal, eds. 1995. *American Sacred Space*. Bloomington: Indiana University Press.

Claval, Paul, Maria Paola Pagnini Alberti, and Maurizio Scaini. 2005. "The Cultural Turn in Human Geography," in Paul Claval and Maurizio Scaini (eds.), *The Cultural Turn in Geography: Proceedings of the Conference, 18–20th of September 2003, Gorizia Campus*, 9–11. Università di Trieste / International Geographical Union.

Deffontaines, Pierre. 1948. *Géographie et Religion*. Paris: Gallimard.

Duncan, Nancy and James Duncan. 2010. "Doing Landscape Interpretation," in Dydia DeLyser, Steve Herbert, Stuart Aitken, Mike Crang, and Linda McDowell (eds.), *The SAGE Handbook of Qualitative Geography*, 225–47. London: Sage Publications.

Dwyer, Claire. 2016. "Why Does Religion Matter for Cultural Geographers?" *Social & Cultural Geography*, 17 (6): 758–62.

Dyas, Dee. 2001. *Pilgrimage in Medieval English Literature: 700-1500*. Cambridge: Brewer.

Eddy, Marjorie E. 1999. *The Precepts of Zion and Joseph Smith's City of Zion Plan: Major Influences for the Planning of Nauvoo*, MA Thesis. Provo, UT: Brigham Young University.

Ellen, Roy. 1988. "Persistence and Change in the Relationship Between Anthropology and Human Geography," *Progress in Human Geography*, 12 (2): 229–62.

Engelke, Matthew. 2010. "Religion and the Media Turn: A Review Essay," *American Ethnologist*, 37 (2): 371–9.

Esplin, Scott C. 2018. *Return to the City of Joseph: Modern Mormonism's Contest for the Soul of Nauvoo*. Urbana: University of Illinois Press.

Farmer, Jared. 2010. *On Zion's Mount: Mormons, Indians, and the American Landscape*. Cambridge, MA: Harvard University Press.

Feld, Steven and Keith H. Basso, eds. 1996. *Senses of Place*. Santa Fe: School of American Research Press.

Feldman, Jackie. 2016. *A Jewish Guide in the Holy Land: How Christian Pilgrims Made Me Israeli*. Bloomington: Indiana University Press.

Francaviglia, Richard V. 1969. "The City of Zion in the Mountain West," *The Improvement Era*, 72: 10–17.

Francaviglia, Richard V. 1970. "The Mormon Landscape: Definition of an Image in the American West," *Proceedings of the Association of American Geographers*, 2: 59–61.

Francaviglia, Richard V. 1971a. "Mormon Central-Hall Houses in the American West," *Annals of the Association of American Geographers*, 61: 65–71.

Francaviglia, Richard V. 1971b. "The Cemetery as an Evolving Cultural Landscape," *Annals of the Association of American Geographers*, 61 (3): 501–9.

Francaviglia, Richard V. 1978a. *The Mormon Landscape: Existence, Creation, and Perception of a Unique Image in the American West*. New York: AMS Press.

Francaviglia, Richard V. 1978b. "The Passing Mormon Village," *Landscape*, 22 (2): 40–7.

Francaviglia, Richard V. 2003. *Believing in Place: A Spiritual Geography of the Great Basin*. Reno: University of Nevada Press.

Francaviglia, Richard V. 2015. *The Mapmakers of New Zion: A Cartographic History of Mormonism*. Salt Lake City: The University of Utah Press.

Grubiak, Margaret M. 2020. *Monumental Jesus: Landscapes of Faith and Doubt in Modern America*. Charlottesville: University of Virginia Press.

Jackson, John B. 1953. "The Westward-Moving House," *Landscape*, 2 (2): 8–21.

Jackson, Richard H. 1979. "Review of: R.V. Francaviglia 1978 The Mormon Landscape: Existence, Creation, and Perception of a Unique Image in the American West," *Utah Historical Quarterly*, 47 (4): 441–2.

Jacobsen, Eric O. 2003. *Sidewalks in the Kingdom: New Urbanism and the Christian Faith*. Grand Rapids: Brazos Press.

Kaell, Hillary. 2014. *Walking Where Jesus Walked: American Christians and Holy Land Pilgrimage*. New York: New York University Press.

Klassen, Pamela E. 2018. *The Story of Radio Mind: A Missionary's Journey on Indigenous Land*. Chicago: University of Chicago Press.

Knott, Kim. 2005. *The Location of Religion: A Spatial Analysis*. London and Oakville: Equinox Publishing.

Knott, Kim. 2010. "Religion, Space, and Place: The Spatial Turn in Research on Religion," *Religion and Society: Advances in Research*, 1: 29–43.

Lane, Belden C. 2001. "Giving Voice to Place: Three Models for Understanding Sacred Space," *Religion and American Culture: A Journal of Interpretation*, 11 (1): 53–81.

Lins, Ribeiro G. 2019. "The Global / Local Tension in the History of Anthropology," *Journal of Global History*, 14: 375–94.

Maddrell, Avril, Veronica della Dora, Alessandro Scafi, and Heather Walton, eds. 2014. *Christian Pilgrimage, Landscape and Heritage: Journeying to the Sacred*. London: Routledge.

Meinig, Donald W., ed. 1979. *The Interpretation of Ordinary Landscapes: Geographical Essays*. New York: Oxford University Press.

Mitchell, Jon. 2020. "How Landscapes Remember," *Material Religion*, 16 (4): 432–51.

Napolitano, Valentina, Nimrod Luz, and Nurit Stadler. 2015. "Introduction: Materialities, Histories, and the Spatialization of State Sovereignty," *Religion and Society: Advances in Research*, 6 (1): 90–7.

Park, Chris C. 2004. "Religion and Geography," in John R. Hinnels (ed.), *Routledge Companion to the Study of Religion*, 439–55. London: Routledge.

Qian, Junski and Lily Kong. 2018. "Buddhism Co. Ltd? Epistemology of Religiosity, and the Re-invention of a Buddhist Monastery in Hong Kong," *Environment and Planning D: Society and Space*, 36 (1): 159–77.

Renan, Ernest. 1863 [2005]. *The Life of Jesus*. The Project Gutenberg EBook, www.gutenberg.net.

Rogers, Stephanie Stidham. 2011. *Inventing the Holy Land: American Protestant Pilgrimage to Palestine, 1865–1941*. Lanham: Lexington Books.

Ron, Amos S. 1989. *Gardens in Cultures: The Garden as a Symbolic Landscape – A Study in Landscape Interpretation*, M.A. Thesis. Hebrew University of Jerusalem, [Hebrew].

Stoddard, Robert. 1982. "Field Techniques and Research Methods in Geography," *Geography Faculty Publications*, 26. https://digitalcommons.unl.edu/geographyfacpub/26.

Street, Alice and Simon Coleman. 2012. "Introduction: Real and Imagined Spaces," *Space and Culture*, 15 (1): 4–17.

Tilley, Christopher and Kate Cameron-Daum. 2017. *An Anthropology of Landscape*. London: UCL Press.

Treviño, Roberto R. and Richard R Francaviglia, eds. 2007. *Catholicism in the American West: A Rosary of Hidden Voices*. College Station: A & M University Press.

Zelinsky, Wilber. 1961. "An Approach to the Religious Geography of the United States: Patterns of Church Membership in 1952," *Annals of the Association of American Geographers*, 51 (2): 139–94.

Zelinsky, Wilber. 1976. "Unearthly Delights: Cemetery Names and the Map of the Changing American Afterworld," in David Lowenthal and Martyn J. Bowden (eds.), *Geographies of the Mind*, 171–95. New York: Oxford University Press.

Zelinsky, Wilber. 1990. "Nationalistic Pilgrimages in the United States," in Gisbert Rinschede and Surinder Mohan Bhardwaj (eds.), *Pilgrimage in the United States*, 253–67. Berlin: Dietrich Reimer Verlag.

Zelinsky, Wilber. 2001. "The Uniqueness of the American Religious Landscape," *Geographical Review*, 91 (3): 565–85.

Chapter 1

Accrocca, Felice and Michele Curto. 2008. *La Grotta di San Michele sul Gargano. Una Meta di Pellegrinaggio dal Medioevo ad Oggi*. Monte Sant'Angelo: Edizioni Michael.

Allegri, Renzo. 1998. *Padre Pio : un santo tra noi*. Milano: Mondadori.

Anon. 2008. "Padre Pio 'Set to Beat Lourdes," *Italy Magazine*, May 8. http://www.italymag.co.uk/italy/puglia/padre-pio-set-beat-lourdes.

Anon. 2017. "Turismo in provincia di Foggia: i dati ufficiali del 2016," *Foggia Today*, July 21. Accessed from www.foggiatoday.it/economia/dati-turismo-provincia-foggia-2016.html on August 14, 2019.

Anon. 2019. "Michael," *Babycenter.com*. Accessed from https://www.babycenter.com/baby-names-michael-462485.htm on August 14, 2019.

Badone, Ellen. 1990. *Religious Orthodoxy and Popular Faith in European Society*. Princeton: Princeton University Press.

Baudrillard, Jean. 1994. *Simulacra and Simulation*, Translated by Sheila Faria Glaser. Ann Arbor: University of Michigan Press.

Bobbio, A. 2006. "I più amati dagli italiani," *Famiglia Cristiana*, LXXVI (45), 5: 66–9.

Bosco, Francesco. 2018. "Papa Francesco, il primo Papa "pellegrino" a Pietrelcina, 17 marzo," *Teleradio Padre Pio*, March 9. Accessed from www.teleradiopadrepio.it/papa-francesco-primo-papa-pietrelcina-piana-romana/ on August 11, 2018.

Campanella, Stefano. 2011. *Obaedientia et pax: La vera storia di una falsa persecuzione*. San Giovanni Rotondo: Edizione Padre Pio da Pietrelcina.

Da Ripabottoni, Alessandro and Alessio Parente. 1996. *Padre Pio of Pietrelcina: Everybody's Cyrenean*. San Giovanni Rotondo: Convento Santa Maria delle Grazie.

Dellios, Rosita. 2003. "Mandala: From Sacred Origins to Sovereign Affairs in Traditional Southeast Asia," CEWCES Research Papers. Paper 8. http://epublications.bond.edu.au/cewces_papers/8.

Delooz, Pierre. 1983. "Towards a Sociological Study of Canonized Sainthood," in Stephen Wilson (ed.), *Saints and Their Cults: Studies in Religious Sociology, Folklore and History*, 189–215. Cambridge: Cambridge University Press.

Di Flumeri, Gerardo. 1977. *La Permanenza Di Padre Pio a Venafro*. San Giovanni Rotondo: Edizioni "Padre Pio da Pietrelcina."

Di Giovine, Michael A. 2011. "Pilgrimage: Communitas and Contestation, Unity and Difference – An Introduction," *Tourism: An International, Interdisciplinary Journal*, 59 (3): 247–69.

Di Giovine, Michael A. 2012a. "A Tale of Two Cities: Padre Pio and the Reimagining of Pietrelcina and San Giovanni Rotondo," *Textus: English Studies in Italy*, 1 (1), 155–67.

Di Giovine, Michael A. 2012b. *Making Saints, (Re-)Making Towns: Pilgrimage and Devotion in the Land of St. Padre Pio of Pietrelcina*, Unpublished diss. Chicago: University of Chicago.

Di Giovine, Michael A. 2012c. "Padre Pio for Sale: Souvenirs, Relics or Identity Markers?" *International Journal of Tourism Anthropology*, 2 (2): 108–27.

Di Giovine, Michael A. 2013 "Sacred Journeys as Spaces for Peace in Christianity," in Antón Pazos (ed.), *Pilgrims and Pilgrimages as Peacemakers in Christianity, Judaism, and Islam*, 1–38. Surrey: Ashgate.

Di Giovine, Michael A. 2014 "The *Imaginaire* Dialectic and the Refashioning of Pietrelcina," in Noel Salazar and Nelson H. H. Graburn (eds.), *Tourism Imaginaries: Through an Anthropological Lens*, 147–71. Oxford: Berghahn Books.

Eade, John and Michael J. Sallnow. 1991. *Contesting the Sacred: The Anthropology of Pilgrimage*. 2nd ed. Urbana: University of Illinois Press.

Eliade, Mircea. 1959. *The Sacred and the Profane : The Nature of Religion*, Translated by Willard R. Trask. New York: Harcourt, Brace.

Fischer, Michael M. J. 2013. "Afterword. Galactic Polities, Radical Egalitarianism, and the Practice of Anthropology: Tambiah on Logical Paradoxes, Social Contradictions and Cultural Oscillations," in Felicity Aulino, Miriam Goheen and Stanley Tambiah (eds.), *Radical Egalitarianism: Local Realities, Global Relations*, 233–58. New York: Fordham University Press.

Frati Minori Cappuccini. n.d. "Gli Altri Luoghi," *Convento Santuario di Padre Pio*, Accessed from http://www.conventosantuariopadrepio.it/it/gli-altri-luoghio on October 8, 2018.

Gaudiose, Dorothy M. 1993. *Mary's House: Mary Pyle: Under the Spiritual Guidance of Padre Pio*. 1st ed. South Williamsport: Alba House.

Grottola, Fortunato. 2009. *Itinerario Di Fede Alla Scuola Di Padre Pio*. San Giovanni Rotondo (Foggia): Edizioni "Padre Pio Da Pietrelcina."

Hertz, Robert. 1983. "Saint Besse: A Study of an Alpine Cult," in Stephen Wilson (ed.), *Saints and Their Cults: Studies in Religious Sociology, Folklore and History*, 55–100. Cambridge: Cambridge University Press.

Holy See. 2009. "Padre Pio da Pietrelcina," www.vatican.va/news_services/liturgy/saints/ns_lit_doc_20020616_padre-pio_en.html.

IAR. 2017. "Record Numbers of Tourists in Kraków," *Radio Poland*. December 15. Accessed from www.thenews.pl/1/11/Artykul/339882,Record-number-of-tourists-in-Krakow on October 10, 2018.

Keane, Colm. 2008. *Padre Pio: The Irish Connection*. Edinburgh and London: Mainstream Publishing.

Luzzatto, Sergio. 2009. *Padre Pio : miracoli e politica nell'Italia del Novecento*. Turin: G. Einaudi.

Maddrell, Avril. 2011. "Praying the Keeills': Rhythm, Meaning and Experience on Pilgrimage Journeys in the Isle of Man," *Landabrefid*, 25: 15–29.

Marianeschi, Paolo Maria, ed. 1988. "La Scomparsa Delle Stimmate Di Padre Pio," in *Atti Del Convegno Di Studio Sulle Stimmate Del Servo Di Dio Padre Pio Da Pietrelcina (San Giovanni Rotondo, 16–20 Settembre 1987)*, 225–57. Padre Pio Da Pietrelcina—Collana "Spiritualità" 2. San Giovanni Rotondo: Edizioni Padre Pio da Pietrelcina, Convento S. Maria delle Grazie.

McArdle, Fr. Jack. 2002. "Father Alessio, Introduction," in *Father Alessio*, www.padrepio.ie/Alessio/Alessio.htm.

Meltzer, Françoise and Jas' Elsner. 2011. *Saints: Faith Without Borders*. Chicago: University of Chicago Press.

NAB. 1995. *The New American Bible*. Wichita: Catholic Bible Publishers.

Neirotti, Marco. 2008. "I mercanti traditi da Padre Pio: 'Tutti attendono l'esposizione della salma, intanto qui gli alberghi sono vuoti,'" *La Stampa*, March 17, sec. CRI.

Pio da Pietrelcina. 2008a. *Epistolario I: Corrispondenza con i direttori spirituali, 1910–1922*, Edited by Melchiorre da Pobladura, Alessandro da Ripabottoni, and Gerardo Di Flumeri. 4th ed. Vol. 1. 4 vols. San Giovanni Rotondo: Edizioni "Padre Pio da Pietrelcina."

Pio da Pietrelcina. 2008b. *Epistolario IV: Corrispondenza con diverse categorie di persone*, Edited by Melchiorre da Pobladura, Alessandro da Ripabottoni, and Gerardo Di Flumeri. 4th ed. Vol. 4. 4 vols. San Giovanni Rotondo: Edizioni "Padre Pio da Pietrelcina."

Raffaele da S. Elia a Pianisi. 1967. "Appunti Su P. Pio Da Pietrelcina in Riguardo Alle Origine Delle Stimmate Espressamente Richiesti Dal Rev.mo P. Clemente Da S. Maria in Punta, Amministratore Apostolico Della Provincia Di Foggia," in Giuseppe Pagnossin (ed.), *Il Calvario Di Padre Pio*, 2: 354–8. Padova: Conselve.

Robinson, Roland and Frank Lechner. 1985. "Modernization, Globalization and the Problem of Culture in World Systems Theory," *Theory, Culture and Society*, 2 (3): 103–17.

Ruffin, C. Bernard. 1991. *Padre Pio: The True Story*. 2nd ed. Huntington: Our Sunday Visitor.

Salazar, Noel B. and Nelson H. H. Graburn. 2014. *Tourism Imaginaries Through an Anthropological Lens*. Oxford: Berghahn Books.

Saldutto, Gerardo. 2001. *Il cammino di Padre Pio*. Casale Monferrato: Piemme.

Tambiah, Stanley J. 1976. "The Galactic Polity: The Structure of Traditional Kingdoms in Southeast Asia," *Annals of the New York Academy of Sciences*, 69–97.

Tambiah, Stanley J. 1977. "The Galactic Polity in Southeast Asia," in Stanley A. Freed (ed.), *Anthropology and the Climate of Opinion*, 69–97. New York: New York Academy of Sciences.

Tambiah, Stanley J. 2013. "The Charisma of Saints and the Cult of Relics, Amulets, and Tomb Shrines," in Felicity Aulino, Miriam Goheen, and Stanley J. Tambiah (eds.), *Radical Egalitarianism: Local Realities, Global Relations*, 233–58. New York: Fordham University Press.

Turner, Victor. 1969. *The Ritual Process: Structure and Anti-Structure (Lewis Henry Morgan Lectures)*. London: Routledge and Kegan Paul.

Turner, Victor. 1973. "The Center Out There: Pilgrim's Goal," *History of Religions*, 12 (3): 191–230.

Turner, Victor and Edith Turner. 1978. *Image and Pilgrimage in Christian Culture*. New York: Columbia University Press.

United States Catholic Conference, and Libreria Editrice Vaticana. 1994. *Catechism of the Catholic Church/English*. Liguori: Liguori Publications.

Villani, Antonio. 2000. "La Sala Di Lettura Padre Pio," *Voce Di Padre Pio*, October.

Voce di Padre Pio. n.d. "The Magazine," Accessed from https://www.padrepio.foundation/en/the-magazine-voce-di-padre-pio/ on October 8, 2018.

Wallerstein, Immanuel. 1974. *The Modern World System I: Capitalist Agriculture and the Origins of the European World-Economy in the Sixteenth Century*. New York: Academic Press.

Weber, Max. 1958. *From Max Weber: Essays in Sociology*, Edited by H. H. Gerth and C. Wright Mills, Translated by H. H. Gerth and C. Wright Mills. Oxford and New York: Oxford University Press.

Wilson, Stephen, ed. 1983. *Saints and Their Cults: Studies in Religious Sociology, Folklore and History*. Cambridge: Cambridge University Press.

Woestman, William H. 2002. *Canonization: Theology, History, Process*. Ottawa: Saint Paul University.

Chapter 2

Albera, Dionigi and John Eade, eds. 2015. *International Perspectives on Pilgrimage Studies: Itineraries, Gaps and Obstacles*. New York and Abingdon: Routledge.

Albera, Dionigi and John Eade, eds. 2017. *New Pathways in Pilgrimage Studies: Global Perspectives*. New York and Abingdon: Routledge.

Badone, Ellen. 2007. "Echoes from Kerizinen: Pilgrimage, Narrative, and the Construction of Sacred History at a Marian Shrine in Northwestern France," *Journal of the Royal Anthropological Institute*, 13 (2): 453–70.

Billet, B. and P. Lafourcade. 1981. *Lourdes Pèlerinage*. Condé-sur-Noireau: C. Corlet.

Carroll, Michael. 1985. "The Virgin Mary at LaSalette and Lourdes: Whom Did the Children See?" *Journal for the Scientific Study of Religion*, 24 (1): 56–74.

Coleman, Simon. 2000. "Meanings of Movement, Place and Home at Walsingham," *Culture and Religion*, 1 (2): 153–69.

Coleman, Simon. 2002. "Do You Believe in Pilgrimage? Communitas, Contestation and Beyond," *Anthropological Theory*, 2 (3): 355–68.

Coleman, Simon and John Eade, eds. 2018. *Pilgrimage and Political Economy*. Oxford and New York: Berghahn.

Dahlberg, Andrea. 1991. "The Body as a Principle of Holism: Three Pilgrimages to Lourdes," in J. Eade and M. Sallnow (eds.), *Contesting the Sacred: The Anthropology of Christian Pilgrimage*, 30–50. London and New York: Routledge.

Eade, John. 1991. "Order and Power: Lay Helpers and the Organization of a Pilgrimage Shrine," in J. Eade and M. Sallnow (eds.), *Contesting the Sacred: The Anthropology of Christian Pilgrimage*, 51–76. London and New York: Routledge.

Eade, John. 2017. "Healing Social and Physical Bodies: Lourdes and Military Pilgrimage," in J. Eade and M. Katic (eds.), *Military Pilgrimage and Battlefield Tourism: Commemorating the Dead*, 15–34. Abingdon and New York: Routledge.

Eade, John and Michael Sallnow. 1991. "Introduction," in J. Eade and M. Sallnow (eds.), *Contesting the Sacred: The Anthropology of Christian Pilgrimage*, 1–29. London and New York: Routledge.

Gesler, Wilbert. 1992. "Therapeutic Landscapes: Medical Issues in Light of the New Cultural Geography," *Social Science and Medicine*, 34: 735–46.

Gesler, Wilbert. 1996. "Lourdes: Healing in a Place of Pilgrimage," *Health & Place*, 2: 95–105.

Gesler, Wilbert. 2003. *Healing Places*. New York: Rowman and Littlefield.

Goldingay, Sarah, Paul Dieppe, and Miguel Farias. 2014. "Nd the Pain Just Disappeared into Insignificance': The Healing Response in Lourdes—Performance, Psychology and Caring," *International Review of Psychiatry*, 26 (3): 315–23.

Hall, David, ed. 1997. *Lived Religion in America: Toward A History of Practice*. Princeton: Princeton University Press.

Harris, Ruth. 1999. *Lourdes: Body and Spirit in the Secular Age*. London: Allen Lane.

Harris, Alana. 2010. "A Place to Grow Spiritually and Socially: The Experiences of Young Pilgrims to Lourdes," in S. Collins-Mayo and P. Dandelion (eds.), *Religion and Youth*, 139–48. Farnham and Burlington: Ashgate.

Harris, Alana. 2013. "Lourdes and Holistic Spirituality: Contemporary Catholicism, the Therapeutic and Religious Thermalism," *Culture and Religion*, 14, 1.

Hazard, Sonia. 2013. "The Material Turn in the Study of Religion," *Religion and Society Advances in Research*, 4: 58–78.

Jansen, Willy and Catrien Notermans. 2011. "Ex-Votos in Lourdes: Contested Materiality of Miraculous Healings," *Material Religion*, 7 (2): 168–92.

Kaufman, Sharon. 2005. *Consuming Visions: Mass Culture and the Lourdes Shrine*. Ithaca and London: Cornell University Press.

Lochtefeld, James. 2010. *God's Gateway: Identity and Meaning in a Hindu Pilgrimage Place*. New York: Oxford University Press.

McDannell, Colleen. 1993. *Material Christianity: Religion and Popular Culture in America*. New Haven: Yale University Press.

Meyer, Birgit. 2012. *Mediation and the Genesis of Presence. Towards a Material Approach to Religion*. Utrecht: Universiteit Utrecht.

Moore, L. 2014. *Le pèlerinage à Lourdes, la fin d'un cycle?* [Pilgrimage to Lourdes, the end of a cycle?], Unpublished Master's thesis. University of Bordeaux.

Morgan, David, ed. 2000. *Religion and Material Culture*. London: Routledge.

Morinis, Alan. 1984. *Pilgrimage in the Hindu Tradition: A Case Study of West Bengal*. New Delhi: Oxford University Press.

Orsi, Robert. 2010. "Introduction to the Second Edition," in *The Madonna of 115th Street: Faith and Community in Italian Harlem, 1880–1950*, xxvii. New Haven and London: Yale University Press.

Orsi, Robert. 2013. *Between Heaven and Earth: The Religious Worlds People Make and the Scholars Who Study Them*. Princeton, NJ and London: Princeton University Press.

Orsi, Robert. 2017. "The Clergy Sex Abuse Crisis Is Good for Thinking about Catholics, Catholicism, and about the Anthropology of Catholicism," in K. Norget, V. Napolitano and M. Mayblin (eds.), *The Anthropology of Catholicism*, 282–92. Oakland: University of California Press.

Petro, Anthony. 2015. "Beyond Accountability: The Queer Archive of Catholic Sexual Abuse," *Radical History Review*, 2015 (122): 160–76.

Reader, Ian. 2007. "Pilgrimage Growth in the Modern World: Meanings and Implications," *Religion*, 37: 210–29.

Reader, Ian. 2015. *Pilgrimage in the Marketplace*. Abingdon and New York: Routledge.

Ronan, Marian. 2008. "The Clergy Sex Abuse Crisis and the Mourning of American Catholic Innocence," *Pastoral Psychology*, 56 (3): 321–39.

Turner, Victor and Edith Turner. 1978. *Image and Pilgrimage in Christian Culture: Anthropological Perspectives*. New York: Columbia University Press.

Tweed, Thomas. 2006. *Crossing and Dwelling: A Theory of Religion*. Cambridge, MA: Harvard University Press.

Vásquez, Manuel. 2010. *More Than Belief: A Materialist Theory of Religion*. New York: Oxford University Press.

Chapter 3

Borhegyi, Stephan F. de. 1954a. "The Cult of Our Lord of Esquipulas in Middle America and New Mexico," *El Palacio: A Review of Arts and Sciences in the Southwest*, 61 (12): 387–401.

Borhegyi, Stephan F. de. 1954b. "The Evolution of a Landscape," *Landscape*, 4 (1): 24–30.

Borhegyi, Stephen F. de and E. Boyd. 1982. *El Santuario de Chimayo*. Reprint ed. Santa Fe: Ancient City Press.

Boyd, E. 1974. *Popular Arts of the Spanish New Mexico*. Santa Fe: Museum of New Mexico Press.

Brading, D. A. 2001. *Mexican Phoenix: Our Lady of Guadalupe: Image and Tradition across Five Centuries*. New York: Cambridge University Press.

Bunting, Bainbridge. 1976. *Early Architecture in New Mexico*. Albuquerque: University of New Mexico Press.

Carrillo, Charles. 1999. "Our Lord of Esquipulas in New Mexico," *Tradición*, 4 (2): 50–54.

Eliade, Mircea. 1957. *The Sacred and the Profane: The Nature of Religion*. San Diego: Harcourt.

Gavin, Robin Farwell, Barbara B. Mauldin, and Helen R. Lucero. 1990. *History and Iconography of the Architecture and Art at Nuestro Señor de Esquipulas Church (Santuario de Chimayó)*. Santa Fe: The Museum of International Folk Art and the Archdiocese of Santa Fe.

González, Julio. 2013. *The Santuario de Chimayo in New Mexico: The Shrine of Our Lord of Esquipulas and the Holy Child*. Chimayó: Sons of the Holy Family.

Gutiérrez, Ramón A. 1995. "El Santuario de Chimayo: A Syncretic Shrine in New Mexico," in Ramón A. Gutiérrez and Geneviève Fabre (eds.), *Feasts and Celebrations in North American Ethnic Communities*, 71–86. Albuquerque: University of New Mexico Press.

Harrington, John Peabody. 1916. *The Ethneogeography of the Tewa Indians*. Twenty-Ninth Annual Report of the Bureau of American Ethnology to the Secretary of the Smithsonian Institution. Washington: Bureau of American Ethnology.

Hendrickson, Brett. 2017. *The Healing Power of the Santuario de Chimayó: America's Miraculous Church*. New York: New York University Press.

Howarth, Sam and Enrique R. Lamadrid. 1999. *Pilgrimage to Chimayó: Contemporary Portrait of a Living Tradition*. Santa Fe: Museum of New Mexico Press.

Kay, Elizabeth. 1987. *Chimayo Valley Traditions*. Santa Fe: Ancient City Press.

Lange, Charles H., Elizabeth M. Lange, and Carroll L. Riley. 1966. *Southwest Journals of Adolph F. Bandelier, 1889–1892*. Vol. 2. Albuquerque: University of New Mexico Press.

Lummis, Charles F. 1952. *The Land of Poco Tiempo*. Albuquerque: University of New Mexico Press.

Martin, Joel W. 2001. *The Land Looks after Us: A History of Native American Religion*. New York: Oxford University Press.

Ortiz, Alfonso. 1969. *The Tewa World: Space, Time, Being, and Becoming in a Pueblo Society*. Chicago: University of Chicago Press.

"Popular Legends Surround Building of Santuario," 1984. *People of God*, 2 (2), April.

Roca, Casimiro. 2007. *A Long Journey for Two Short Legs: My Album of Memories*. Chimayó: Sons of the Holy Family.

Sheldrake, Philip. 2001. *Spaces for the Sacred: Place, Memory, and Identity*. Baltimore: Johns Hopkins University Press.

Smith, Jonathan Z. 1992. *To Take Place: Toward Theory in Ritual*. Chicago: University of Chicago Press.

Spicer, Edward H. 1962. *Cycles of Conquest: The Impact of Spain, Mexico, and the United States on the Indians of the Southwest, 1533–1960*. Tucson: University of Arizona Press.

Turner, Victor and Edith Turner. 1978. *Image and Pilgrimage in Christian Culture*. New York: Columbia University Press.

Twitchell, Ralph Emerson. 1914. *The Spanish Archives of New Mexico*. Vol. 1. Cedar Rapids: The Torch Press.

Usner, Don J. 1995. *Sabino's Map: Life in Chimayó's Old Plaza*. Santa Fe: Museum of New Mexico Press.

Chapter 4

Bross, Kristina. 2011. "A Wilderness Condition: The Captivity Narrative as Christian Literature," in Catherine A. Brekus and W. Clark Gilpin (eds.), *American Christianities: A History of Dominance and Diversity*, 307–26. Chapel Hill: University of North Carolina Press.

Castiglia, Christopher. 1996. *Bound and Determined: Captivity, Culture-Crossing, and White Womanhood from Mary Rowlandson to Patty Hearst*. Chicago: University of Chicago Press.

Derounian-Sotdola, Kathryn Zabelle. 2009. "Ann Eliza Webb Young (Denning)," *Legacy*, 26, 150–59.

Dowling, Claudia Glenn. 2012. "Ann Eliza and the Prophet," *American History*.

Ebersole, Gary L. 1995. *Captured by Texts: Puritan to Post-Modern Images of Indian Captivity*, Charlottesville: University Press of Virginia.

Eliason, Eric Alden. 1998. *Celebrating Zion: Pioneers in Mormon Popular Historical Expression*, PhD diss. University of Texas at Austin.

Eliason, Eric A. 2013. "Pioneers and Recapitulation in Mormon Popular Historical Expression," in Eric A. Eliason and Tom Mould (eds.), *Latter-day Lore: Mormon Folklore Studies*, Salt Lake City: The University of Utah Press.

"Elizabeth Smart: Autobiography Part 1," 2017. *A&E, Aired*, November 12.

Farmer, Jared. 2008. *On Zion's Mount: Mormons, Indians, and the American Landscape*. Cambridge, MA: Harvard University Press.

Firmage, Edwin Brown and Richard Collin Mangrum. 1988. *Zion in the Courts: A Legal History of the Church of Jesus Christ of Latter-day Saints, 1830–1900*. Urbana: University of Illinois Press.

Flake, Kathleen. 2004. *The Politics of American Religious Identity: The Seating of Senator Reed Smoot, Mormon Apostle*. Chapel Hill: The University of North Carolina Press.

Fluhman, J. Spencer. 2012. *"A Peculiar People" Anti-Mormonism and the Making of Religion in Nineteenth-Century America*. Chapel Hill: University of North Carolina Press.

Givens, Terryl L. 1997. *The Viper on the Hearth: Mormons, Myths, and the Construction of Heresy*. New York: Oxford University Press.

Gordon, Sarah Barringer. 2002. *The Mormon Question: Polygamy and Constitutional Conflict in Nineteenth Century America*. Chapel Hill: University of North Carolina Press.

Reeve, W. Paul. 2015. *Religion of a Different Color: Race and the Mormon Struggle for Whiteness*. Oxford: Oxford University Press.

Reynolds v. United States. 1879.

Samyn, Mary Ann. 1999. *Captivity Narrative*. Columbus: The Ohio State University Press.

Shipps, Jan Shipps. 1987. *Mormonism: The Story of a New Religious Tradition.* Urbana: University of Illinois Press.
Smart, Elizabeth Smart with Chris Stewart. 2013. *My Story.* New York: St. Martin's Press.
Sriknth, Rajni. 2002. "Ventriloquism in the Captivity Narrative: White Women Challenge European American Patriarchy," in Samina Najmi and Rajini Srikanth (eds.), *White Women in Racialized Spaces: Imaginative Transformation and Ethical Action in Literature.* Albany NY: State University of New York Press.
Turner, John G. 2012. *Brigham Young: Pioneer Prophet.* Cambridge, MA: The Belknap Press of Harvard University Press.
Van Wagoner, Richard S. 1989, *Mormon Polygamy: A History,* Salt Lake City: Signature Books.
www.ldsliving.com/Elizabeth-Smart-Shares-How-Chastity-Lessons-in-Our-Culture-Can-Have-Harmful-Lasting-Effects on July 5, 2018.
www.thecut.com/2016/09/elizabeth-smart-is-speaking-out-against-the-mormon-church.html on July 5, 2018.
Young, Ann Eliza. 2014. *Wife No. 19: The Story of a Life in Bondage, Being a Complete Expose of Mormonism, and Revealing the Sorrows, Sacrifices and Sufferings of Women in Polygamy,* Enhanced Ebooks.

Chapter 5

Adediran, Biodun. 1994. *The Frontier States of Western Yorubaland 1600-1889.* Ibadan: IFRA.
Asiwaju, A. I. 1976. *Western Yorubaland under European Rule 1889–1945. A Comparative Analysis of French and British Colonialism.* London: Longman.
Bateson, Gregory. 1972. *Steps to an Ecology of Mind: Collected Essays in Anthropology, Psychiatry, Evolution, and Epistemology.* Chicago: University of Chicago Press.
Bateson, Gregory. 1979. *Mind and Nature: A Necessary Unity.* New York: Bantam Books.
Bateson, Gregory and Mary Catherine Bateson. 1987. *Angels Fear: An Investigation into the Nature and Meaning of the Sacred.* New York: Macmillan.
Bony, Jean. 1983. *French Gothic Architecture of the Twelfth and Thirteenth Centuries.* Berkeley: University of California Pres.
Bourdieu, Pierre. 1984. *Distinction.* London : Routledge.
Buck, Edward John. 1904. *Simla, Past and Present.* Simla: Thacker & Spink.
Chua, Liana. 2012. *The Christianity of Culture. Conversion, Ethnic Citizenship, and the Matter of Religion in Malaysian Borneo.* New York: Palgrave Macmillan.
Coleman, Simon. 2000. *The Globalisation of Charismatic Christianity.* Cambridge: Cambridge University Press.
Coleman, Simon. 2002a. "The Faith Movement: A Global Religious Culture?" *Culture and Religion,* 3 (1): 3–19.

Coleman, Simon. 2006. "Materializing the Self. Words and Gifts in the Construction of Charismatic Protestant Identity," in F. Cannell (ed.), *The Anthropology of Christianity*, 163–84, Durham: Duke University Press.

Coleman, Simon and John Eade, eds. 2004. *Reframing Pilgrimage. Cultures in Motion*. London: Routledge.

Ebron, Paulla. 1999. "Tourists as Pilgrims: Commercial Fashioning of Transatlantic Politics," *American Ethnologist*, 26: 910–32.

Eck, Diana. 2012. *India: A Sacred Geography*. New York: Harmony.

Engelke, Matthew. 2010. "Past Pentecostalism: Notes on Rupture, Realignment, and Everyday Life in Pentecostal and African Independent Churches," *Africa: The Journal of the International African Institute*, 80 (2): 177–99.

Flynn, Donna K. 1997. "'We Are the Border': Identity, Exchange, and the State Along the Benin-Nigerian Border," *American Ethnologist*, 24 (2): 311–30.

Frey, Nancy L. 1998. *Pilgrim Stories: On and Off the Road to Santiago*. Berkley: University of California Press.

Gibson, Erin. 2007. "The Archaeology of Movement in a Mediterranean Landscape," *Journal of Mediterranean Archaeology*, 20 (1): 61–87.

Gifford, Paul. 2015. "Unity and Diversity within African Pentecostalism: A Comparison of the Christianities of Daniel Olukoya and David Oyedepo," in M. Lindhardt (ed.), *Pentecostalism in Africa. Presence and Impact of Pneumatic Christianity in Postcolonial Societies*, , 115–35. Leiden: Brill.

Gordon-Cumming, C. F. 1884. *In the Himalayas and on the Indian Plains*. London: Chatto and Windus, Piccadilly.

Graburn, Nelson H. 1983. "The Anthropology of Tourism," *Annals of Tourism Research*, 10 (1): 9–33.

Heidegger, Martin. 1971. *Poetry, Language, Thought*, Translated by A. Hofstadter. New York: Harper Colophon Books.

Ingold, Tim. 2000. *The Perception of the Environment: Essays on Livelihood, Dwelling and Skill*. London: Routledge.

Ingold, Tim. 2010. "Footprints Through the Weather-World: Walking, Breathing, Knowing," *Journal of the Royal Anthropological Institute*, 16: S121–39.

Ingold, Tim. 2011. *Being Alive: Essays on Movement, Knowledge and Description*. London: Taylor & Francis.

Ingold, Tim. 2015. *The Life of Lines*. Abingdon: Routledge.

Ingold, Tim. 2016. *Lines: A Brief History*. Abingdon: Routledge.

Keane, Webb. 2008. "The Evidence of the Senses and the Materiality of Religion," *Journal of the Royal Anthropological Institute*, 14: S110–27.

Keltner, Dacher and Jonathan Haidt. 2003. "Approaching Awe, a Moral, Spiritual, and Aesthetic Emotion," *Cognition and Emotion*, 17 (2): 297–314.

Kennedy, Dane. 1996. *The Magic Mountains: Hill Stations and the British Raj*. Berkley: University of California Press.

Lobo, Lancy. 2002. *Globalisation, Hindu Nationalism, and Christians in India*. Jaipur: Rawat Publications.

Marshall, Ruth. 2009. *Political Spiritualities. The Pentecostal Revolution in Nigeria*. Chicago: University of Chicago Press.

Maxwell, David. 2008. *African Gifts of the Spirit. Pentecostalism and the Rise of a Zimbabwean Transnational Religious Movement*. Oxford, Harare, Athens, OH.: James Currey, Weaver Press, Ohio University Press.

Mayrargue, Cedric. 2001. "The Expansion of Pentecostalism in Benin: Individual Rationales and Transnational Dynamics," in A. Corten and R. Marshall-Fratani (eds.), *Between Babel and Pentecost. Transnational Pentecostalism in Africa and Latin America*, 274–92, London: Hurst & Company.

Mayrargue, Cedric. 2005. "Dynamiques Transnationales et Mobilisations Pentecôtistes dans l'Espace Publique Béninois," in L. Fouchard, A. Mary and R. Otayek (eds.), *Entreprises Religieuses Transnationales en Afrique de l'Ouest*, 243–65, Ibadan: IFRA, Karthala.

Merton, Thomas. 2008. *An Introduction to Christian Mysticism: Initiation Into the Monastic Tradition*. Michigan: Cistercian Publications.

Meyer, Birgit. 1998. "'Make a Complete Break with the Past': Memory and Postcolonial Modernity in Ghanian Pentecostal Discourse," in R. Webner (ed.), *Memory and the Post-colony. African Anthropology and the Critique of Power*, 182–208, London and New York: Zed Books.

Meyer, Birgit. 2004. "Christianity in Africa: From African Independent to Pentecostal-Charismatic Churches," *Annual Review of Anthropology*, 33: 447–74.

Miles-Watson, Jonathan. 2012. "The Cathedral on the Ridge and the Implicit Mythology of the Shimla Hills," *Suomen Antropologi: Journal of the Finnish Anthropological Society*, 37 (4): 30–46.

Miles-Watson, Jonathan. 2013. "Pipe Organs and Satsang: Contemporary Worship in Shimla's Colonial Churches," *Culture and Religion*, 14 (2): 204–22.

Miles-Watson, Jonathan. 2015. "Ruptured Landscapes, Sacred Spaces and the Stretching of Landscape Capital," in H. Sooväli-Sepping, H. Reiner and J. Miles-Watson (eds.), *Ruptured Landscapes: Landscape and Identity in Times of Social Change*, 149–65, Dordrecht: Springer.

Miles-Watson, Jonathan. 2016. "Teachings of Tara: Sacred Place and Human Wellbeing in the Shimla Hills," *Anthropology in Action*, 23 (3): 30–42.

Miles-Watson, Jonathan. 2019. *Christianity and Belonging in Shimla*. London: Bloomsbury.

Miles-Watson, Jonathan, Hugo Reinert, and Helen Soovali-Sepping. 2015. "Introduction—Ruptured Landscapes," in H. Sooväli-Sepping, H. Reinert and J. Miles-Watson (eds.), *Ruptured Landscapes: Landscape and Identity and Social Change*, 1–7, Dordrecht: Springer.

Noret, Joel. 2010. "On the Inscrutability of the Ways of God: The Transnationalisation of Pentecostalism on the West African Coast," in A. Adogame and J. V. Spickard (eds.), *Religion Crossing Boundaries. Transnational Religious and Social Dynamics in Africa and the New African Diaspora*, 107–22. Leiden-Boston: Brill.

Oyedepo, David. 2005. *Understanding Financial Prosperity*. Lagos: Dominion Publishing House.
Prasad, Marehelli. 2015. "Conch-Shells, Bells, and Gongs in Hindu Temples," *The Journal of the Acoustical Society of America*, 137 (4): 2427.
Pubby, Vipin. 1996. *Shimla Then and Now*. Delhi: Indus Publishing.
Robbins, Joel. 2007. "Continuity Thinking and the Problem of Christian Culture: Belief, Time, and the Anthropology of Christianity," *Current Anthropology*, 48 (1): 5–38.
Sax, William Sturman. 1991. *Mountain Goddess: Gender and Politics in a Himalayan Pilgrimage*. Oxford: Oxford University Press.
Sheldrake, Philip. 2007. "Placing the Sacred: Transcendence and the City," *Literature and Theology*, 21 (3): 243–58.
Turner, Victor. 1969. *The Ritual Process. Structure and Antistructure*. London: Routledge.
van Wyk, Ilana. 2015. *The Universal Church of the Kingdom of God in South Africa*. Cambridge: Cambridge University Press.
Wylie, John. 2007. *Landscape*. Abingdon: Routledge.

Chapter 6

Ardener, Edwin. 2007. *The Voice of Prophecy and Other Essays*. Oxford: Berghahn.
Bialecki, Jon. 2011. "No Caller ID for the Soul: Demonization, Charisms, and the Unstable Subject of Protestant Language Ideology," *Anthropological Quarterly*, 84 (3): 679–703.
Burridge, Kenneth. 1960. *Mambu: A Study of Melanesian Cargo Movements and Their Social and Ideological Background*. London: Methuen.
Elisha, Omri. 2017. "Proximations of Public Religion: Worship, Spiritual Warfare, and the Ritualization of Christian Dance," *American Anthropologist*, 119 (1): 73–85.
Evans-Pritchard, E. E. *Witchcraft, Oracles and Magic Among the Azande*. Oxford: Oxford University Press.
Gluckman, Max. 1972. *The Allocation of Responsibility*. Manchester: Manchester University Press.
Harding, Susan. 2000. *The Book of Jerry Falwell: Fundamentalist Language and Politics*. Princeton: Princeton University Press.
Jenkins, Timothy. 2013. *Of Flying Saucers and Social Scientists: A Re-Reading of When Prophecy Fails and of Cognitive Dissonance*. New York: Palgrave Macmillan.
Keller, Eva. 2004. "Towards Complete Clarity: Bible Study among Seventh-Day Adventists in Madagascar," *Ethnos*, 69 (1): 89–112.
Laidlaw, James. 2010. "Agency and Responsibility: Perhaps You Can Have Too Much of a Good Thing," in Michael Lambek (ed.), *Ordinary Ethics: Anthropology, Language, and Action*, 143–64. New York: Fordham University Press.
Laidlaw, James. 2014. *The Subject of Virtue: An Anthropology of Ethics and Freedom*. Cambridge: Cambridge University Press.

McAlister, Elizabeth. 2016. "The Militarization of Prayer in America: White and Native American Spiritual Warfare," *Journal of Religious and Political Practice*, 2 (1): 114–30.
Mooney, James. 1965 [1896]. *The Ghost Dance Religion and the Sioux Outbreak of 1890*. Chicago: Chicago University Press.
Sahlins, Marshall. 1996. "The Sadness of Sweetness: The Native Anthropology of Western Cosmology," *Current Anthropology*, 37 (3): 395–428.
Smiderle, Carlos and Mesquita, Wania. 2016. "Political Conflict and Spiritual Battle: Intersections between Religion and Politics among Brazilian Pentecostals," *Latin American Perspectives*, 43 (3): 85–103.
The Temple Institute. Accessed on February 26, 2018. www.templeinstitute.org
van Wyk, Ilana .2014. *The Universal Church of the Kingdom of God in South Africa: A Church of Strangers*. Cambridge: Cambridge University Press.
Webster, Joseph. 2013a. "The Eschatology of Global Warming in a Scottish Fishing Village," *Cambridge Anthropology*, 31 (1): 68–84.
Webster, Joseph. 2013b. *The Anthropology of Protestantism: Faith and Crisis among Scottish Fishermen*. New York: Palgrave Macmillan.

Chapter 7

Abrams, Andrea C. 2014. *God and Blackness: Race, Gender, and Identity in a Middle Class Afrocentric Church*. New York: New York University Press.
Berlant, Lauren. 1998. "Intimacy: A Special Issue," *Critical Inquiry*, 24 (2): 281–8.
Bialecki, Jon. 2017. *A Diagram for Fire: Miracles and Variations in an American Charismatic Movement*. Berkeley: University of California Press.
Bowler, Kate. 2013. *Blessed: A History of the American Prosperity Gospel*. New York: Oxford University Press.
Boyarin, Jonathan. 2009. *The Unconverted Self: Jews, Indians, and the Identity of Christian Europe*. Chicago: University of Chicago Press.
Boyer, Paul. 1992. *When Time Shall Be No More: Prophecy Belief in Modern American Culture*. Cambridge, MA: Harvard University Press.
Cahn, Peter. 2011. *Direct Sales and Direct Faith in Latin America*. New York: Palgrave Macmillan.
Cobb, James C. 2005. *Away Down South: A History of Southern Identity*. New York: Oxford University Press.
Coleman, Simon. 2000. *The Globalization of Charismatic Christianity: Spreading the Gospel of Prosperity*. Cambridge: Cambridge University Press.
Coleman, Simon. 2011. "Prosperity Unbound?: Debating the 'Sacrificial Economy,'" *Research in Economic Anthropology*, 31: 23–45.
Daswani, Girish. 2013. "On Christianity and Ethics: Rupture as Ethical Practice in Ghanaian Pentecostalism," *American Ethnologist*, 40 (3): 467–79.

Deloria, Philip J. 1998. *Playing Indian*. New Haven: Yale University Press.
Dulin, John. 2013. "Messianic Judaism as a Mode of Christian Authenticity: Exploring the Grammar of Authenticity through Ethnography of a Contested Identity," *Anthropos*, 108: 35–51.
Dulin, John. 2015. "Reversing Rupture: Evangelicals' Practice of Jewish Rituals and Processes of Protestant Inclusion," *Anthropological Quarterly*, 88 (3): 601–34.
Eaves, Latoya E. 2017. "Black Geographic Possibilities: On a Queer Black South," *Southeastern Geographer*, 57 (1): 80–95.
Elisha, Omri. 2008. "Faith beyond Belief: Evangelical Protestant Conceptions of Faith and the Resonance of Anti-Humanism," *Social Analysis*, 52 (1): 56–78.
Elisha, Omri. 2011. *Moral Ambition: Mobilization and Social Outreach in Evangelical Megachurches*. Berkeley: University of California Press.
Emerson, Michael O. and Christian Smith. 2001. *Divided by Faith: Evangelical Religion and the Problem of Race in America*. New York: Oxford University Press.
Engelke, Matthew. 2010. "Number and the Imagination of Global Christianity; or, Mediation and Immediacy in the Work of Alain Badiou," *South Atlantic Quarterly*, 109 (4): 811–29.
Frederick, Marla. 2013. "For the Love of Money?: Distributing the Go$pel beyond the United States," *Callaloo*, 36 (3): 609–17.
Frykholm, Amy. 2004. *Rapture Culture: Left Behind in Evangelical America*. New York: Oxford University Press.
Furey, Constance M. 2012. "Body, Society, and Subjectivity in Religious Studies," *Journal of the American Academy of Religion*, 80 (1): 7–33.
Goldman, Shalom. 2010. *Zeal for Zion: Christians, Jews, and the Idea of the Promised Land*. Chapel Hill: University of North Carolina Press.
Green, Rayna. 1988. "The Tribe Called Wannabee: Playing Indian in America and Europe," *Folklore*, 99 (1): 30–55.
Handman, Courtney. 2011. "Israelite Genealogies and Christian Commitment: The Limits of Language Ideologies in Guhu-Samane Christianity," *Anthropological Quarterly*, 84 (3): 655–77.
Harding, Susan. 2000. *The Book of Jerry Falwell: Fundamentalist Language and Politics*. Princeton: Princeton University Press.
Haynes, Naomi. 2012. "Pentecostalism and the Morality of Money: Prosperity, Inequality and Religious Sociality on the Zambian Copperbelt," *Journal of the Royal Anthropological Institute*, 18 (1): 123–39.
Imhoff, Sarah and Hillary Kaell. 2017. "Lineage Matters: DNA, Race, and Gene Talk in Judaism and Messianic Judaism," *Religion and American Culture: A Journal of Interpretation*, 27 (1): 95–127.
Kaell, Hillary. 2013. "Evangelical Ketubah, Messianic Mezuzah: Judaica for Christians," *Religion & Politics*, March 12. Accessed from http://religionandpolitics.org/2013/03/12/evangelical-ketubah-messianic-mezuzah-judaica-for-christians/ on May 7, 2014.

Kaell, Hillary. 2016. "Under the Law of God: Mimesis and Mimetic Discipleship among Jewish-affinity Christians," *Journal of the Royal Anthropological Institute*, 22 (3): 496–515.

Kollontai, Pauline. 2004. "Messianic Jews and Jewish Identity," *Journal of Modern Jewish Studies*, 3 (2): 195–205.

Lovett, Laura L. 1998. "'African and Cherokee by Choice': Race and Resistance under Legalized Segregation," *American Indian Quarterly*, 22 (1/2): 203–20.

Lugo, Luis, Alan Cooperman, Gregory A. Smith, Erin O'Connell, and Sandra Stencel. 2013. "A Portrait of Jewish Americans," *Pew Research Center*, October 1. Accessed from http://www.pewforum.org/files/2013/10/jewish-american-full-report-for-web.pdf on May 6, 2014.

Luhrmann, Tanya. 2012. *When God Talks Back: Understanding the American Evangelical Relationship with God.* New York: Vintage Books.

Martin, Craig. 2014. *Capitalizing Religion: Ideology and the Opiate of the Bourgeoisie.* New York: Bloomsbury.

Merkley, Paul. 2001. *Christian Attitudes toward the State of Israel.* Montreal: McGill-Queens Press.

Poloma, Margaret. 1998. "The Spirit Movement in North America at the Millennium: From Azusa Street to Toronto, Pensacola and Beyond," *Journal of Pentecostal Theology*, 12: 83–107.

Power, Patricia. 2011. "Blurring Boundaries: American Messianic Jews and Gentiles," *Nova Religio: The Journal of Alternative and Emergent Religions*, 15 (1): 69–91.

Robbins, Joel. 2007. "Continuity Thinking and the Problem of Christian Culture: Belief, Time, and the Anthropology of Christianity," *Current Anthropology*, 48 (1): 5–38.

Sandmel, David Fox. 2010. "Philosemitism and 'Judaizing' in the Contemporary Church," in Franklin T. Harkins and John Van Engen (eds.), *Transforming Relations: Essays on Jews and Christians throughout History in Honor of Michael A Signer*, 405–20. Notre Dame: University of Notre Dame Press.

Shelton, Jason E. and Michael O. Emerson. 2012. *Blacks and Whites in Christian America: How Racial Discrimination Shapes Religious Convictions.* New York: New York University Press.

Smith, Jonathan Z. 2004. *Relating Religion: Essays in the Study of Religion.* Chicago: University of Chicago Press.

Spector, Stephen. 2009. *Evangelicals and Israel: The Story of American Christian Zionism.* New York: Oxford University Press.

Springwood, Charles Fruehling. 2004. "'I'm Indian Too: Claiming Native American Identity, Crafting Authority in Mascot Debates," *Journal of Sports and Social Issues*, 28 (1): 56–70.

Wasserman, Jeffery, S. 2000. *Messianic Jewish Congregations: Who Sold This Business to the Gentiles?* Lanham: University Press of America.

Weber, Timothy P. 1979. *Living in the Shadow of the Second Coming: American Premillennialism 1875–1925.* New York: Oxford University Press.

Weber, Timothy P. 2005. *On the Road to Armageddon: How Evangelicals Became Israel's Best Friend*. Grand Rapids: Baker Academic.

Webster, Joseph. 2013. *The Anthropology of Protestantism: Faith and Crisis among Scottish Fishermen*. New York: Palgrave Macmillan.

Chapter 8

Agnew, Vanessa. 2007. "History's Affective Turn: Historical Reenactment and Its Work in the Present," *Rethinking History*, 11 (3): 299–312.

Agnew, Vanessa. 2014. "Gooseflesh: Somatosensation in the Making of Historical Experience," Paper presented at the Varieties of Historical Experience conference, Chicago, IL.

Basso, Keith H. 1996. "Wisdom Sites in Places: Notes on a Western Apache Landscape," in Steven Feld and Keith H. Basso (eds.), *Senses of Place*, 53–90. Santa Fe: School of American Research Press.

Beal, Timothy K. 2012. *The Rise and Fall of the Bible: The Unexpected History of an Accidental Book*. New York: Mariner.

Bielo, James S. 2018. *Ark Encounter: The Making of a Creationist Theme Park*. New York: New York University Press.

Bowman, Glenn. 1991. "Christian Ideology and the Image of a Holy Land: The Place of Jerusalem Pilgrimage in the Various Christianities," in John Eade and Michael Sallnow (eds.), *Contesting the Sacred: The Anthropology of Christian Pilgrimage*, 98–121. London: Routledge.

Coleman, Simon. 2004. "Pilgrimage to "England's Nazareth": Landscapes of Myth and Memory at Walsingham," in Ellen Badone and Sharon Roseman (eds.), *Intersecting Journeys: The Anthropology of Pilgrimage and Tourism*, 52–67. Urbana: The University of Illinois Press.

Davis, John. 1996. *The Landscape of Belief: Encountering the Holy Land in Nineteenth-Century American Art and Culture*. Princeton: Princeton University Press.

Feld, Steven and Keith H. Basso, eds. 1996. *Senses of Place*. Santa Fe: School of American Research Press.

Kark, Ruth and Seth J. Frantzman. 2010. "The Protestant Garden Tomb in Jerusalem, Englishwomen, and a Land Transaction in Late Ottoman Palestine," *Palestine Exploration Quarterly*, 142 (3): 199–216.

Leatherbarrow, David. 1987. "The Image and Its Setting: A Study of the Sacro Monte at Varallo," *RES: Anthropology and Aesthetics*, 14: 107–22.

Long, Burke O. 2003. *Imagining the Holy Land: Maps, Models, and Fantasy Travels*. Bloomington: Indiana University Press.

Promey, Sally M. 2001. "The Public Display of Religion," in David Morgan and Sally M. Promey (eds.), *The Visual Culture of American Religions*, 27–48. Berkeley: University of California Press.

Ron, Amos S. and Jackie Feldman. 2009. "From Spots to Themed Sites – The Evolution of the Protestant Holy Land," *Journal of Heritage Tourism*, 4 (3): 201–16.
Supp-Montgomerie, Jenna. 2015. "Affect and the Study of Religion," *Religion Compass*, 9 (10): 335–45.
Tilley, Christopher and Kate Cameron-Daum. 2017. *An Anthropology of Landscape*. London: UCL Press.

Chapter 9

Aggelomatē-Tsougarakē, Elenē. 2007. "Το φαινόμενο της ζητείας κατά τη Μεταβυζαντινή περίοδο," in Theodosēs Pylarinos (ed.), *Ιόνιος λόγος*, 247–93. Corfu: University of the Ionian.
Andriotis, Konstantinos. 2009. "Sacred Site Experience: A Phenomenological Study," *Annals of Tourism Research*, 36 (1): 64–84.
Badone, Ellen and Sharon Roseman. 2004. "Approaches to the Anthropology of Pilgrimage and Tourism," in Ellen Badone and Sharon Roseman (eds.), *Intersecting Journeys: The Anthropology of Pilgrimage and Tourism*, 1–23. Urbana and Chicago: University of Illinois Press.
Bajc, Vida, Simon Coleman, and John Eade. 2007. "Introduction: Mobility and Centering in Pilgrimage," *Mobilities*, 2 (3): 321–9.
Baldovin, John. 1987. *Urban Character of Christian Worship: The Origins, Development, and Meaning of Stational Liturgy*. Rome: Pontifical Oriental Institute Press.
Berger, Albrecht. 2001. "Imperial and Ecclesiastical Processions in Constantinople," in Nevra Necipoglu (ed.), *Byzantine Constantinople: Monuments, Topography and Everyday Life*, 73–88. Leiden: Brill Academic Publishers.
Chatzēphōtēs, Iōannēs. 1977. *Agion Oros: Anthologia logotechnikōn keimenōn*. Athens: Ekdoseis Kritikōn Phyllōn.
Chatzēphōtēs, Iōannēs. 2002. *Ē kathēmerinē zōē tōn Ellēnōn stēn Tourkokrateia*. Athens: Ekdoseis Dēmētriou Papadēma.
Christo, Gus George. 2005. *The Consecration of a Greek Orthodox Church According to Eastern Orthodox Tradition: A Detailed Account and Explanation of the Ritual*. Lewiston: E. Mellen Press.
Cohen, Eric. 1992. "Pilgrimage Centres: Concentric and Excentric," *Annals of Tourism Research*, 19: 33–50.
Coleman, Simon and John Eade. 2004. *Reframing Pilgrimage*. London: Routledge.
della Dora, Veronica. 2011a. *Imagining Mount Athos: Visions of a Holy Mountain from Homer to World War II*. Charlottesville: University of Virginia Press.
della Dora, Veronica. 2011b. "Turning Holy Mountains into Ladders to Heaven: Overlapping Topographies and Poetics of Space in Post-Byzantine Sacred Engravings of Sinai and Mount Athos," in Sharon Gerstel and Robert Nelson (eds.),

Approaching the Holy Mountain: Art and Liturgy at St. Catherine's Monastery in the Sinai, 505–35. Turnhout: Brepols.

della Dora, Veronica. 2016. *Landscape, Nature and the Sacred in Byzantium*. Cambridge: Cambridge University Press.

Deluga, Waldemar and Iwona Zych. 2002. "Greek Church Prints," *Print Quarterly*, 19 (2): 123–35.

Du Boulay, Juliet. 2009. *Cosmos, Life, and Liturgy in a Greek Orthodox Village*. Limni: D. Harvey.

Dubisch, Jill. 1995. *In a Different Place: Pilgrimage, Gender and Politics of a Greek Island*. Princeton: Princeton University Press, Princeton.

Eade, John and Michael Sallnow, eds. , 1991. *Contesting the Sacred: The Anthropology of Christian Pilgrimage*. New York and London: Routledge.

Eliade, Mircea. 1959. *The Sacred and the Profane: The Nature of Religion*. New York: Harcourt, Brace and World.

Evangelical Christendom. 1872. *Evangelical Christendom: A Monthly Chronicle of the Churches and Record of the Transactions of the Evangelical Alliance*, 25 (13): 85–6.

Frangos, George. 2005. "The Largest Piece of the True Cross Of Christ, Holy Monastery of Xeropotamou, Mount Athos," Accessed from http://holymountain-agionoros.blogspot.it on February 10, 2018.

Frey, Nancy. 1998. *Pilgrim Stories: On and Off the Road to Santiago*. Berkeley: UC Press.

Gothóni, René, ed. 2013. *Pilgrims and Travellers in Search of the Holy*. Oxford: Peter Lang International Academic Publishers.

Greenfield, Richard, trans. and ed. 2000. *The Life of Lazaros of Mt. Galesion: An Eleventh-Century Pillar Saint*. Washington: Dumbarton Oaks Research Library and Collection.

Gregory of Nyssa. 1978. *On the Life of Moses*, Translated by Abraham Malherbe et al. New York: Paulist Press.

Ignatios, Archimandrite, ed. 1998. *Aghiou Iōannou tou Sinaitou Klimax*. Ōropos Attikēs: I. M. Paraklētou.

Ioustinos Simonopetrētēs, Hieromonk. 1987. *Ἄξιον Εστίν: Η θαυματουργική εικόνα του Πρωτάτου. Αγιορείτικα τετράδια*. Agion Oros: Ekdoseis Panselēnos.

John of Damascus. 1997. *On the Divine Images*, Translated by David Anderson. Crestwood: St Vladimir Seminary.

Kishovsky, Sophia. 2011. "In Russian Chill, Waiting Hours for Touch of the Holy Belt," *New York Times*, November 23. Accessed from http://www.nytimes.com/2011/11/24/world/europe/virgin-mary-belt-relic-draws-crowds-in-moscow.html on February 10, 2018.

Kotsi, Filareti. 1999. "The Enchantment of a Floating Pilgrimage: The Case of Mount Athos, Greece," *Vrijetijdstudies*, 17: 5–20.

Kourilēs, Eulogiou Metropolitan. 1953. "Η επίσημος λιτανεία της Παναγίας Άξιον Εστί εν Καρεαίς κατά την Δευτέρα ημέραν του Πάσχα," *Agioreitikē Bibliothēkē*, 18 (2): 63–72.

Lane, Belden. 1998. *The Solace of Fierce Landscapes: Exploring Desert and Mountain Spirituality*. New York and Oxford: Oxford University Press.

Lidov, Alexei. 2006. "Spatial Icons: The Miraculous Performance with the Hodegetria of Constantinople," in Alexei Lidov (ed.), *Hierotopy: Creation of Sacred Spaces in Byzantium and Medieval Russia*, 325–72. Moscow: Progress-tradition.

Maddrell, Avril et al. 2014. *Christian Pilgrimage, Landscape, and Heritage: Journeying to the Sacred*. London: Routledge.

Malpas, Jeff. 1999. *Place and Experience: A Philosophical Topography*. Cambridge and New York: Cambridge University Press.

Mamalakēs, Iōannēs. 1971. *Το Άγιον Όρος (Άθως) δια μέσω των αιώνων*. Thessaloniki: Etaireia Makedonikōn Spoudōn.

Mayer, Wendy. 1998. "The Sea Made Holy: The Liturgical Function of the Waters Surrounding Constantinople," *Ephemerides Liturgicae*, 112 (6): 459–68.

Morinis, Alan, ed. 1992. *Sacred Journeys: The Anthropology of Pilgrimage*. New York: Greenwood Press.

Myribēlēs, Stratēs. 1995 [1949]. *Ē Panaghia ē gorgona*. Athens: Bibliopoleio tēs Estias.

N. a. 2012. "Με τιμές αρχηγού κράτους υποδέχθηκαν στην Θεσσαλονίκη την εικόνα της Παναγίας «Αξιον Εστί»," *Iefimerida*, October 13. Accessed from http://www.iefimerida.gr/news/72043/ on February 10, 2018.

N. a. 2016. "Πῶς συμμετέχουμε στὶς λιτανεῖες," *Ο Σωτήρ*, February 15. Accessed from https://christianvivliografia.wordpress.com/2016/02/22/%CE%BF%CE%B9-%CE%BB%CE%B9%CF%84%CE%B1%CE%BD%CE%B5%CE%B9%CE%B5%CF%83/ on February 10, 2018.

Nikodēmos, Agioreitēs. 2001. *The Supplicatory Canon to Our Lady Quick to Hear*, Translated by Holy Transfiguration Monastery. Boston: Holy Transfiguration Monastery.

Papastratou, Dory. 1990. *Paper Icons: Greek Orthodox Religious Engraving, 1665–1899*, 2 vols. Athens: Papastratos S.A. Publications.

Polyviou, Miltiadēs. 1992. "Η ζητεία τού Καισαρίου Δαπόντε για τήν ανοικοδόμηση του καθολικού τής μονής Ξηροποτάμου," *Κληρονομιά*, 24: 183–203.

Ron, Amos. 2012. "Revisiting Holy Land and Spiritual Maintenance," *Loch Lectures: Spirituality and the Life Cycle*. Ouranoupoli, Halkidiki.

Savvas Philotheitēs, Hieromonk. 1936. *Πανηγυρικαί τελεταί του Ιερού Ναού του Πρωτάτου εν Καρυαίς του Αγίου Όρους*. Agion Oros: Kallitechniko Typographeio tēs Ieras Koinotētos.

Scriven, Richard. 2014. "Geographies of Pilgrimage: Meaningful Movements and Embodied Mobilities," *Geography Compass*, 8 (4): 249–61.

Sheldrake, Philip. 2001. *Spaces for the Sacred: Place, Memory, and Identity*. Baltimore: John Hopkins University Press.

Sideropoulos, Georgios. 2010. "The Contribution of the Cartographic Visualisation in Understanding the Historical Geography of an Old Land Property Regime in Mount Athos (Karyes)," *The Cartographic Journal*, 47 (3): 270–7.

Speake, Graham. 2002. *Mount Athos: Renewal in Paradise*. New Haven and London: Yale University Press.
Taft, Robert. 1992. *The Byzantine Rite: A Short History*. Collegeville: Liturgical Press.
Talbot, Alice-Mary. 1996. "Women and Mt Athos," in Anthony Bryer and Mary Cunningham (eds.), *Mount Athos and Byzantine Monasticism*, 67–80. Aldershot: Ashgate Variorium.
Talbot, Alice-Mary. 2001. "Les saintes montagnes a Byzance," in Michel Kaplan (ed.), *Le sacre et son inscription dans l'espace a Byzance et en Occident*, 263–75. Paris: Byzantina Sorbonensia.
Thomas, John, et al. eds. 2000. *Byzantine Monastic Foundation Documents: A Complete Translation of the Surviving Founders' Typika and Testaments*, 1–5. Washington: Dumbarton Oaks Research Library and Collection.
Turner, Victor and Edith Turner. 1978. *Image and Pilgrimage in Christian Culture: Anthropological Perspectives*. Oxford: Blackwell.
Varvounēs, Manolēs. 2014. "Η λαογραφία μεταξύ Αποκριάς και Μεγάλης Εβδομάδας," *Pemptousia*, 12 April.
Walker White, Andrew. 2015. *Performing Orthodox Ritual in Byzantium*. New York: Cambridge University Press.
Ware, Timothy. 1963. *The Orthodox Church*. New York: Penguin Books.

Chapter 10

Barkay, Gabriel. 1986. "The Garden Tomb: Was Jesus Buried Here?" *Biblical Archaeology Review*, 12 (2): 40–56.
Barrie, Thomas. 2010. *The Sacred In-between: The Mediating Roles of Architecture*. London: Routledge.
Barrie, Thomas. 2012. "Sacred Space and the Mediating Roles of Architecture," *European Review*, 20 (1): 79–94.
Beckford, James A. and John Walliss. 2017. *Theorising Religion: Classical and Contemporary Debates*. London and New York: Routledge.
Bielo, James S. 2018a. "Biblical Gardens and the Sensuality of Religious Pedagogy," *Material Religion*, 14 (1): 30–54.
Bielo, James S. 2018b. "Flower, Soil, Water, Stone: Biblical Landscape Items and Protestant Materiality," *Journal of Material Culture*, 23 (3): 368–87.
Bitton, Michal. 2012. "The Garden as Sacred Nature and the Garden as a Church: Transitions of Design and Function in the Garden of Gethsemane, 1800–1959," *Cathedra*, 146: 27–66 (in Hebrew).
Bitton, Michal. 2016. *Between Authenticity of a Sacred Place and a Universal Message: The Creation of the Garden Tomb – A Protestant Prayer Garden*. PhD diss. Hebrew University of Jerusalem, Jerusalem.

Chen, Lior. 2019. "Authentication and Competition at Sacred Sites," *The Reflective Practitioner*, 4: 23–36.

Cohen, Erik. 1972. "Toward a Sociology of International Tourism," *Social Research*, 39 (1): 164–82.

Conan, Michel. 1999. "From Vernacular Gardens to a Social Anthropology of Gardening," in Michel Conan (ed.), *Perspectives on Garden Histories*, 21: 181–204. Washington: Dumbarton Oaks.

Conan, Michel. 2007. "Introduction: The Cultural Agency of Gardens and Landscapes," in Michel Conan (ed.), *Sacred Gardens and Landscapes: Ritual and Agency*, 3–14. Washington: Dumbarton Oaks.

Cosgrove, Denis E. 1984. *Social Formation and Symbolic Landscape*. London and Sydney: Croom Helm.

Dafni, Amotz. 2002. "Why are Rags Tied to the Sacred Trees of the Holy Land?" *Economic Botany*, 56 (4): 315–27.

Dafni, Amotz. 2006. "On the Typology and the Worship Status of Sacred Trees with a Special Reference to the Middle East," *Journal of Ethnobiology and Ethnomedicine*, 2 (26): doi:10.1186/1746-4269-2-26.

Dafni, Amotz. 2011. "On the Present-day Veneration of Sacred Trees in the Holy Land," *Electronic Journal of Folklore*, 48: 7–30.

Davidson, Linda Kay and David M. Gitlitz. 2002. *Pilgrimage: From the Ganges to Graceland: An Encyclopedia*. Santa Barbara: CA. ABC-CLIO.

Deil, Ulrich, Heike Culmsee, and Mohamed Berriane. 2005. "Sacred Groves in Morocco: A Society's Conservation of Nature for Spiritual Reasons," *Silva Carelica*, 49: 185–201.

Duncan, Nancy and James Duncan. 2010. "Doing Landscape Interpretation," in Dydia DeLyser, Steve Herbert, Stuart Aitken, Mike Crang, and Linda McDowell (eds.), *The SAGE Handbook of Qualitative Geography*, 225–47. London: Sage Publications.

Feldman, Jackie. 2016. *A Jewish Guide in the Holy Land: How Christian Pilgrims Made Me Israeli*. Bloomington: Indiana University Press.

Fontanari, Martin and Berit Berger-Risthaus. 2020. "Problem and Solution Awareness in Overtourism: A Delphi Study," in Harald Pechlaner, Elisa Innerhofer and Greta Erschbamer (eds.), *Overtourism: Tourism Management and Solutions*, 43–66. Abingdon and New York: Routledge.

Galbraith, David B., D. Kelly Ogden, and Andrew C. Skinner. 1996. *Jerusalem: The Eternal City*. Salt Lake City: Deseret Book Company.

Guter, Yael. 2004. *Aspects of Christian Pilgrimage to the Holy Land: The Pilgrim's Experience*. PhD diss. Bar-Ilan University, Ramat Gan.

Halevi, Masha. 2009. *Reshaping a Sacred Landscape: Antonio Barluzzi and the Rebuilding of the Catholic Shrines in the Holy Land: Political, Geographical and Cultural Influences*. PhD diss. Hebrew University of Jerusalem, Jerusalem (in Hebrew).

Halevi, Masha. 2012. "An Italian Nationalist and Religious Artist: Antonio Barluzzi, the Agent of Italian Interests in the Holy Land," *Cathedra*, 144: 75–106 (in Hebrew).

Hall, Stuart. 1973. *Encoding and Decoding in the Television Discourse.* CCCS Stencilled Occasional Paper no. 7. Centre for Contemporary Cultural Studies, University of Birmingham.

Hepper, F. Nigel. 1997. *Planting a Bible Garden.* London: HMSO.

Hoade, Eugene. 1962. *Guide to the Holy Land.* Jerusalem: Franciscan Press.

Hunt, John D. 2000. *Greater Perfections: The Practice of Garden Theory.* Philadelphia: University of Pennsylvania Press.

Hunt, John D. 2004. *The Afterlife of Gardens.* Philadelphia: University of Pennsylvania Press.

Ikutegbe, Victoria Ufuoma. 2016. *A Phenomenological Study of Gardening Practices and Invasive Plant Management in the Sydney Basin.* PhD diss. University of Wollongong, Wollongog, Australia. Accessed from https://ro.uow.edu.au/cgi/viewcontent.cgi?article=5871&context=theses on September 9, 2020.

Jones, Lindsay. 2000. *The Hermeneutics of Sacred Architecture.* Volume 2. Cambridge, MA: Harvard University Press.

Koeditz, Malte. 2011. *Timelessness in Architecture: Perception, Interpretation, Function.* Accessed from http://www.maltekoeditz.com/pages/timelessness-essay.html on September 9, 2020.

Lane, Belden C. 2001. *Landscapes of the Sacred: Geography and Narrative in American Spirituality.* 2nd Expanded ed. Baltimore and London: The Johns Hopkins University Press.

Lewis, Pearce K. 1979. "Axioms for Reading the Landscape: Some Guides to the American Scene," in Donald W. Meinig and John B. Jackson (eds.), *The Interpretation of Ordinary Landscapes*, 11–31. Oxford: Oxford University Press.

Lioy, Daniel T. 2010. "The Garden of Eden as a Primordial Temple or Sacred Space for Humankind," *Conspectus: The Journal of the South African Theological Seminary,* 10: 25–7.

Nasr, Seyyed Hossein. 1987. *Islamic Art and Spirituality.* Albany NY: State University of New York Press.

Prest, John. 1981. *The Garden of Eden: The Botanic Garden and the Re-Creation of Paradise.* New Haven and London: Yale University Press.

Relph, Edward. 1976. *Place and Placelessness.* London: Pion.

Ron, Amos S. 1989. *Gardens in Cultures: The Garden as a Symbolic Landscape – A Study in Landscape Interpretation,* M.A. Thesis. Hebrew University of Jerusalem, [Hebrew].

Ron, Amos S. 1993. "The Gardens of Persia and the Gardens of Islam," *Garden & Landscape,* 13: 44–6 (in Hebrew).

Ron, Amos S. 2001. "Summer Holy Land Study Tour, June 6–22," *Private Collection of Itineraries,* 1–4.

Ron, Amos S. 2007. "Family Holy Land Tour, June 19–30," *Private Collection of Itineraries,* 1–4.

Ron, Amos S. and Dallen J. Timothy. 2019. *Contemporary Christian Travel: Pilgrimage, Practice and Place.* Clevedon: Channel View Publications Ltd / Multilingual Matters (Aspects of Tourism Series).

Rubin, Miri. 2009. *Mother of God: A History of the Virgin Mary*. New Haven and London. Yale University Press.

Schachter, Lifsa. 2013. "The Garden of Eden as God's First Sanctuary," *Jewish Bible Quarterly*, 41 (2): 73–7.

Semple, Ellen C. 1929. "Ancient Mediterranean Pleasure Gardens," *Geographical Review*, 19 (3): 420–43.

Semple, Ellen C. 1971. "Ancient Mediterranean Pleasure Gardens," in Christopher L. Salter (ed.), *The Cultural Landscape*, 192–6. Belmont: Duxbury Press.

Singh, Sushma, Youssouf Mudasir, Malik Zubair A., and Rainer W. Bussmann. 2017. "Sacred Groves: Myths, Beliefs, and Biodiversity Conservation—A Case Study from Western Himalaya, India," *International Journal of Ecology*, Article ID 3828609, 12 pages, Accessed from https://doi.org/10.1155/2017/3828609 on September 9, 2020.

Stidham Rogers, Stephanie. 2011. *Inventing the Holy Land: American Protestant Pilgrimage to Palestine, 1865–1941*. Lanham MD. Lexington Books.

Storrs, Ronald. 1937. *The Memoirs of Sir Ronald Storrs*. New York: G. P. Putnam's Sons.

Swisher, David J. 2017. *Vantage Point: Using Narrative and Discourse Analysis of Jesus' Sermon on the Mount to Improve Discipleship Outcomes*. DMin diss. George Fox University, Newberg, Oregon. Accessed from http://digitalcommons.georgefox.edu/dmin/238 on April 5, 2021.

Verdi, Laura. 2005. "Review of John Dixon Hunt, *The Afterlife of Gardens*, London: Reaktion Books, 2004," *International Journal of Cultural Studies*, 8 (3): 375–81.

Wilson, Mervyn. 2007. "The Vicar and the Vicar's Garden," *Rural Theology*, 5 (2): 101–9.

X. Malcolm. 2001. *The Autobiography of Malcolm X: As Told to Alex Haley*. New York: Penguin Books.

Zeng, Lily. 2018. "Problematizing Ideas of Purity and Timelessness in the Conservation Narratives of Sacred Groves in Xishuangbanna, China," *Journal for the Study of Religion, Nature and Culture*, 12 (2): 172–200. Accessed from https://doi.org/10.1558/jsrnc.34555 on September 10, 2020.

Zoran, A. 2020. *God's Gardens in the Holy Land*. Ramat Hasharon: Sfat Em Publishers (in Hebrew).

Afterword

Coleman, Simon. 2002. "From the Sublime to the Meticulous: Art, Anthropology and Victorian Pilgrimage to Palestine," *History and Anthropology*, 13 (4): 275–90.

Coleman, Simon. 2010. "Constructing the Globe: A Charismatic Sublime?" in Gertrud Hüwelmeier and Kristine Krause (eds.), *Traveling Spirits: Migrants, Markets and Mobilities*, 186–202. New York: Routledge.

Dempster, Murray W., Byron D. Klaus, and Douglas Petersen, eds. 1999. *The Globalization of Pentecostalism: A Religion Made to Travel*. Oxford: Regnum.

Eade, John and Sallnow, Michael, eds. 1991. *Contesting the Sacred: The Anthropology of Christian Pilgrimage*. London: Routledge.

Encyclopaedia Britannica (no author given). 1911. *Seddon, Thomas*. Chicago: Horace Hooper.

Hirsch, Eric. 1995. "Introduction: Landscape Between Place and Space," in Eric Hirsch and Michael O'Hanlon (ed.), *The Anthropology of Landscape: Perspectives on Place and Space*, 1–30. Oxford: Clarendon Press.

Hummel, Ruth and Thomas Hummel. 1995. *Patterns of the Sacred: English Protestant and Russian Orthodox Pilgrims of the Nineteenth Century*. Jerusalem: Scorpion Cavendish.

Hunt, William Holman. 1905. *Pre-Raphaelitism and the Pre-Raphaelite Brotherhood*, Volume I. London: Macmillan and Co.

Lousteau, Marc and Kate DeConinck. 2019. "Editors' Introduction," *Journal of Global Catholicism*, 3 (1): 13–25.

Smith, Jonathan Z. 1987. *To Take Place: Toward Theory in Ritual*. Chicago: Chicago University Press.

Tambiah, Stanley J. 1977. "The Galactic Polity: The Structure of Traditional Kingdoms in Southeast Asia," *Annals of the New York Academy of Sciences*, 293: 60–97.

Contributors

James S. Bielo is Associate Professor of Anthropology at Miami University (Oxford, Ohio, USA). He is the author of five books, most recently *Materializing the Bible: Scripture, Sensation, Place* (2021).

Simon Coleman is Chancellor Jackman Professor at the Department for the Study of Religion, University of Toronto, and past-president of the Society for the Anthropology of Religion. His research interests include Pentecostalism, pilgrimage, cathedrals, and the construction of religious infrastructure, and he has conducted fieldwork in Sweden, England, and Nigeria. His most recent book is *Powers of Pilgrimage: Religion in a World of Movement* (2021).

Veronica Della Dora is Professor of Human Geography at Royal Holloway, University of London, and a fellow of the British Academy. She is the author of *Imagining Mount Athos: Visions of a Holy Place from Homer to World War II* and *Landscape, Nature, and the Sacred in Byzantium* (2016).

Michael A. Di Giovine is Associate Professor of Anthropology in the Department of Anthropology and Sociology at West Chester University, and the Director of the West Chester University Museum of Anthropology and Archaeology. He is the author of *The Heritage-Scape: UNESCO, World Heritage, and Tourism* (2009).

John Eade is Professor of Sociology and Anthropology at the University of Roehampton, Research Fellow at the Department for the Study of Religion, University of Toronto and co-founder of the Routledge Religion, Travel and Tourism series. His research interests and publications focus on the anthropology of pilgrimage, global migration, and urban ethnicity.

Brett Hendrickson is Associate Professor of Religious Studies at Lafayette College. He is the author of three books, most recently *Mexican American Religions: An Introduction* (2021).

Rebekka King is Associate Professor in the Department of Philosophy and Religious Studies at Middle Tennessee State University. Her first book is *The New Heretics: Secularism, Skepticism, and the End of Christianity*.

Kim Knibbe is Associate Professor of Anthropology and Sociology of Religion at the University of Groningen. She is the author of *Faith in the Familiar: Religion, Spirituality and Place in the South of the Netherlands* (2013).

Jonathan Miles-Watson is Associate Professor of the Anthropology of Religion in the Department of Theology and Religion, Durham University. He is the author of *Christianity and Belonging in Shimla: Sacred Entanglements of a Himalayan Landscape* (2020).

Sara M. Patterson is Associate Professor of Theological Studies at Hanover College. She is the author of two books, most recently *Pioneers in the Attic: Place and Memory along the Mormon Trail* (2020).

Sitna Quiroz is Assistant Professor of the Study of Religion in the Department of Theology and Religion, Durham University. Her primary research interests focus on Benin, Mexico, Christianity, Pentecostalism, Kinship, and Gender.

Amos S. Ron a retired independent researcher specializing in the geography of religions, Christian travel and pilgrimage, religious culinary tourism, religious themed-environments, and sacred site place-making and management. He is currently a research fellow at the department of French Culture at Bar Ilan University. He is the author or of *Contemporary Cristian Travel: Pilgrimage, Practice and Place* (2019, with DJ Timothy).

Joseph Webster is Lecturer in the Study of Religion at Cambridge University. He is the author of two books, most recently *The Religion of Orange Politics: Protestantism and Fraternity in Contemporary Scotland* (2020).

Index

Actor Network Theory 130
affordances 13, 158, 165, 167, 221, 227
agency 1, 7, 56, 101, 121, 128, 130, 140, 159, 222, 228
anthropology
 of Christianity 11, 101, 115, 138, 222
 of ethics 130
apocalypticism 11–12, 121, 140
archeology 29, 62, 168–9, 205, 208–9, 213
architecture 15, 23, 42, 106, 119, 161, 169, 202, 205, 219, 227
authenticity 12, 49, 138, 147, 169, 208–12, 224
authority 12, 22–5, 38, 51, 91, 94, 133, 139, 147, 222, 224

Basilica of Our Lady of Guadalupe (Mexico) 67
Bateson, Gregory 102, 115, 117
biblical sand sculptures (Maryland) 166
botanicals 70, 110, 132, 160, 163, 169, 174, 181, 188, 201, 203, 219

captivity narratives 78
charisma 23, 31, 36, 40–1, 44, 176, 178, 191, 193, 223–5
Christian Zionism 123, 126, 128–9, 131, 144, 152
circulation 37, 39, 43, 73, 119–20, 190–1
colonialism 7, 23, 61, 101, 116, 226–7
commodification 2, 113, 116–17, 142
communitas 24, 102, 117–18

devotional labor 157, 165, 167, 170, 172, 223
dwelling 1–2, 13, 72, 101, 104, 115–16, 159, 222, 226

Eastern Orthodox Christianity 6, 8, 13, 169, 176–9, 182–7, 190–5, 200, 208–11, 228, 236
Esquipulas (Guatemala) 64, 69
exotic capital 147–8

Francaviglia, Richard V. 3–4

Garden of Gethsemane 207, 220
Garden of Hope (Kentucky) 167–70
gardens 107, 160, 183, 188, 202
Garden Tomb (Jerusalem) 168, 202, 208, 224
gender 78, 86, 89, 94, 176
geography of religion 2–4, 6
geophagy 70, 73
Grotto of the Redemption (Iowa) 168

Hall, Stuart 204
healing 7, 10, 46–7, 49, 54, 58, 60, 62, 64–76, 104, 115, 188, 224
heritage ix, 20, 28, 34, 36, 42, 119
Holy House of Loreto 163
Holy Land 2, 129, 162–3, 168, 181, 201, 220–1
Holy Land Experience (Orlando) 210
Holy Land USA (Connecticut) 157, 174

identity 1, 12, 78, 80, 81, 93, 111, 114, 137–39, 142, 147–8, 151, 154, 164, 180, 189, 225, 228, 234
ideology 2, 7, 11, 23–5, 49, 117, 151, 158, 160, 175, 223
indigeneity 61, 64–7, 70, 78, 138, 142, 146, 159, 223, 227
infrastructure ix, 7, 9, 46–8, 170, 180, 225

Jewish Affinity Christianity 137–42, 223

landscape, as process x, 6–7, 101, 107, 159, 221
Latter-Day Saints 4, 77, 208, 217, 225–6
 and federal legislation 83
 and whiteness 84
liminality 48–9, 162, 177, 185–6, 189
Lourdes 7, 9, 10, 46–59, 224, 225, 231, 237

materiality ix–xi, 2, 8, 12, 15, 36, 46, 54, 59, 107, 121, 148, 157, 164, 169, 187, 221

mediation   7, 158, 222
mega-churches   ix, 6, 20, 150
miracles   10, 39, 50, 118, 164–5, 181, 184–5, 191, 193, 196
Mormonism, *see* Latter Day-Saints
mountains   4, 32, 45, 47, 49–50, 60, 65, 93, 110, 112, 117–18, 159, 162, 176, 202
Mount Athos   8, 13, 14, 176–8, 182, 184–92, 195–8
Mount of Beatitudes   207
Mount of Olives   219–20
Museums   34, 36, 160–3, 170, 172
music   3, 52, 104–5, 110, 113–14, 152, 170, 173–4, 183, 185, 187, 193, 195, 197–8, 234

nature-culture   1–2, 13, 45, 49, 159, 219
Nazareth Village   163, 169

Padre Pio of Pietrelcina   223
   globalization of   34–7, 43
   map of shrines   30, 43
   and San Giovanni Rotondo   29–33
   sites associated with youth   26–9
Palestine Park   162
Pentecostal and charismatic Christianity   ix, 102–4, 120, 136, 139, 142–3, 150, 222, 226, 228
pilgrimage   8–9, 15, 19–20, 24–6, 30, 32, 45, 51, 60, 70, 101, 107, 116, 132, 168, 176–7, 185, 191, 193–4, 201, 206, 212, 216, 224, 227
politics   x, 11, 21, 43, 46, 61, 123, 129, 139, 146, 158
Pope Francis   19, 29, 41, 224
Prosperity Gospel   12–13, 102, 105–07, 118–19, 143, 145, 151, 153–4, 188, 226, 234–5

racialization   78–80, 146, 149
reception theory   204
replication   10, 22–6, 36, 43, 64, 71, 141, 160–4, 167–70, 224
Roman Catholicism   19–29, 47–57, 60–75, 106, 119, 142, 157, 160, 163–9, 208–10, 217, 223–7
rurality   148, 150–1, 155, 160, 163–5, 175–6, 181, 186, 193, 204–6, 215, 221

sacralization   7, 45, 47, 61, 112, 176, 198, 202
Sacred Mount of Varallo   162
Santiago de Compostela   51
secularity   10, 16, 22, 57–8, 61, 63, 68, 70, 153, 159–60, 179, 186, 192, 236–7
senses   8, 46–7, 55, 106, 161, 170, 177, 187, 193, 197, 213–15, 224
sexuality   51, 56, 78–9, 82, 86–8, 90–1, 94–6, 146, 152, 177, 225–6
smell   88, 169, 177, 185, 193
soil   10, 60, 75, 164, 221, 227
souvenirs   26, 43, 49, 63, 191
spatial turn   1, 4–5
Stations of the Cross   31, 48, 164–5

Tambiah, Stanley   21–2
Temple Institute   129
temporality   11, 24–5, 43, 120, 123, 129, 135, 138–42, 147–8, 154, 167, 184–5, 200, 204–5, 221–2, 228–9
theology   2, 4, 6, 8, 24, 29, 85, 88, 92, 94–6, 118–19, 123, 140, 142, 164, 167, 174, 202, 226
topography   7, 14, 23, 76, 157, 160, 178–80, 183–4, 188, 196–200
tourism   9, 13, 15, 45, 107, 116, 166, 174, 194, 201, 203, 213
transmedial   161, 223
Turner, Edith and Victor   24, 68, 116

UNESCO   20
urban   18, 104, 116, 125, 153, 175, 179–80, 191–4, 204, 206, 218, 225, 237

Vatican   23, 25, 30, 51

Walsingham (England)   163–4, 167, 174
water   7, 10, 47–50, 53–6, 60, 74, 91–2, 126, 163, 180, 183, 193, 198, 224
weather   56, 108, 110–13, 124, 126, 128, 133, 164, 166, 173, 213
wilderness   45, 89, 92, 176, 196, 202

Young, Brigham   11, 78, 82, 85–8, 90

Zelinsky, Wilbur   3

www.ingramcontent.com/pod-product-compliance
Lightning Source LLC
Chambersburg PA
CBHW052219300426
44115CB00011B/1753